Keith Waterhouse

Keith Waterhouse is one of our most distinguished and popular writers. He has produced a large range of work for television, cinema and the theatre, and writes an award-winning column for the *Daily Mail*. His recent plays *Jeffrey Bernard is Unwell* and *Our Song* (adapted from his novel) have been successful productions on the London stage. His novels, which include BILLY LIAR, BIMBO and most recently UNSWEET CHARITY, have been published to great acclaim. Keith Waterhouse is also the author of several works of non-fiction, including THE THEORY AND PRACTICE OF TRAVEL and SHARON & TRACY & THE REST (a collection of his journalism).

SCEPTRE

Also by Keith Waterhouse and published by Sceptre

There is a Happy Land
Our Song
Bimbo
Unsweet Charity
Sharon & Tracy & the Rest

City Lights

A Street Life

KEITH WATERHOUSE

SCEPTRE

Copyright © 1994 Keith Waterhouse Ltd

First published in 1994 by Hodder and Stoughton
First published in paperback in 1995 by Hodder and Stoughton
A division of Hodder Headline PLC
A Sceptre Paperback

The right of Keith Waterhouse to be identified as the Author of
the Work has been asserted by him in accordance with the
Copyright, Designs and Patents Act 1988.

10 9 8 7 6 5 4 3 2 1

British Library Cataloguing in Publication Data
Waterhouse, Keith
City Lights: Street Life
I Title
823.914 [F]

ISBN 0 340 62463 9

Printed and bound in Great Britain by
Cox and Wyman Ltd, Reading, Berkshire

Hodder and Stoughton
A Division of Hodder Headline PLC
338 Euston Road
London NW1 3BH

ACKNOWLEDGMENTS

I should like to thank the many friends and relations who have strolled with me down Back Memory Lane during the composition of this book, notably Barry Cryer, the late Guy Deghy, Willis Hall, the late Dennis Haywood, Jack Higgins, Ray Hill, the Rt Hon Gerald Kaufman PC MP, Stella Lawson, Peter O'Toole, Robert E. Preedy, Donald Tate, Frank Walker, Dennis Waterhouse and George Young. I am further indebted to Gerald Kaufman for kind permission to quote from his book *My Life in the Silver Screen*. My thanks are also due to the staff of Leeds Central Reference Library for their help and patience.

Any errors, however, are mine. These are impressions of growing up in a certain place at a certain time but I have not set out to compile a geographical and historical record. While I have checked facts where I could, memory does play tricks and when I have gone back to a particular location to remind myself of this or that detail, I have often found, in Gertrude Stein's words, that I have got there only to find no there there.

NB For the three sections of this book, covering childhood, adolescence and late youth, I have borrowed the titles of three of my novels — *There Is A Happy Land, Billy Liar, and In The Mood*. This is not to say that those novels were autobiographical. Nor is it to say that this autobiographical fragment is fictional.

K.W.

ONE

There is a Happy Land

'You had to crawl through a big drain pipe at the edge of the park, it was an old sewer I think, and where it brought you out was in a long road with houses that had been there for ages, made out of stone. You were clean out of the estate then. You just had to walk up this road and there was a coal mine with a lot of slag heaps, and railway lines that went right over the street, so that lorries bumped when they went over them. The houses were all in long rows and made of black stone, and all the streets were just rough cobbles with sooty grass growing through them. Not like our blinking street.'

— THERE IS A HAPPY LAND, 1957

1 In the stifling August of 1936 the black American athlete Jesse Owens arrived in Berlin to claim four gold medals at Hitler's Olympic Games; the King took Mrs Wallis Simpson on an Adriatic cruise; the *Queen Mary* regained the Blue Riband for Britain with an Atlantic crossing of three days, twenty-three hours, fifty-seven minutes from the Ambrose Light, New York, to the Bishop Rock, Scilly Isles; and I, aged seven and a half, set off on an expedition to a faraway country, clutching a borrowed cardboard suitcase.

I was reassured in some measure, as we assembled for our journey into the unknown at the departure point outside the offices of the Leeds Poor Children's Holiday Camp Association, by the discovery that our mode of transport was to be one of Saml Ledgard's navy blue charabancs. For Sammy Ledgard, as he was familiarly known to all his passengers, could be trusted. And while he was unlikely to be driving his coach personally, he had at least signed it.

Just about everything of any significance in Leeds at that time, it seemed, bore a signature that was at once frighteningly authoritarian yet comforting, like the word of God. The trams were signed, and in gold leaf at that, by W. Vane Morland, General Manager, Leeds Corporation Transport Dept; so that when you read the notice "No Spitting, By Order", you were left in no doubt by whom the order had been given. Council rent books and notices prohibiting ball games and the hanging out of bed linen were signed by the Housing Director, with his impressive array of initials front and back — R.A.H. Livett, ARIBA. The dense acreage of park bye-laws was signed by a municipal celebrity, none other than Thos Thornton, Town Clerk & Clerk to the Council. Anything to do with hospitals or clinics was signed, as I would have cause to remember, by J. Johnstone Jervis, Medical Officer of Health.

But the most famous signature of all was that of Geo Guest,

3

Director of Education, whose Christian name I thought to rhyme with Leo (the name my father had wanted to bestow on me, until dissuaded by my mother), just as I thought the Saml who had signed my charabanc rhymed with enamel. Geo Guest's signature, rubber-stamped in heliotrope, sent quivers of fear through generations of Leeds schoolchildren, to whom it was as familiar in its ubiquitous facsimile – on reports, on playground notices, on circulars to parents, even on school dinner menus – as that of Elizabeth I or Guy Fawkes after torture. I was amazed to read in the usually memory-perfect Richard Hoggart's autobiography, where he recalls actually being summoned personally before this awesome figure as a student, that "I think his name was George Guest." It was as if someone granted an audience by the Italian dictator of the time had written, "I think his name was Mussolini."

It was Geo Guest's signature stamped on a cyclostyled chit from Middleton Council School that had delivered me up to serve fourteen days in the Poor Children's Holiday Camp at Silverdale in Lancashire, a grassy promontory inhabited only by gulls and temporary orphans, overlooking Morecambe Bay. I was terrified.

I took what solace I could from the spiritual presence, via his waiting charabanc, of Saml Ledgard, whose name was almost as familiar to me as Geo Guest's. A publican who had diversified into steam wagons to service the beer tents of the north-eastern racecourses, he had gradually built up a bus and coach fleet to rival the de luxe operation of Wallace Arnold – another Leeds enterprise – and was a local legend, like Mr Scarr of Scarr's Stores who had come to the city with only one clog to his feet, or Harry Ramsden, the self-crowned King of Fish and Chips, or Tommy Wass who was famous for running a famous pub which was famous for being known as Tommy Wass's, to which folk came from far and wide simply to have been there.

These were swaggering days when every city had its larger than life figures, not only its Tommy Liptons and Jesse Boots but hosts of lesser luminaries who had started with one greengrocery stall and now ran twelve, or who had evolved from bicycle repairs to a chain of filling stations, and who smoked cigars and wore straw boaters and gave racy interviews to the evening papers on matters of the day; and it was to this grade that our Sammy Ledgard belonged. And now here was his dark blue charabanc, signed, outside the Leeds Poor Children's Holiday Camp Association offices which were housed

4

where they are still housed (though in these euphemistic days the adjective "poor" has long been quietly dropped), in the upper rooms of a humble converted shop quite out of keeping with its grand surroundings – the spanking new Portland stone Civic Hall, the domain of Thos Thornton, Town Clerk & Clerk to the Council; the equally pristine and ultra-modern Brotherton Wing of Leeds Infirmary, in the charge of J. Johnstone Jervis; and, so close across the square that it threw a looming shadow over the pavement where our huddle of pinched-faced refugees blinked and squinted in the morning sunlight, the brooding, soot-black headquarters of Leeds Education Department with the words SCHOOL BOARD etched in the uncompromising stone above a row of tall upper windows from the most imposing of which – the one with the curtains – Geo Guest was doubtless inspecting his ragamuffin charges. All was safe – for those not venturing beyond the city boundaries.

My mother, of course, had escorted me thither, on one of the new streamlined trams that didn't make you sick, known as Lance-corporals because of the chevron adorning their fronts. It was my second tram-car expedition of the week, the other having been on one of the old open-fronted bone-rattlers, plastered with enamelled advertisements for Melbourne Ales and Tizer, that positively did make you sick and whose conductor kept a bag of sawdust under the stairs against that contingency. I had been brought into Town – the city centre was always known as Town, with a vocalised capital T – to acquire the new shoes that now chafed my ankle bones and bruised my toes, even though they were a size too big to allow for my growing into them. We had gone to the Public Benefit Shoe Co. which, despite its imposing fascia and superior location in a popular shopping street (it was just a few doors from the Murder Shop, so-called because "We don't cut prices, we murder 'em"), I imagined, by virtue of its name and the fact that my mother paid for my shoes with a Board of Guardians voucher, to be a charity affair – probably an offshoot of the Boots for the Bairns Fund.

To tell the truth I did not have a great deal of time for the Boots for the Bairns Fund, for all that it was organised by the *Yorkshire Evening Post*, the paper that twelve years later was to employ me, and to which its readers adhered with fierce brand loyalty (the only time its rival, the *Yorkshire Evening News*, came into our house was when it was wrapped round the fish and chips). Earlier in the year, while playing choo-choo trains in the school playground, I had been

5

hauled out of the game by a teacher and in front of all my classmates reprimanded as an ingrate for abusing what she assumed, because it was charity grey in colour, to be a Boots for the Bairns Fund jersey. I was too tongue-tied to explain that we were not Boots for the Bairns clientele, being a family of shoe-wearers. (In the pecking order of our community, shoes were favoured by those who "kept themselves to themselves" and did not frequent the pawnshop. Boots were worn by the rougher element, then came clogs, with plimsolls at the bottom of the social heap. The ragged throng now shuffling on to Sammy Ledgard's charabanc were predominantly plimsoll-wearers.) When I recounted the experience to my mother she was indignant and all for going down to the school. I persuaded her to drop it — she would only have compounded my embarrassment, which was what I had endured rather than humiliation. I do not think humiliation figured much in our lives — it would have been a daily occurrence had we allowed it. Certainly when my best friend Jackie Allerdyce had a birthday party and everyone in our class but me was invited to it, his excuse for my exclusion, namely that his mother had said I was too dirty, seemed to me an altogether reasonable explanation, my only cavil being that there were at least two guests who were dirtier.

Neither did any humiliation attach to assembling outside the Poor Children's Holiday Camp Association with the next-door neighbours' suitcase containing my brother's pyjamas (mine were too patched). It was, anyway, one up on its rival good cause, the Leeds Never Seen The Sea Fund, which boasted that it had despatched "2,000 poor bairns and many tired mothers" to Scarborough. To be accompanied by a tired mother would have been the last straw. It was bad enough being kissed goodbye by one — a rare and fleeting gesture, for we were not a demonstrative family.

This token display of affection signalled the end of one huge adventure — two trips into Town in the same week, two glimpses of the Black Prince on his granite plinth in City Square, surrounded by an improbable coterie of naked bronze nymphs; two glimpses of one of the wonders of the world, the rotating news scanner atop the Majestic Cinema which flashed out the headlines in electric light bulbs: HALFPENNY ON FOUR POUND LOAF — and the beginning of another, for which I had no stomach. No one had consulted me as to where I wished to take my holiday. Had they done so, I would never have opted for fresh air — I should have gone for the fetid air of Leeds, rising in a sulphurous haze over the cloth mills. I had yet to

6

make the acquaintanceship of Wordsworth, but Earth had not anything to show more fair than the view from Leeds Bridge of a swirling palette of factory dye drifting down the River Aire. A daily tram ride into Town, even on one of the rocking street galleons that made you sick, would have been holiday enough for me.

But now we were off, leaving the waving mothers to disperse themselves among the arcades and department stores and pork shops and markets of the busy city. Lucky mothers. We bowled along a western-bound trunk road past civic buildings, suites of Victorian office chambers with gold lettering on their frosted windows, chapels and tabernacles, factories, rows of shops, pubs, terrace-ends, and then there were municipal pebbledash housing estates dispiritingly like my own, and municipal grass.

Even before the Silverdale experience I already had a strong aversion to grass, especially where it had been grown deliberately, as in the pointless verges and roundabouts, big enough to stage the Olympic Games, which were such a feature of the council estates where I was to grow up. It would be a long time before I knew anything about the work of Ebenezer Howard, the garden city pioneer with his vision of "the marriage of town and country" in the ratio of twelve houses to the acre; but what I did know was that so far as I was concerned the experiment didn't work. I was only two years old when we were decanted from the southern fringe of the city, so I could no longer remember having lived anywhere else; but I must have retained an Ur-memory of those sardine-packed mean streets, for so long as I lived in Leeds I was always drawn to them, and my heart always quickened at the sight of a row of red-brick terraces with donkey-stoned steps, and sank at the sight of pebbledash and grass.

The grass was getting serious now. We had left the tramlines behind – I had always understood that you could go all the way from Leeds to Manchester and beyond by tram, with only a fifty-yard walk between the various termini; but perhaps we were going a different route – and we were climbing. This would be the moorland I had heard about, somewhat like the rolling field that led down to the railway lines back home, but more of it. Craning your neck and gazing over the drystone walls you had a tantalising view of crowded rooftops and tall mill chimneys far below – the curlew's-eye image caught by Priestley in the opening pages of *The Good Companions*, the big thick library book I had already had a stab at reading: "The

7

roof of the Midland Railway Station glitters in the sun, and not very far away is another glitter from the glass roof of the Bruddersford Market Hall . . ." There were stifled sniffles as the younger of us thought of our mothers tucking into boiled ham sandwiches and hot sweet tea at the oilcloth-covered tables of Birkbeck's café in the covered Market.

To keep our peckers up as we tilted over the Pennines, one of our accompanying adults, a Rover Scout if ever I saw one, began goading us into singing campfire ditties – "Ten Green Bottles", "They'll be Coming Round the Mountain", and "A Tisket A Tasket" which fizzled out because it was a popular wireless hit so none of the plimsoll-wearers knew the words (no wireless set). Then, from the back of the charabanc, two or three bullet-headed urchins who were evidently old Silverdale hands began to pipe up what I was to learn was our unofficial camp song:

> *There is a happy land, far, far away,*
> *Where they have jam and bread three times a day,*
> *Eggs and bacon they don't see,*
> *They get no sugar in their tea,*
> *Miles from the familee, far, far away.*

I found this so unbearably poignant that my eyes pricked with tears. But I was not homesick, I was Town sick, city sick, street sick. (And twenty years on, I did get the title of my first novel out of that moment.)

The landscape was full of sheep and I longed for bricks and mortar. I was grateful even for a stray cluster of farm buildings; then came a straggle of stone cottages, and then bungalows and semis with bay windows – what we council house dwellers called "bought houses". These heralded our proximity to one of the Lancashire mill towns, and my spirits lifted to see, presently, gasometers, fish and chip saloons, cobbled streets with the trams back where they belonged although in an unfamiliar livery, gabled blank walls painted with advertisements for Bile Beans; but it was only a small town and soon my heart sank again. More grass.

But it was not as desolate as the endless, curlew-circling moors. This was fair-to-decent scrubland, enlivened by gravel pits and cinder heaps and allotments with their attendant shanty towns of lean-to shacks cobbled together out of old doors, railway sleepers, corrugated iron and tarpaulin. It was semi-urban, and after a few miles I began cautiously to warm to it as even now I warm to a car dump in some interminable tract of natural beauty.

Not for long. Soon we were among potato fields, getting on for real countryside, and then forlorn acres of reeds, relieved only by the friendly pylons, and then by a cheerful settlement of caravans; and then there was the sea, as grey as zinc. It was not the sea as I understood it. I had seen the proper sea – I had been taken by my Uncle Edward and Auntie Orrie in their little Singer four-seater with the celluloid windows to Bridlington, where the proper sea, pea-green, had been alive with pleasure boats and there had been donkeys and ice-cream carts on the beach, and the shore had been lined with amusement arcades and funfairs and Crazy Golf. Not here. This was Silverdale.

Had I possessed any knowledge of prisoner-of-war camps – all I knew on the subject was that my father had spent most of the Great War in one, where he had been fed on black bread, which from my mother's hushed tones when she recounted this oft-told tale I took to be a vicious Hun punishment diet – I should have made the comparison with Silverdale. A collection, at that time, of connecting wooden huts – dormitories, refectory, ablutions and recreation hall (wet weather only) – with colonial-looking verandahs, it had the air of being surrounded by barbed wire, although that may be a detail I have invented. Certainly it would have been a difficult establishment to break out of. Ahead, across the ubiquitous grass, was a sheer drop down to the sands on the scale, to a seven-year-old, of Beachy Head. Behind was the hut settlement, patrolled by a sergeant-majorly Warden. On either side were boggy-looking fields containing animals – sheep, goats and horses. The Association's publicity material has always played up the enchantment in store for back-street waifs setting eyes on cattle for the first time; all I can say on behalf of our intake is that we steered well clear of all these four-footed enemies, apart from feeding lumps of coke to the goats.

I must not be hard on Silverdale, which is remembered with affection by generations, and is still looked forward to by children who would otherwise never get a holiday. But it was no place for misfits, loners or urban agoraphobics, and I fell into all three categories.

The Warden saw it as his mission to send his whey-faced, rickets-riddled charges home as brown as nuts and filled with as many cubic feet of fresh air as their little lungs could accommodate. Skulking indoors was therefore discouraged. One day, tiptoeing into the deserted recreation hall with its school gymnasium smell of lavender Mansion polish and a linoleum floor you could ice-skate on, I discovered a locked, glass-fronted bookcase, crammed with thick, embossed editions of *The Fifth Form at St Dominic's*, *The Last of the Mohicans* and the like. The Warden arriving to flush me out into the open air, I made so bold as to ask if I might borrow a book. He was genuinely baffled. It wasn't raining, he explained, as to an idiot. Books were for bad weather.

There was no bad weather. The sun beat down remorselessly for the full fourteen days, and I thought longingly of tar bubbles, the Stop-me-and-buy-one man, and the echoing, white-tiled corporation swimming baths. The camp being full of boys — I imagine the girls took up occupation on alternate fortnights — the days were spent in boyish pursuits such as cricket, rounders, birds' nesting and splashing about in the sea; but so long as you were getting your quota of fresh air and sunshine, nobody seemed to mind if you involved yourself in these activities or not. I took to spending most of my time mooning around on the cliff edge, gazing across the bay to where distant Morecambe shimmered like a mirage in the summer haze. I could see the promenade, the pier, tall white wedding-cake buildings, a helter-skelter — an edifice previously sighted only in the pages of the *Film Fun* comic — and buses like Dinky toys.

Or so I now imagine. Maybe I could see very little at all, and this elusive Mecca on the far horizon was what I fervently wished to see. What I do remember is that late one night when I got up to spend a penny I crept out on to the verandah and behold, the sky across the bay was ablaze with a dancing aurora borealis of red neon, and in the forefront was a wide arc of fairy lights twinkling like an illuminated necklace. I stared at this vision, mesmerised, until I began to shiver in the chill night air, when I went to bed and dreamed of the enchanting prospect of my once and future city, so accessible yet so tantalisingly out of reach.

That became a recurrent dream, and I have been experiencing it regularly ever since, for over fifty years, but with a difference. I am still there on the Silverdale clifftop but that is no longer Morecambe across the bay. I have outgrown Morecambe. My Mecca on the opposite side of Morecambe Bay has become an amalgamation, an accumulation, of all the cities I have come to know and love.

10

Shimmering there in the heat haze are the Chrysler Building from New York, the Sears Tower from Chicago, the Sydney Opera House, the Galleria Vittorio Emanuele II from Milan, the Boulevard du Montparnasse, the Piazza san Marco, the Tivoli Gardens, the Savoy . . . a jostling architectural cornucopia linked to my side of the bay by the Golden Gate Bridge.

But the bridge is too high up: from my perch on the clifftop its near view looks like the towering underside of the Brooklyn Bridge. I can't reach it, can't get up to the Golden Gate Bridge to cross to my golden city.

2   This was by no means the first time I had stayed away from home. There had been the Bridlington jaunt with Uncle Edward and Auntie Orrie, when I had been brought along as company for my contemporary, Cousin Jeffrey – and also, I dare say, because like whichever acolyte of Geo Guest had entered my name for Silverdale, my Auntie Orrie – Oriel, my mother's sister – had divined that with my peaky face and skeletal limbs I could do with a holiday. We stayed in a rented caravan at Flamborough Head, hard by the lighthouse, where any prospective resemblance to the Silverdale clifftop was relieved by the wafting stench of fish and chips and mushy peas from the stall across the cinder track, the reassuring, richocheting rat-a-tat of a tin-roofed pintable arcade, and the proximity of the lights of Bridlington, only twenty petrol-fumed minutes away in the Singer saloon with the celluloid windows.

And then there had been St James's Hospital.

When I was about three a great craze for circumcision swept our neighbourhood, probably instigated by Dr Sugare, our exotic, faintly mysterious half-Indian panel doctor who, practising from the front room of a privet-hedged council house next to the Thrift Stores, brought a whiff of the Orient to our humdrum estate. Acting upon advice from Dr Sugare, although I did not at the time see the connection, my mother one day told me that she was taking me into Town to see Mickey Mouse.

I was already well acquainted with Mickey Mouse, having been taken by my sister to a fleapit cinema nestling among my beloved terraces, called the Rex, to see a Walt Disney Silly Symphony, and later to a so-called "bug-hutch", the Pavilion in the same neighbourhood (our own super-cinema, the Tivoli – pronounced to rhyme with Jolly – was, with its ancillary Chocolate Cabin, still being built) where Mickey Mouse was also appearing, together with Laurel and Hardy and a cowboy, probably Tom Mix.

13

I had cracked the miracle of cinematography to my satisfaction by much the same logic as I had used, at the age of two and a half, to work out the principles of aviation. In August 1931 the German airship *Graf Zeppelin*, looking like a great discoloured cucumber, caused a sensation by flying over Leeds. Even more sensationally, it floated over our house in Middleton Park Grove where I was in the back garden, digging a hole to Australia. Somewhere around that time, too, there was an air display of sorts on the big clearing in the middle of the Murder Woods, as Middleton Park Woods had been known ever since the dismembered body of a young woman, distributed in sacks, had been found among the bluebells. As I watched a bright yellow Tiger Moth take off and loop the loop, I was interested to observe that the higher it went up, the smaller it got. The same principle applied to the *Graf Zeppelin*. It did not take me long to work out the explanation. There was, I reasoned, something in the atmosphere, a gas or mysterious impulse like gravity, that caused aircraft to diminish in size, together with their passengers, once they were off the ground. This Tom Thumb process helped these hitherto top-heavy machines and their personnel to stay up in the air. As they descended, they passed out of this sphere of influence and reverted to their normal size.

Cinematography was altogether a simpler and much less phenomenal process. The screen consisted of a giant magnifying glass in front of which these characters, Laurel and Hardy, Tom Mix and Mickey Mouse – a man in costume – would perform. When they were in close-up they were in fact very close up to the magnifying screen, and kneeling down. Tom Mix's horse was on a conveyer belt, with the scenery behind them on a roller (little did I realise that I had invented back projection). As to how the whole pack of them came to be appearing at five cinemas simultaneously, it was obvious that they flitted from one venue to another just as, so my mother had told me, Nellie Wallace and the old music-hall comics used to do. I could see a cinema manager raising his bowler hat to Mr Laurel and Mr Hardy as he tapped on the door of their dressing room at the Rex. "Excuse me, gentlemen, but since you're in the district, I wonder if you'd care to oblige my colleagues at the Pavilion, the Gem, the Crescent, and the People's Picture Palace? There will be something in it for you, of course."

Only one aspect of this latest cinematic expedition gave me cause for concern, and that was the possibility of the MGM lion escaping from the travelling cage in which he was transported from cinema to cinema, or worse still bursting through the screen and eating my mother. Otherwise it was with a jaunty step that I set off for the tram stop, trustingly clutching my mother's hand.

I was enthralled. The journey involved not one tram ride but two – the No. 12 Lance-corporal from Middleton up past the Black Prince and his attendant nymphs plus the magic Majestic news scanner, then the No. 11 bone-rattler from the glass-roofed tram shelters opposite the Corn Exchange, above which, over a brightly lit oyster bar, gleamed an enormous sign for Bovril, its letters picked out in white electric light bulbs that flickered on and off. I had no theories about this phenomenon other than that there must be a man sitting in a little room behind the sign, flicking the light switch on and off all day long.

Mickey Mouse was a long time coming but even as we reached the gates of St James's Hospital I did not realise that I was the victim of a hoax, for all that I had visited St James's before, and in distressing circumstances. Only a few months earlier my father had died there, probably from residual war wounds, aged forty-nine. I keenly recalled the event of his death. Leaving me in the care of my Auntie Lizzie, my mother and sister had gone to see him, perhaps in response to one of the hospital bulletins which in those telephoneless days appeared daily in the evening papers – "Dangerously ill 361; Poorly but making satisfactory progress 393 196 412" etc. My sister came running down the street with the tearful news, "Me dad's dead, me dad's dead!" It was the first time I had ever seen my sister cry and so, in my childish incomprehension of the situation, I pointed a triumphant finger at her and chortled, in the local vernacular of the time, "Hoo-hoo, our lass is roaring!", whereupon my Auntie Lizzie, who was my father's sister, fetched me a resounding clip over the ear. Aunties were supposed to be kindly souls who gave you sweets and money; they were certainly not entitled to strike you and I was filled with burning resentment. I went out into the back garden and continued digging to Australia.

That I remembered, and also my mother coming home with my father's brown suit, from the pockets of which she unearthed a halfpenny, his total estate, which passed to me; but I did not remember the hospital.

St James's, now St James's University Hospital and known to television audiences as Jimmy's, was then a grim-looking edifice, formerly the Union Workhouse, and it is difficult to see with hindsight how even at that tender age I could possibly have mistaken it for a cinema. All I can say in mitigation is that the fifty-odd picture palaces of Leeds came in all shapes and sizes, from tin shacks and former miners' institutes which accepted jam jars as payment, to the de luxe super-cinemas with their Wurlitzer organs. There was a cinema, St Patrick's, in a converted church; another, the Gem, under the railway arches. Why should not the gaunt yet imposing frontage of St James's house a cinema too, bigger even than the Paramount?

Even I cannot have mistaken the children's ward for an auditorium but I do recall being assured by the nurse to whom I was delivered up that I was indeed going to the theatre — a wicked play on words, for of course she meant the operating theatre. I am happy to say that upon waking up later back in the ward, the deed done, I promptly wet the bed, when I was bundled off into a freezing bath. Upon my complaining about the icy cold water the same nurse retorted smugly, "That's what you get for wetting your bed." Had she been more of a psychologist she might have troubled to explain that the only reason the water was cold, as I did not realise for years, was that at that hour all the hot water had been run off the boilers.

All in all the St James's episode should have been a deeply traumatic experience, yet while in later childhood I did develop, for a while, a mild fear that our house and everyone in it would disappear off the face of the Earth while I was at infants' school, I do not believe any lasting harm was done. Indeed, once the operation was over and done with, my stay in hospital was hugely enjoyable. We had dorm feasts like the ones I was to read about in public school stories when I was old enough to join the library, and every day the paper seller would come round with the latest comics. Although I was not myself in funds I did manage to borrow from an extraordinarily kind and apparently wealthy older boy — the organiser of the midnight tuck-ins who spoke with what I took to be an upper-class accent, which is probably to say that he pronounced the occasional aitch — all the exciting twopenny coloured comics like *Rainbow*, *Bubbles* and *Tiger Tim's Weekly* that had always been outside our household's price range.

But the real pleasure of St James's was that we were snugly cocooned in what no one had yet learned to call the inner city. All day I could hear the clanging of the trams and at night the shunting of trains from the nearby marshalling yards, and in the small hours the parish church clock chiming, and in the morning the clatter of horses' hooves, the rumble of wagons and lorries, the distant street cries from the Market, the droning trams again, the factory hooters, the clanking of brewers' drays delivering their crates and barrels, the small thunder of cattle on their way to the slaughterhouse, the revving-up of buses, the shouts of the newsvendors, the voices of workmates exchanging banter, the bolting back of doors, the whistling of porters and errand boys, the rat-a-tat of postmen, the far-off tinkling of the arcade carillons, and all the instruments of the city, brass, strings, timpani and woodwind that gradually orchestrated themselves into the concerto of the day-long hubbub.

3 And even from the earliest age I was no stranger to the city. One of the only two memories I have of my father is of being scooped out of bed in the middle of the night (it would have been about five in the morning, adult time), swaddled in a potato-sack and jogged through the sweating cobbled streets to the wholesale Market on the back of his horse and cart. (The other is of him standing magisterially astride the fireplace, like God in a brown suit, while my sister badgered him for her Saturday penny. He dug deep into his pocket and flung a handful of coins across the room – an upturned cornucopia of pennies, threepenny bits, sixpences, shillings, florins, even a half-crown or two. As we scrambled for the treasure I thought what a wonderfully mad, larger-than-life gesture; but I saw that my mother was not impressed, and she impounded the lot as housekeeping money. It was not until I reached the maturity of six or seven that I guessed, from guarded remarks, that he must have drunk a lot.)

My father, Ernest by name, was a costermonger, selling fruit, veg and unskinned rabbits from a horse and cart all over south Leeds. His interest in the trade must have come from his mother Sarah, who despite being unable to read or write had run a greengrocer's shop among the back-to-backs of Hunslet. His father Henry and grandfather Job were cloth fullers – that is, engaged in the thickening of raw cloth as it was pulled through rollers lubricated by troughs of stale urine (their own) – probably at Armley Mills, then the world's largest woollen mill and now a prestigious industrial museum.

Neither Job nor his wife could read or write either (although Job's cross on the marriage certificate is altogether more dashing than bride Elizabeth's). Illiteracy, indeed, seems to have run on both sides of the family. My maternal grandfather, a colliery labourer living all his life in Bolsover near Chesterfield, reached the age of ninety-five

19

without being able even to sign his name. After the death of my grandmother, my mother kept in touch with him by sending him, each week, a self-addressed stamped envelope which he would promptly post back to her. When one week he neglected to return the envelope − he had stuck a gardening fork in his foot and developed gangrene − she put on her coat, took the train down to Chesterfield, and buried him.

From the tales told about him, my father, born 1884, had led something of an adventurous life. He joined the King's Own Yorkshire Light Infantry as a boy soldier and saw service in India before being bought out by his mother. He seems to have called himself an engineer at one point − he is so described on the marriage certificate − but that probably means only that he was a machine hand for one of the many Leeds engineering companies. With the outbreak of the 1914−18 war he was recalled to the colours, wounded and taken prisoner at Mons, and escaped twice from German POW camps, on the second attempt nearly reaching the Belgian border before he was recaptured. After his death I used often to look at his Mons Star, a campaign medal which I believed was an award for valour only a little below the Victoria Cross. We had some bound volumes of the *Vivid War Weekly* and I would pore over them looking for a picture of my father among the gruesome battle scenes, and reading over and over again the legend of the Angel of Mons and how the filthy Huns were supposed to have tied nuns by the heels to the bellropes of the cathedral and used them as human clappers.

But just now Father in his brown suit and his shock of iron-grey hair, too unruly to accommodate the cloth cap of his calling, was still very much with us and here we were bowling into Town on a cart painted like a fairground carousel by the dawn's early light.

Father gave employment to at least three horses in his time, or "Gallawas" as he apparently always called them, from a tradition that the best Yorkshire and Lancashire pack horses were bred in Galloway, south-west Scotland: a bomb-happy ex-army nag which would shy and bolt at any loud noise; Peter, who would not budge from the kerb until fed with two of mother's home-made buns, but who when bored with waiting would find his own way home from the most distant pub; and Tommy, stabled in the field that ran down to the railway lines where it was my brothers' pre-breakfast task to catch him, who took life at the trot. This must have been Tommy for it was at a spanking pace that we approached Kirkgate Market, as the covered Market, retail and wholesale, is properly named, although it has always been universally known simply as "t'Market".

"Aladdin's Cave" is now an expression usually applied to the clearing-house of burglars, but at that time it still had its fairytale connotations as exemplified by the lavish scenery and glittering props of the Leeds Grand Theatre pantomime; and while I had yet to see a panto I did know Aladdin's Cave when I saw it and this, as we rode into its depths under a high wide iron arch, was out of the story books. All was light and dazzle and noise and the Christmas smell of oranges. In those disorganised days the wholesale and retail markets were all of a cheek-by-jowl jumble so that around the corner from the potato merchants' stockpile of King Edwards, as high as slag heaps it seemed, was Game Row with its multi-tiered racks of poultry, and across from the wholesalers' pyramids of apples was Pets' Row where budgerigars tweeted and canaries sang sweetly, and there were rabbits to feed with cabbage leaves rescued from underfoot. Granelli's sarsaparilla stall must have been somewhere near at hand but for me it was a beaker of milky cocoa and a doorstep of bread and dripping from the wooden-sided workmen's café, pushed into my hands by a gentle giant in a stained white overall and a straw boater.

I was to roam the Market times without number in my childhood and youth and have never subsequently visited Leeds without making the pilgrimage to these domed and turreted halls of plenty with their glazed brick walls, ornate balconies embellished with cast-iron dragons, and Corinthian columns adorned with the city's coat of arms (what appears to be a dead sheep, although it is in reality a fleece, between a pair of owls), supporting a glittering glass roof. Yet whenever I think of Kirkgate Market I see in my mind's eye what was indelibly stamped on it by that first confused and dreamlike impression – a shimmering crazy-mirror montage of burnished scales, brass weights, marble slabs, naptha lamps, mountains of pomegranates, horses' breath, billy-cans, iron-clad wheels, squashed blood oranges, and big men with pencil stubs behind their ears shouting the price of carrots. My father's cart piled high with replenished produce, I rode home on top of a sack of Brussels sprouts still nibbling my wedge of bread and dripping and feeling, as we passed out into the awakening streets, that I had been in a grotto, the personal guest of a wizard.

It was that dawn outing to the Market, I would guess, when I was less than the height of a cart wheel, that awoke in me my lifelong love affair with cities. It was theatre, it was the circus come to town, it was promise, it was enfolding warmth, it was light brighter than the Bovril sign, it was life. I was home where I belonged.

4   I was an only child, the youngest of five.

My brother Kenneth was the eldest, my senior by ten years. Then, over a seven-year span, came Stella, Dennis and Stanley. I was an afterthought, or perhaps an accident, three years later. Accordingly I was the lone one of the family, the odd boy out. Because of the age gap I did not get to play much with my brothers who understandably did not want a snivelling moppet (I had a head of ash-blond Fauntleroy curls) traipsing after them on their secret expeditions to relieve the Clerk of Works' compound of a handful of nails and staples, or to chomp the rhubarb growing in forbidden fields (Leeds was, and is, the rhubarb capital of the universe).

Besides, from my perspective they were adults. At twelve or thirteen Kenneth seemed a grown man. Indeed, at the age of fourteen upon leaving school, a grown man he perforce became: we had fallen on hard times by then and Kenneth, working for the tailoring firm of Sumpter & Barge, was the sole breadwinner. To mark his first day at work my mother determined to give him a proper workman's tea. The only funds in the house consisted of a three-halfpenny stamp, so the rest of the family were despatched to the post office to sell it back. We bought a tin of sardines with the proceeds and clustered round the scullery table to watch our grown-up brother make short work of it.

I was born at No. 17 Low Road next to the receiving office for Beeston Laundry and two doors from the Hunslet Baptist Tabernacle. Low Road, now largely urban desert, was one of the tram-rattling arteries running from the city centre, all of them lively thoroughfares lined with ironmongers' shops, newsagents and tobacconists, small grocers, family butchers, fish and chip shops, pawnshops, public houses without number, breweries, foundries, obscure little factories and workshops, and countless sooty red-brick terraces which stemmed off the main road on either side like herring bones.

Because of Low Road's position between the Aire and Calder Navigation and the railway lines, and its generally insalubrious reputation, I grew into adolescence imagining that I must have been born in one of the city's notorious back-to-backs (mean little terraces backing on to a common spinal wall to save the cost of bricks and the space consumed by an alley), and that it was as victims of the slum clearance scheme that we had been deported to Middleton "housing scheme" as council estates used to be called. Seemingly not. The family's older hands recall that 17 Low Road had been the residence of a doctor. It was a double-fronted house backing on to the Nelson pub cricket ground, with rooms to spare in which my mother had gas meters installed with a view to taking in lodgers. There was even a playroom — the former surgery — and a large walled garden where for some unfathomable reason my father chose to keep a donkey. It had evidently been a seaside donkey since it would give us rides to the bottom of the garden, but not back again.

It would have been pleasant to have grown up at No. 17 but the property stood in the way of a road-widening scheme — Leeds in the early thirties was a veritable beehive of civic works — and so to Middleton we went. There we lived until I was nine. I do not know what the council thought it was about, since it had only lately launched a vigorous programme against overcrowding, for No. 41 Middleton Park Grove was far too small for us and I had to sleep three in a bed with my brothers Dennis and Stanley, sandwiched between them.

Although we always called No. 41 a house, and it boasted front and back gardens and a privet hedge, it was in fact a ground floor flat, one of a block of four built to a pattern then popular with our multi-initialled Housing Director R.A.H. Livett ARIBA, in cunning imitation of a pair of semi-detached houses. The respectability lent by the style of architecture was largely negated by the type of tenant, many of whom came from the bona fide slums of Hunslet and Holbeck. They included a drunken ex-miner whose enraged post-pub cries of "Who's in bed with his boots on?" and "Which of you's put rabbit bones under t' pillow?" were widely imitated; and a slummocking family of plimsoll-wearers who put us to shame by necessitating our evacuation from the block while it was "stoved" — fumigated — for bed-bugs. Another family was evicted for non-payment of rent and lived for a while on the pavement, in a tent made from a clothes-horse draped with blankets.

Upstairs from us was an enormous family of tuberculosis sufferers who, one by one, were carried off to the sanitorium with the regularity of Brontës. "Galloping consumption", as it was known, was common in the neighbourhood, as was rickets (I nursed a secret desire to have my leg clamped in iron callipers, which to me at least had the glamour of a sling or eye patch). These were, after all, the Hungry Thirties. If the inhabitants of No. 41 were not yet hungry, it was because my father brought home the rabbits and pomegranates he could not sell.

Our turn was to come. Shortly before his death my father, a man of somewhat grandiose dreams by all accounts, much given to saying "When my ship comes in . . .", borrowed some money either with the idea of expanding his business from one horse and cart to two horses and carts, or – another theory – of setting himself up as the Cucumber King of Kirkgate Market. Neither enterprise materialised and no one knows what happened to the money, except that he did like a drink and his interest in horses extended beyond those which pulled fruit and veg carts for a living. At any rate, after he died penniless – his last words, according to my mother, being "My ship's come in" – the bailiffs arrived and took away all the furniture except the mattresses and a stool for my mother to sit on. There was no war pension. He had forfeited it by omitting to wear a surgical belt at an army medical for the war-wounded. We were in the hands of the Board of Guardians.

I vaguely, though by no means vividly, remember there being nowhere to sit down except on the bare floorboards. My mother nevertheless always seemed to be receiving visitors – welfare agents of one kind or another, who came into the house without knocking, examining the rent book and other documents that were kept with Father's Mons Star in a biscuit tin, and shining torches into the bed linen. One of them was the Means Test man who ordered my mother to sell her few remaining possessions, including a pair of electro-plated fairground vases, known proudly as "the ornaments", which I always imagined to be silver. Instead of selling them – she would have died rather than go into the pawnshop – she hid them under the coal. This I thought quite a lark.

Another survivor was a handsome harp zither which my father had bought on the instalment plan from a man at the door. Although I loved to play with it, and could pick out tunes from the time I was three, the harp zither was barred to me in case the Means Test man returned, and hidden away in the airing cupboard. There being little else in the denuded household to detain a small boy, I turned to outdoor pursuits: the digging of my hole to Australia in the back garden, and expeditions, a fixation with me ever since I had been strong enough to work the iron catch of the garden gate.

The simple object of these expeditions was to see how far I could get before the search party caught up with me. I had no idea where I was going, for the very good reason that I had no idea where I was: Middleton might have been at the North Pole for all I knew. Yet although I could have set off in any of a dozen directions I was always magnetically drawn to but two alternative areas of exploration – the Murder Woods or the park.

The Murder Woods route was a straightforward matter of following the tram track which cut through them – just as all roads lead to Rome I knew that all tramlines led to Town, to the Black Prince, the Majestic Cinema electric news scanner, and the Bovril sign. As for the park, that did not in itself much interest me, apart from the boating lake where in the snowy winter I tried to launch myself on a floating piece of ice and all but drowned. But at the far side of the park, at the end of a creepy-looking lane through the rhododendron bushes, was a storm drain through which a four-year-old of slight build could easily wander. It led out into a new housing development, at which point I was usually rounded up by my breathless pursuers.

Since one council housing estate looks much like another, I had no particular interest in this neighbourhood beyond the storm drain and could not explain to my exasperated mother why I was so inexplicably drawn to it, like Alice going down the rabbit hole. It was not until I was old enough to wander off by myself with parental approval or anyway lack of active disapproval, and I had formed the Middleton Hiking Club (membership: one) that I realised, as the circumference of my explorations got wider and wider, where I had invariably been heading.

Like a cat finding its way back to its old home across miles of unfamiliar countryside, I was making unerringly for a long straight thoroughfare called Balm Road which led across the railway to Hunslet, the terraces, and No. 17 Low Road.

5 Had they survived, the proceedings of the Middleton Hiking Club, meticulously entered in a penny notebook, would have shown that while the club's membership remained static, the sphere of its activities expanded. The club's aims were to see what was around the next corner or beyond the near horizon, a mission that led me farther and farther afield.

The club would meet either on Saturday morning or immediately after Sunday midday dinner, when I would roam until driven home by hunger. Thirst was never a problem: under a far-ranging unwritten constitution governing the care and protection of Leeds minors, every child was entitled to knock on any door and request a cup of water. If you were lucky, you might get a glass of Tizer ("the Appetiser") instead.

As with my unauthorised earlier ramblings, these journeys usually began either at the park or the Murder Woods − or, presently, both: for one serendipity-touched Sunday in the search for a new route out of the park after finding my storm drain about a foot deep in rainwater, and descending a grassy valley I had never known was there, I stumbled across the pit wheels and waste tips of Middleton Colliery on the northern fringe of the park. I had never been so close to a coal mine before, although I knew that seams ran under the whole of Middleton, and the earliest sound of the day, before even the blackbird, was the clomping of miners' clogs. I drank in the sight of the old brick sheds, the chimneys, the winding gear, the washing-line of overhead tip-up tubs like a fairground ride, the cartloads of pit props, the cogs and cranks of ancient machinery, all but the steam pumps idle on a Sunday, and marvelled that below my feet when the pit cage rattled down again tomorrow morning, neighbours of ours would be burrowing beneath the rhododendron bushes and rolling lawns of Middleton Park.

I was almost as fascinated by the railway lines that carried the old

Puffing Billy steam engine that pulled the trucks that carried the coal. I knew enough of our local history — everybody did: it was passed on by your parents, long before you got the official version at school — to be aware that this was probably, after its fashion, the first steam traction railway system in the country if not in the world, certainly the first to be established by Act of Parliament. It was the Industrial Revolution I was looking at here, and while Middleton Colliery and its coal railroad were still and silent on this butterfly-fluttering Sunday afternoon, and while I knew little about the Industrial Revolution beyond the story of James Watt and his steaming kettle, it was in my bones and I could smell the cindery excitement of it.

I decided to follow the railway lines and see where they took me. Where they went, I was to discover, was through the Murder Woods, emerging in a donkey-grazing scrubland area of Hunslet known as Parkside, home of the greyhound stadium and the Hunslet Rugby League ground; then over an acre or so of flattened cinders known as Hunslet Moor, where a great fair — Hunslet Feast — was held every August Bank Holiday; and via a succession of viaducts, cuttings and tunnels above and below and beneath the high mill walls, to the coal barges on the River Aire and the Leeds and Liverpool Canal.

I half recognised the district from my occasional tram rides into Town — the tramlines and the railway lines crossed at Parkside, and now I remembered the coal train waiting for our tram to pass, steam evidently giving way to electric — and from the annual family visit, a keenly anticipated compulsory ritual, to Hunslet Feast.

I could confirm at once my previous fleeting impression that here was a neighbourhood of great liveliness. Even on a Sunday afternoon when just about everything was closed, there were still people abroad, chatting at street corners or in doorways, looking in shop windows, waiting at tram stops or drifting towards Hunslet Moor for a constitutional around the cinders. The dingy streets were made even livelier by their richness in what conservationists now call street furniture — public clocks; shop signs suspended from wrought-iron brackets; glass pavement canopies; white blinds painted with the names of grocers, chemists and drapers; barbers' poles; iron bollards; newspaper placards and lurid cinema posters, and enamelled advertisements for Mazawattee Tea and Bisto, and the names of Turog and Hovis picked out in golden letters over the bakers' shops, and every blank wall plastered with fly-posters or painted with huge slogans — "Uncle Joe's Mint Balls. They Keep You All Aglow"; and a medley of overhanging lamps and pub signs, horse troughs, statues of benefactors, public lavatories resembling family tombs, and, surpassing all, a great ornamental drinking fountain to rival the Albert Memorial.

Whenever I glance at those Then and Now photographs comparing the way a particular locality looks now with the way it looked thirty or forty or fifty years ago, the modern picture always looks sadly barren, stripped as it almost invariably is of all the features that gave the streets their colour, all the details that have been tidied up and planned out of existence. And denuded, too, of people: it did not take much precocious perception on the part of the sole member of the Middleton Hiking Club to divine that it was the environmentally busy air of Hunslet that gave the place its vitality, and that drew the people into the streets.

Not that we lacked for street life in Middleton Park Grove. While separated from the soot and grime of industrial Leeds by a *cordon sanitaire* of trees and greenery, we were townies by nature, children of the terraces from which we sprang. Accordingly, although there were fields in plenty a mere two minutes' walk away, nobody ever played in them. Cricket was a street game, with the lamppost as wicket. Football was played down the middle of the road with heaps of pullovers for goalposts, just as it had been in the cobbled past. Hide and seek — "hiddy" — and Relieve-oh were played not in the nearby woods where there was ample scope for concealment, but through a trampled series of back gardens, which were regarded, at any rate by us, as the public domain. Our territory for street activities extended between one so-called "opening" — a street turning — and another, beyond which it was not done to venture. Was it by coincidence that this stretch was the length of the average Hunslet terrace?

Nor was our street life by any means all our own creation. Lacking corner shops (although one enterprising woman did illicitly sell small grocery items from her sideboard drawer, this venture being known as "the house shop") we probably had more pedlars and itinerant traders than Hunslet and Holbeck where no one was more than a hundred yards away from the shops.

Not a day went by without a handbell, a street cry or a knock on the door announcing the presence of, say, the fried fish man, the pea and pie man, the firewood man, the bread man, the pop man who dispensed lemonade (and for some reason slabs of pork dripping) on Sunday mornings, the gypsies hawking clothes pegs and lavender, the scissors grinder, the chair mender, the Indian herbal medicine man, the legitimate ice-cream man (Walls's stop-me-and-buy-one) and the non-legitimate ice-cream man (a cupful of ice-cream, a villainous yellow in hue, for a halfpenny, manufactured in a corrugated iron shack in the vendor's back yard), the roundabout man who gave rides on a mobile carousel in exchange for jam jars, the tingle-airy man with his barrel organ and attendant monkey; and even a muffin man, or more accurately a pikelet man, who true to tradition carried his basket on his head.

The most venerable of all our street hawkers was the Tea Man, a walking bazaar, a one-man Woolworth's, who would stand patiently on the doorstep, a heavy tray slung from his shoulders by thick canvas straps, while his customers browsed among his display of pins and needles, razor blades, press studs, bobbins of cotton, bootlaces, hair slides, tapes and ribbons. Whatever he didn't have he would fetch the next week, committing effortlessly to memory a hundred tiny orders for combs and collar studs, cards of elastic and gramophone needles. The one thing the Tea Man did not dispense was tea — this was delivered each Saturday by the firm of Rington's in a shiny green brougham drawn by a smart black horse with plumes, a ritual on a ceremonial par for us with the Changing of the Guard.

Yet despite all these comings and goings the street never felt properly alive. This was to no small degree down to the dead hand of the council estate architect who in common with most of his brethren had not only placed an obsessional stress on aimless breathing space but, with a view to relieving the dullness of his own design, had garnished the development with an entirely pointless and ultimately dreary series of curves and crescents following no known contours. A simple grid would have done it. But mainly, the problem was that there was little to do in Middleton except live there.

It would be years before Jane Jacobs wrote *The Death and Life of Great American Cities* but while I could not have articulated her principles I had already, from my meanderings around Hunslet, an instinctive understanding of what she would be driving at — that what gives a neighbourhood the vibrancy that my council housing estate almost completely lacked was what planners disparagingly call "mixed use". Hunslet had mixed use in abundance. "Housing", to use another planning expression, was but one ingredient, if a major one, of a rich mixture which, with its accompanying mishmash of street ornamentation, included small factories and great foundries, shops, warehouses, offices, schools, swimming baths and wash houses, public libraries, churches, chapels and mission halls, pubs, recreation grounds, coke dumps, scrap yards, coal staithes, police stations, fire stations, cinemas, billiard halls, cemeteries, railway shunting yards, dog racing tracks, football grounds, breweries, workmen's cafés, savings banks, temperance hotels, garages, stables, hairdressing salons, gasworks, Territorial Army barracks, tailoring establishments, steam laundries, allotments and even a smallholding or two with pigs and hens, all within the same crowded square mile.

While delighted to have discovered Hunslet, I was puzzled as to how it was possible to set off in precisely opposite directions – the storm drain at the edge of the park, and the railway line through the Murder Woods – and arrive at the same place. Putting the solution down to the curvature of the Earth, I set about exploring the parish where I was born, originally with the intention of locating No. 17 Low Road. That proving elusive from this particular end of Hunslet, and it never occurring to me to acquire or at least consult a map, I abandoned my mission after one or two tries and took to rambling about the district more or less aimlessly, always relying on the tramlines to guide me home again.

Curiously for one who from infancy was determined never to work in one, come what may (despite the assertion of Jackie Allerdyce's mother, I had an aversion to getting dirty), I discovered that I had an affinity with factories, of which there was a profusion in Hunslet and its environs, ranging from the Yorkshire Relish works at one end of my perambulations to the Hunslet Printing Sheds at the other. Leeds at that time was known, or claimed to be known, as the City of a Thousand Trades, and most of them seemed to be represented in Hunslet. Many of them were nook-and-cranny businesses crammed into small yards or down narrow alleys or "ginnels": organ builders, oyster merchants, penholder manufacturers, shroud makers, coffin makers, Welsh slate merchants, skin factors, horse harness dealers, blacksmiths, lard refiners, lamp dealers, a Berlin Wool depository, in what was itself a depository of now long-lost trades.

In contrast to these back-street enterprises were the great set-piece mills and factories, sturdy and substantial and standing out like steel engravings against the sulphurous yellow sky: Thwaite Mills; the chemical works; the sweet-smelling coffee works; the fireclay and brick works; Hudswell Clarke's Railway Foundry, shipping locomotives to the Argentine and every dominion in the Empire; a nail mill; a soap factory; Alf Cooke's mighty Printing Works where I would often linger, already savouring and unaccountably excited by the smell of printer's ink; and Marshall's Mill, an exact replica of one of the temples of the Nile, on whose grass-covered roof sheep were supposed to graze, although I never saw them doing so nor solved the mystery of how they got up there in the first place.

Probably from my search for overhead sheep, I learned early Gropius's dictum that one must always gaze up to a building's roof level; and it was there above their frowning porticos that I would find the names of these great industrial dynasties chiselled in the stone, as if they expected to be there for ever.

The same air of permanence attached to the shops, whose monograms or colophons would be picked out in polished granite mosaic in their recessed doorways, and whose elaborate fascias – tiled representations of farmyard scenes for the butcher's and the dairy, sober varnish and deeply etched lettering in gold for the chemist's – were integral to the fabric rather than a glued-on afterthought. The tram-cars droned by and it all looked as if everything would still be the same in a hundred years' time. The motorway cuts through Hunslet now.

I gradually got to know these streets of the Leeds 10 postal district well, and to me their names were as romantic as that of the Silk Road to Samarkand (which I was to travel less than twenty years later). Meadow Lane, South Accommodation Road, Pepper Road, Sweet Street, Balm Road, Beza Street, Joseph Street . . . and at last I stumbled upon Low Road, only to find No. 17 and its neighbours demolished. The Hunslet Baptist Tabernacle, miraculously, was still standing, and I put this down to a mysterious rubric on the wall, "Ancient Lights", which I imagined protected it from the wrecker's ball. (Even more miraculously, the Tabernacle stands to this day, although by now, surrounded by fresh air, it has all the Ancient Lights it could possibly desire.)

I discovered that Low Road, as it pursued the No. 25 tram route into Town, became Hunslet Road; and Hunslet Road, a lively two-mile strip of small shops, took me past Joshua Tetley's Brewery with its magnificent shire dray horses (another survival) to Leeds Bridge, where Town began.

Now that I had located it, I rarely ventured beyond this point. The city bustle was different from the Hunslet bustle: it was a cash-register-ringing, mercenary, metropolitan kind of hubbub. Instinctively I must have known that at not yet eight years old, poorly clad and penniless, I was not yet ready for these lush pastures. Instead, I would content myself with a wistful look up Briggate, the long and busy shopping thoroughfare that runs from one side to the other of the city centre; and I would linger just long enough to take in the golden time ball atop Dyson's the jeweller's, which glided up and down to mark off the hours for all that there was a perfectly good clock beneath it, and a famous one at that, surmounted by a model of Father Time and the motto *Tempus Fugit*, a Leeds landmark and the meeting place for courting couples going back to the 1870s. And then the Middleton Hiking Club would turn back.

I did, none the less, achieve the odd jaunt into Town, in company with my mother. Often these would be but tantalising cross-city journeys, when we would descend from the No. 12 tram only to board the Sammy Ledgard bus that would transport us to Sunday tea with Auntie Orrie, in what is now a Leeds suburb but which then seemed a remote country village, Horsforth, in my eyes saved from the stigma of Silverdale only in that Auntie lived in a terrace house and the main street was known as Town Street. Or, but this was only once a year, we would change to the No. 3 from Briggate to the many acred, lake-endowed and, so we believed, world-famous Roundhay Park for the annual Children's Day, a Germanic orgy of athletics and gymnastics. I was never a competitor and the sports bored me, but oddly for one who had roamed a good part of the city by now, I took care to stay close to my mother for fear of ending up in the Lost Children's tent.

Luckily for me my mother was herself to some degree under the magnetic influence of Town, to which she was drawn compulsively every Friday morning, returning always with two ounces of mint imperials, a quarter of polony and half a pound of tomato sausages from Redman's pork shop, lights for the cat (which would always meet her at the tram stop), a bag of broken biscuits and sometimes a bargain remnant from the back of the Market such as a bit of oilcloth or a piece of chipped crockery. And on school holidays, as a prudent alternative to leaving me at home to "mind the house" when in the absence of my sister and brothers I was apt to occupy myself in such pastimes as sticking the poker in the fire until it became red hot and then burning holes in pieces of wood, she would occasionally take me with her. Or, on the odd occasion, a promised trip to Town would be an inducement to lure me to the school dentist, presumably because I was no longer of an age to be taken in by the Mickey Mouse ploy. I went willingly: the dental clinic was deep in the heart of my beloved Hunslet, and I would have had all my blackened teeth extracted one by one for one more visit to those blackened terraces.

I must have been a tiresome companion for my mother, since our ideas of what constituted the attractions of Town differed. Hers veered towards the cheap clothing stores and cut-price shops; mine, reasoning that one could get all that sort of thing in Hunslet, towards the municipal grandeur of City Square, the Majestic news scanner, the Bovril sign and suchlike wonders of the world. I would allow myself to be dragged away from the Majestic's electric headlines – BALDWIN RESIGNS: CHAMBERLAIN NEW PREMIER – only on condition that she took me to one of the splendid Edwardian arcades which were, and are, a feature of Leeds – either Thornton's and its celebrated animated clock with Robin Hood, Friar Tuck, Richard Coeur de Lion and Gurth the swineherd from Sir Walter Scott's *Ivanhoe*, striking the quarter hours with their fists; or, preferably, the Grand Arcade where, above an inscription from *Macbeth*, "Come what may, time and the hour runs through the roughest day", two knights with battleaxes would bash out the hour, whereupon the doors of a Windsor Castle straight out of the Theatre Royal panto would creak open, and out would whirr a saluting guardsman followed by the bowing figures of a kilted Scotsman, an Irishman with his shillelagh, a Canadian trapper, and an obsequious Indian, the tableau being completed by a cockerel which flapped its wings and crowed like the one in the Pathé newsreel.

My mother had seen all this a hundred times and would grow impatient if we had to hang around the Arcade for more than ten minutes to see the action begin. But our tastes did converge in our next port of call – a leisurely wander around Kirkgate Market, with which I believe she felt almost as close an affinity as I. Then to Woolworth's where she came by her mint imperials. Only if pestered would she take me up Briggate to Lewis's, the big and still spankingly newish department store – there was nothing in there my mother could afford and she most likely felt it was all a bit too grand for her. It was certainly not too grand for me – it was like being aboard the *Queen Mary* – and I resolved, as I rode its moving staircase (the first in the north of England, so we proudly learned), to return in my own time and on my own terms.

By a combination of sheer good luck, initiative and brass nerve I was able to do this far sooner than I anticipated, and with gratifying frequency.

6 One of my regular calls was down through the rhubarb fields to watch the *Flying Scotsman* go by. A stone wall overlooking the railway gave me a grandstand seat. A survival from when Middleton was farmland, it was one of the traditional drystone walls that you can still see all over the Yorkshire Dales, although less so now that the farmers have taken to selling the stone by the truckload to building contractors. The drystone method, so we learned at school, goes back to pre-cement and indeed pre-Roman days and relies on a simple dovetailing formula to hold the heavy slabs of undressed stone together. Properly constructed, a drystone wall can last for centuries.

This one can't have been properly constructed. As the *Flying Scotsman* thundered by leaving a rocket trail of steam and sparks and cinders, and my friend the fireman waved to me as he always did, the wall collapsed beneath me, no doubt weakened by the vibrations of one too many express trains. To my surprise, lying there among the debris, I seemed to be unhurt, although had the stones landed on me instead of the other way round, I should unquestionably have been seriously injured or even killed. As it turned out, I sustained only minor grazes and a dislocated rib.

My mother took me to Dr Sugare, who painted my wounds with iodine and referred me to Leeds Infirmary for an X-ray. Another trip to Town. The outcome was that although medical science could do nothing for my bent second left rib, the doctors wanted to keep an eye on it as I grew up, and to this end my mother was given a white printed card requiring me to report to the X-ray department every six months. Signed J. Johnstone Jervis, Medical Officer of Health.

The white card was lodged among a mélange of picture postcards, public library tickets, Co-op vouchers and soap coupons behind the mantelpiece clock, where I discovered it during the course of one of the routine ransackings of the house on which I embarked every time my mother was out, in the hope of turning up something interesting such as my father's death certificate or – a rare find, this – a photograph of my late-Victorian mother wearing trousers, when she was working at the Barnbow munitions factory during what we then called the Great War.

I was intrigued to note that the frequency of my Infirmary appointments was not specified – the card simply directed my mother to a particular reception room where, upon its presentation, I would be processed for examination. I at once impounded it, perceiving immediately that here was my passport to freedom. Whenever I fancied a few hours off school – I must not, of course, overdo it – all it required was to show the teacher my official white card and then it would be heigh-ho for the No. 12 tram and the bright white lights of the Bovril sign.

That I could get away with it I had not the slightest doubt. A cunning and devious child, I had a low opinion of the teaching staff's intelligence, not to mention that of my schoolfellows, and frequently put my assessment to the test. On one occasion I had chalked the legend KW IS A FOOL under the headmaster's window and then loitered by my graffito until he came by, solely so that when accused of defacing the wall I could point out with a sigh that I was unlikely to incriminate myself by chalking up my own initials, let alone accuse myself of being a fool. Baffled by this warped logic the headmaster went on his way, whereupon I turned back to my handiwork and underlined it for good measure, judging correctly that he would not remember whether it was underlined or not.

Then there was the affair of the cruet. This was in my first year at school, or rather in my pre-year, for, already able to read and write, I had been admitted to the infants' department at aged four. On the first day of the winter term our teacher, Miss Pease, turned up in class with a ceramic salt, pepper and mustard set in the form of a donkey and fruit-cart. I have no idea how she came by it or what possessed her to offer a cruet as a suitable prize for children barely weaned off rusks; but offer it she did. It was to go to the boy or girl judged by Miss Pease to have been the best behaved during the term. I craved that donkey-and-cart cruet and determined to have it.

So did most of the other children in the class, so perhaps it was not such a bizarre idea after all. But I was smarter than they were. I reasoned that being of such tender years they would quickly forget why they were behaving so nauseatingly well, and would lapse into their old disruptive ways. I, however, would remember. Instead of wasting my energies being indistinguishably well behaved along with everybody else, I would continue being routinely naughty until the last couple of weeks of term, by which time all my classmates would have fallen by the wayside. I would then bring myself to Miss Pease's attention with a sustained spurt of angelic behaviour, and so win the prize. The ploy worked, as never for a second did I doubt it would. I bore the donkey-and-cart cruet home with smug pride and it stood on my mother's mantelpiece, between the coal-dented ornaments, for the rest of her life.

So there was no doubt in my mind that with the aid of my trusty white card I could fool all of my teachers all of the time. Or as much of the time as was prudent. Once a month, I reckoned, would be about right, this arrangement to incorporate the non-fictional six-monthly visit with my mother, which could not be avoided (and when she looked for the white card behind the mantelpiece clock I would deny all knowledge of it. What would I want with an Infirmary appointment card?). I would make them afternoon expeditions, so that my regular absences would not show up on the school attendance register, which was marked up only in the mornings. That would prevent my name from coming to the attention of Geo Guest, Director of Education.

The only lessons I really hated were woodwork and metalwork, and so I would always choose a woodwork or metalwork period from which to embark on my city excursions. The drawback was that I had to set off for afternoon school wearing my woodwork apron rolled up under my jacket – an obvious giveaway to any eagle-eyed truant officer, or Board Man as he was known. The apron being too bulky to stuff into my pocket I had to find a hiding place for it. The hole I was digging to Australia was too risky in case my mother caught me red-handed, and so I chose the depths of a privet hedge near the tram shelter. If it went missing I could always claim to have left it in the school cloakroom, from whence it had disappeared. But my luck was always in.

The Board Man, a dreaded figure dressed all in black like an undertaker, loomed large in my calculations from the start. It was universally understood that persistent truants were sent to the reformatory, a stark-looking institution standing high on a hill in the sinister-sounding suburb of Shadwell on the other side of Roundhay Park, without hope of reprieve or remission. The inmates were said to be beaten daily as part of their punishment; I was not sure I believed this but I did put Shadwell on the Middleton Hiking Club's agenda, when I went and stared through the railings. There were some shaven-headed boys in grey jerseys, grey shorts and grey stockings being marched from one building to another. While not looking abject they did not seem too happy and I resolved to keep out of the reformatory if I could.

Not so much from paranoia as from prudence, I took the view from my first white card outing onwards that I was being followed by Geo Guest's representative the Board Man. Getting off school had been all too easy: the teacher had barely glanced at the appointment card and had only half listened to my explanation of having to go for an X-ray. But this could be a trap — he could be in collusion with the Board Man, who was frequently to be seen hanging around the school premises. Accordingly, after getting off the tram at the Swinegate terminus near the Yorkshire Relish factory, pausing only to glance at the Majestic news scanner — EUROPEAN POWERS SIGN MUNICH PACT — and making but the slightest detour to go and gaze at my treasured Bovril sign opposite the Corn Exchange, I headed firmly for the Infirmary in case I was being tailed by the Board Man.

I was only too well aware, as I crossed the expanse of civic grass on the approach to the Brotherton Wing of the Infirmary, that I was in dangerous territory. To my left were the offices of Geo Guest himself, Director of Education. To my right, guarded by two seven-foot gold-leafed owls, was the Civic Hall, housing the no doubt palatial chambers of Thos Thornton, Town Clerk & Clerk to the Council. Behind me was the ramshackle HQ of the Leeds Poor Children's Holiday Camp, whose manager's filing cabinet almost certainly contained a classified report on my failure to inhale the proper quota of fresh Silverdale air. And ahead of me was the Brotherton Wing itself, named after one of the city's host of local benefactors, and the dominion not only of J. Johnstone Jervis, Medical Officer of Health, but of a mysterious and powerful-sounding figure known as the Lady Almoner, whose title I had seen on a polished door on my first and only visit, printed in gold. And these mighty personages were here and now in their various inner sanctums, surrounding me. All this and the Board Man too. Putting on a limp to convince any of them who might be watching that I was a bona fide invalid, and brandishing my white card, I entered the

Infirmary's reception hall with as much boldness as I could muster.

Once inside, my trepidation eased. The place was milling with people, including several children of around my own age, and it was easy to mingle myself into invisibility. I liked the Infirmary, or anyway that portion of it I had visited with my mother, which reminded me, with its brilliantly white exterior and railed, rounded balconies, of a Mediterranean cruise liner I had seen a picture of somewhere. It smelled more like a public library than a hospital; and as my mother and I had discovered, it had its very own milk bar, next to the Lady Almoner's office. Here, on this and subsequent visits, among the old biddies wobbling in on their bad feet to nurse thick mugs of tea and boast that the finest specialist in the country had been unable to do anything for them, or that they had refused to be put on a port wine diet, I was able to buy a glass of milk and an individual custard pie for twopence – no doubt it was subsidised. This deliciously illicit snack consumed – illicit because I knew perfectly well that the little cafeteria was for genuine patients and their friends only, and the Lady Almoner might come out of her office at any moment and, having examined my spurious credentials, denounce me to J. Johnstone Jervis – I would strike out confidently along the corridors until the lavender polish smell gave way to disinfectant and the streamlined decor of the Brotherton Wing's emulsion paint, parquet and concealed lighting handed over to age-crazed buff and green tiles and I knew I was in the original part of the Infirmary, a Gothic, collegiate-looking pile to the immediate west of the Town Hall. Having thus shaken the Board Man off, I was free to commence my wanderings.

My first exploration was of the Town Hall itself. This noble municipal pile, in whose otherwise completely unfunctional tower curlews were reputed to nest, had commended itself to my attention when my mother had brought me into Town on the first leg of my exile to the Poor Children's Holiday Camp a few months earlier; and on our recent visit to the Infirmary I had heard organ music wafting out of the Town Hall as we went by. The only serious organ music I had so far ever heard being of an ecclesiastical nature (as distinct from the frivolous I-do-like-to-be-beside-the-seaside stuff we got on the wireless), I had therefore concluded that the Town Hall, as well as being where the Lord Mayor had his parlour – I already knew that from school civics lessons – must also double as a church or perhaps, given its size and architectural stature, a cathedral even.

My mother put me right on that, then told me enough about what went on in the Town Hall to leave me burning with curiosity to see its interior.

Mounting the back steps, then — the front steps, leading up from Victoria Square, were altogether too exposed, and the Board Man might be lurking behind one of the stone lions flanking them — I already knew that as well as housing a mighty concert chamber, Victoria Hall, the Town Hall was also (at that time) an Assize Court where wife-poisoners and other murderers were tried by a judge in scarlet robes and wig, and twelve good men and true.

It was into Victoria Hall that I ventured first, simply because the great doors happened to be open. I was suitably impressed by its opulence, the richly decorated semicircular ceiling, the coloured window glass, the giant pillars surmounted by yet more civic owls, and particularly by the fifty-foot-high organ, which made the organ of the Holy Cross Church, Middleton, look like a set of Pan pipes out of a lucky bag. Then there were the various improving mottoes around the frieze — "Good Will Towards Men", "Forward", "Weave Truth With Trust", "Honesty is the Best Policy" and, oddly, "Trial by Jury". Or perhaps not so oddly, for this legend was a reminder that the Town Hall played Nemesis to all the wife-poisoners in the West Riding; and fascinated though I was to find the grandiloquent source of the organ music I had heard, I was even more fascinated by wife-poisoners.

Murder was a popular preoccupation of the time, part of the theatre of city life. George Orwell got it right in his celebrated essay, "Decline of the English Murder". Many was the raw evening I was sent pelting out in my stockinged feet at the cry of "Special! Special!" from the paper boy racing down the street with the late, late extra of the Buff Final, as the last edition of the *Yorkshire Evening Post* was known. It was nearly always a murder — it would have been a swindle had it been anything less, such as Hitler annexing Austria; with any luck it would be human remains found wrapped in brown paper parcels at a left-luggage office, or perhaps even another dismembered corpse in our very own Murder Woods. As to editorial content, these "Specials" somewhat short-changed the reader: all you got for your penny was a duplicate of the same paper you had had pushed through your letter-box a few hours earlier, plus an inch or two of cable-ese in the Stop Press column. No matter: it would all be fleshed out in the *News of the World* on Sunday.

All human death was there and we feasted upon it, the mass communication age equivalents of the crowds at Tyburn. We would have made a good audience for the *Police Gazette* had it still existed. Buck Ruxton was the most recent murderer to seize the popular imagination, and the subject of a school playground song: "Red stains on the carpet, red stains on your knife, Oh Dr Buck Ruxton, you murdered your wife. The nursemaid she saw you, and threatened to tell, Oh Dr Buck Ruxton, you killed her as well." But Dr Crippen, hanged 1910, was still alive in our minds. So was the Thompson-Bywaters case, seven years before I was born. Charles Peace, known affectionately and anarchistically as Charlie Peace, tried at these very Leeds Assizes and hanged at Armley Jail fifty years before my birth, was still a local legend because of his audacious escapes from the police when he was supposed to have dressed up as a woman to elude arrest. (Armley Jail, quite near Hunslet and built to resemble a mediaeval castle, was almost as much an object of my morbid fascination as Shadwell Reformatory, and the Middleton Hiking Club was to lay on a special expedition to go and stare at it.)

While it had been easy enough to get into the Town Hall – I had feared a major-domo asking name and business – I was not so unrealistic as to suppose that at my tender age I would be allowed into the Assize Courts to watch the trial of a trunk murderer or two. I loitered for a while outside the tall wooden doors of No. 1 Court, guarded by sentinels who from their uniform and general demeanour could have been park rangers, in the vain hope of catching a glimpse of the prisoner at the bar. I did see one or two beefy-faced men in wigs and black gowns – judges, they would be, I expected – stalking the high tiled corridors, but no trunk murderers being frogmarched into court between two policemen.

Of policemen, however, there was no shortage. The Town Hall, I now noticed to my alarm, was milling with them. Clearly, if any one of them paused to question me, it was going to be a Shadwell Reformatory job. Like some juvenile bit-player in a Pinter film adaptation of Kafka, I scurried along the outer corridor as fast as I dared, keeping close to the wall and looking for an exit. The corridor proved to be circular and I was back where I began. Under the eyes of what by now seemed to be the ranks of the entire Leeds City constabulary, I sauntered out, with as much sangfroid as a wanted truant could muster in the very shadow of the courts of justice, the way I had come. I was not to enter the Town Hall again until I was sixteen, when I learned that you could get a bargain Woolton Pie in the basement British Restaurant.

7   The two main thoroughfares of central Leeds, Briggate and
    the Headrow, form a St George's cross. Once the visitor
    has established this, as I quickly did, it is easy to fit their
adjacent cross-streets, lanes, arcades and passages into position.
Thus I never once got lost.

The Town Hall lies at the top of the Headrow, up Park Row, the
banking quarter (where I was impressed to notice the Bank of
England) from City Square. Next to it is the Central Library which I
placed off limits on account of its uncomfortable proximity to Geo
Guest's Department of Education – they then actually backed on to
one another, and for all I knew there was a secret pass door between
the two. Then comes the Art Gallery, equally out of bounds in case I
bumped into a school party being taken to look at the pictures. I was
not, in any case, at the time all that taken with art, which from what
I had seen of it in old magazine illustrations consisted entirely of
rural scenes featuring village ponds and haywains. Had I ever heard
of Atkinson Grimshaw whose Leeds cityscapes adorn its walls, I
should have been up the Art Gallery steps two at a time and taken the
risk.

For the present, however, I was far more interested in the next
building in line, the modernistic head office of the Leeds Permanent
Building Society. I had learned from an answers to correspondents
paragraph in the *Leeds Mercury*, the popular morning paper for
those who found the *Yorkshire Post* too indigestible, the explanation
of that curious word "permanent". The original building societies
had always automatically wound themselves up after the last
subscriber had been paid out. The Leeds had been the first society to
establish itself on a perpetuating, permanent basis. For some reason
I found this information deeply fascinating and relayed it to anyone
who would listen. The new red brick and Portland stone fabric of the
Leeds Permanent Building Society was therefore favoured with a

45

prolonged, scrutinising stare before I passed on.

The only other attraction in the Headrow, apart from the Scout Shop whose window display featured far too much camping and outdoor equipment for my taste, was Lewis's department store at the junction of the Headrow and Briggate, as fleetingly visited in the reluctant company of my mother. But Lewis's could wait, as could Briggate with its arcades and their striking clocks; for if I kept on going down the Headrow I would reach Vicar Lane and the northernmost entrance to Kirkgate Market, in other words the one in closest proximity to the wholesale Market.

It was the first time I had ever ventured into the Market alone and I felt immediately at home. Far from any fear of being recognised and reported to the Board Man by traders who could have known my father – they might, after all, spot the family resemblance even if they did not remember my sole visit in his company when I was half the size I was now – I actively wanted to be recognised, wanted to be hailed and hugged and to have a bread and dripping doorstep and a mug of cocoa pushed gruffly into my hands, wanted to be welcomed into that masonic temple of pomegranates and blood oranges.

I had already worked out that the Market was laid out in the form of streets, like a miniature indoor Hunslet consisting entirely of brilliantly lit shops and stalls, where the terraces were paved with sawdust. Each row, while not necessarily as slavishly devoted to a particular branch of produce as Game Row, Butchers' Row or the fish market, had its speciality.

On one row I could find the crumbly Cheshire – though my own preference was for processed cheese triangles – that my mother always bought (invariably, like everyone else to this day, from the specific stall of her choice, although to my untutored eye at least there would be the same crumbly Cheshire at the same price on five different stalls, and with shorter queues); and Red Leicester, Wensleydale, Derby Sage, and another kind of crumbly in three versions labelled Mild, Medium and Tasty; and blue-veined Stilton that was said to have maggots running through it; and cartwheels of Double Gloucester, and slabs of butter the size of the granite speakers' podium in Middleton Park where fanatics in salt-and-pepper suits frothed and fulminated; and mountains of brown eggs, and basins of green duck eggs nestling in straw.

On another would be hams swinging from brass rails and stuck with cloves like mapping pins; and below them white enamel trays piled high with chitterlings, polonies, Yorkshire ducks, stand pies, Aintree pies, whist pies, pork sausages, beef sausages, tomato sausages, Cumberland sausages, black pudding, white pudding, boiled ham, tongue, corned beef, sliced roast beef, salt beef, brawn, pigs' trotters − the same robust fare, in short, as could be found in any of the dozens of pork shops dotted around the city, which then as now could rival any Soho delicatessen or even Harrods Food Hall itself.

The top row, being dedicated to such preoccupations of the ladies as felt hats, Liberty bodices, surgical stockings and skeins of wool, held little to detain me, save only the glassed-in Invisible Mender's with an animated model of a seamstress sewing away in the window and, I was half ready to believe, the invisible mender himself (it would have to be a he, like H.G. Wells's *Invisible Man* at the Tivoli cinema) lurking somewhere on the premises. But below this comparatively tranquil corridor of haberdashery and ribbons and bows were the cakes and fancies and sweets and confectionery rows, where as well as a tabernacle Whitsun treat of barm cake, Long John cobs, Dunster spiced loaf, iced buns, cream horseshoes, parkin, currant teacakes, gingerbread men, Sally Lunns and twelve kinds of slab cake; and humbugs, treacle toffee, licorice allsorts, Pontefract cakes, cough candy and buttered Brazils, there was one stall selling nothing but broken biscuits and yesterday's buns at a penny a bag, and another awash with broken chocolate, broken nougat, broken bars of fudge and broken coconut ice. This was sold by the pound; I cannot recall the price but it was way beyond my empty pocket. I would press my nose waif-like against the glass ledge that prevented this toothsome merchandise from spilling out on to the flagstones, in the hope that the lady would take pity and give me a chocolate misshape. She never did.

And just below the broken chocolate stall, and across the way from Birkbeck's café where I could have murdered a boiled ham sandwich in a Yorkshire teacake, was Stringer's bookstall, trading in second-hand magazines and comics, as well as American comic books and Canadian Sunday newspaper supplements imported to these shores as ballast. These literary curiosities I would browse among until requested by the management to move on. I was also intrigued by back numbers of a peculiar-looking magazine called *Punch*, the cover of which, depicting Mr Punch himself and an advertisement for Fry's Pure Concentrated Cocoa, was exactly the

47

same week after week. I thought this decidedly odd.

This first solo visit to the Market then took me down through the pungently smelling fish hall in search of the corporation slaughterhouse, another morbid preoccupation. Although I didn't want to see any animals actually being put to death I did want to give the slaughterhouse a good long stare. With any luck, too, I might be witness to one of the occasional stampedes of veal calves that sometimes occurred as they were being herded over from the railway marshalling yards across the way, whence they had travelled from the flat wastes of the East Riding. I had heard stories of terrified passengers being marooned on their tram-cars while fear-maddened cattle rampaged all around them.

The slaughterhouse was right at the end of the Market opposite the parish church with its graveyard full of victims of the Black Death, a plague which it was popularly believed would break out anew if the graves were ever dug up – the parish church too was on my visiting list. But somehow, having been deflected from my mission by a flower market I had never known existed, and in which I could see no commercial purpose since no one in Leeds ever bought flowers except at the gates of cemeteries, I found myself in the Tatters Market – "t' back o' t' Market" as it was known to all who patronised it – an open-air shambles of tarpaulin-sheltered stalls that functioned every Tuesday and Saturday. So my first white card afternoon must have been a Tuesday.

The blue-jowled hawkers in their sharp pinstriped suits and cocky hats seemed a different breed from the solid straw-boatered and white-aproned traders in the indoor Market; they called their wares in different accents too – had I yet travelled to any of these places I should have recognised the voices of Nottingham, Liverpool, Newcastle, Sheffield, London even. They were travelling men with a fairground aura about them, employing the same mock auction patter to sell their dinner services and rolls of linoleum that always so mesmerised me on my annual outings to Hunslet Feast.

Some, in a haze of menthol, eucalyptus, glycerine and wintergreen, were noisily peddling elixirs and potions and cures for barber's rash. Others were demonstrating patent varnishes and quick-drying enamel paints: I have an image, whether from this first visit or no I could not begin to remember, of a hawker so engrossed in painting a kettle bright blue that he quite forgot his spiel, yet he continued to attract an audience who watched him with the encouraging attention they would have given to a rather good pavement artist.

Then, on the periphery of this peripheral open market, there was a shanty town of tattooists' and fortune tellers' booths, pea and pie stalls, and tumbledown little lock-up shops housing barbers, cobblers, knife-grinders, dubious-looking chemists and "family planning" establishments, whatever they might have been, all clustered around this teeming northern souk like pedlars' tents around the walls of a mediaeval town. I liked it here. It had an unsettlingly transient air that made me itch to join this gaudy, gimcrack caravan and see where its rag-tag-and-bobtail band of itinerants led me.

But with my time strictly limited – allowing myself the customary half hour or so of dawdling after school, I had better be no later than five o'clock in getting home if my mother were not to wonder where I'd been – I had to be moving on before they did.

My Bovril sign was only just around the corner from the Markets and so there I repaired for the second time that truant afternoon, to stand on the steps of the Corn Exchange opposite, quite transfixed by the glowing battery of white electric light bulbs winking on and off as they responded to the man in his little room behind the sign manipulating what I had come to suppose, for so large a consumption of power, would be a big lever rather than a conventional light switch like the ones at home.

Hitherto I had regarded our Victorian Corn Exchange as little more than a tram stop. I had no idea, and little curiosity about, what went on in this great elliptical domed structure (popularly believed to be round) except that when I was about five it had staged the world's biggest mouse show, but neither my mother nor my sister would take me, on the incredible grounds that they did not like mice. Now, temporarily sated with my Bovril sign and perhaps emboldened by my successful sortie into the Town Hall, I decided to explore the place.

To my surprise and delight there was a corn market going on. Stone steps led to an iron-railed balcony under the partly glassed dome, where coal merchants and estate agents had their offices. Creeping up them I had a bird's-eye view of about a hundred gaitered or tweeded farmers and corn chandlers clustered around black wooden stands that somewhat resembled kitchen dressers, with their names printed on them in gold (all the names in Leeds seemed

49

to be printed in gold), holding hushed and important conversations with flour merchants and manufacturers of cattle cake as they trickled maize, oats and Yorkshire barley judiciously through their fingers. A ray of sunlight illuminated a big clock framed in golden sheaves of corn. Serendipity.

The Corn Exchange at once went on my list of regular ports of call on my white card excursions. But the next time I crept in I was disappointed to find the huge oval hall eerily deserted – I hadn't realised that the Corn Market, like the Tatters Market, functioned only on market days. It did give me chance, though, to peruse the Bye-laws (I was an avid reader of all kinds of bye-laws, which I studied to make my own flesh creep like an introspective Fat Boy from Pickwick): "A person shall not bring a dog into the Market Place . . . A person shall not smoke tobacco or any like substance in the Market Place . . ." Signed, Joseph Hepworth (of Hepworth's the clothiers, I rightly surmised), April 1907. The Bye-laws are still in position; and the Corn Exchange, while now prettily restored and given over to candle boutiques and cafés, is a corn market still, although the kitchen dresser stands are by now reduced to a bare dozen.

From the Corn Exchange I struck out up Briggate, resisting the temptation to get there through Woolworth's. Although Woolworth's was a powerful draw – they had a counter of lead model sheep, cattle and milkmaids going for a penny each, good to suck meditatively or lick the paint off when you were playing at farmyards – it was notoriously a hotbed of young shoplifters, and I should most assuredly be taken for one and delivered up to Shadwell Reformatory by the private detectives who were known to patrol the store.

Instead I had a quick look around Marks and Spencer's, a store I had yet to enter in my mother's company without her recounting the story of how Mr Marks had started his great enterprise with a penny bazaar in Kirkgate Market. It was a saga I never tired of hearing, better than any fairy tale. But Marks and Spencer's soft furnishings, hardware and ladies' clothing failed to fascinate, and I quickly resumed my walk up Briggate, heading now for one of the arcades – not Thornton's or the Grand but the County Arcade, which, while lacking little men striking the hour, was (and remains, although now tarted up into "the Victoria Quarter") a multi-domed riot of Sienna marble, wrought iron, gold-capitalled columns and allegorical mosaics.

The attraction for me, however, was Banks's Music Arcade, the big double-fronted store that stood on the corner of the County Arcade and the smaller Cross Arcade that was the approach to the Mecca Locarno opposite. Banks's windows featured grand pianos and clarinets and accordions and, the centrepiece, a big gleaming xylophone which I craved, as played by Teddy Brown, a wireless performer of enormous girth whose picture I had seen in the *Radio Times* and who had once honoured Leeds by appearing in person at the Empire.

But even more than I wanted to play the xylophone, I wanted to write music. Along with the piano scores of Haydn, Mendelssohn and other unpronounceables which adorned the foot of Banks's windows, there were always a few folios of blank manuscript paper which I longed to fill with clefs, quavers, crotchets and other pleasing squiggles. The very moment I set eyes on these enticing virgin staves I resolved to teach myself how to compose music. It never occurring to me for a second that there would be textbooks on the subject in the reference library − for a bright child I could be extraordinarily stupid at times − I set about painstakingly compiling my own dictionary of musical terms and symbols, copying them from the sheaves of old sheet music freely available in the horsehair-covered piano stools of Middleton Park Grove; whenever I came across an interesting expression such as *allegro* or *andante*, I would search out a translation and jot it down.

Meanwhile I had begun to compose simple tunes on the harp zither my father had bought at the door. While I have never been able to play a musical instrument properly I found that I had a musical ear and to this day can pick out any tune with one finger, although only in the key of C. Having taught myself the rudiments of musical notation I began writing my compositions down, first on blank paper which I ruled out into staves myself, and then on proper manuscript paper, for as a treat my mother one Friday brought me back from Town a whole twenty-four-page Banks's manuscript book. An expensive buy, but the family circumstances had improved a little by now. Helped either by the Board of Guardians or relatives or both, she had scraped enough together to buy a few sticks of furniture on the hire purchase, the first of these purchases being a stool, "the buffet" as it was always called, which the entire family went down to collect from a cut-price shop at the bottom of Middleton Ring Road, four of us bearing it home like a trophy, one to each leg. Although my mother would frequently sit on the buffet by the fireside with her lips moving as she juggled the family finances in a little notebook, our fortunes, with the prospect of four out of five of us reaching the working age of fourteen, were gradually if modestly on the mend.

My first compositions were variations (a word I had picked up from the *Radio Times*) on the little tunes I had made up. I then embarked on a full-scale opera, scored not only for piano but for brass and two kinds of strings, on the theme of Robin Hood. This fragment, for of course this ambitious work was quickly abandoned, was never played, and indeed for all I know was unplayable, for I was more concerned with the busy appearance of the symbols on the page than with the practical harmonics. I also found myself more interested in the libretto than in the music, which I blamed for the vicious cuts and calluses on my thumb sustained by plucking out the melody on the harp zither with a home-made plectrum fashioned out of a strip cut out of a cocoa tin with my mother's scissors, the original having been lost. Before long my career as a composer languished and I went back to my first love, writing stories.

From the County Arcade there was time now only for a quick look around Lewis's and a ride up and down the escalators. Lewis's, completed only three or four years earlier, was in my estimation the most modern building on the face of the Earth. Everything about it dazzled with streamlined up-to-dateness, from the reflecting chrome of its purring escalators to the shining bronze of its silent lifts, from the pristine tiles of its American soda fountain to the burnished glass of its Ladies' and Gentlemen's Hairdressing Establishments.

But the reason Lewis's was a must on all my white card outings was that it was a rare week when there was not something going on in this go-ahead store, where novelties like American soft ice-cream were being introduced, and where girls with Roundhay High School accents in white smocks would demonstrate egg whisks patented in Kalamazoo or the latest thing in potato peelers. Lewis's had recently surpassed itself by exhibiting on its ground floor – how they had got it through the doors I puzzled over at length – the Bluebird, the racing car with which Sir Malcolm Campbell had established the new land speed record of 301.7 mph. I could not hope for another Bluebird on this occasion but at least there was sure to be something new in the kitchen gadget line and indeed there was, although I cannot now remember what it was. I remember only tearing myself with reluctance from the basement demonstration, taking one more

52

ride on the escalators and then making for the tram stop.

At home my mother asked me how I had got so dirty – in those pre-Clean Air Act days, if the wind in Town were blowing in the wrong direction, it snowed flakes of soot from the cluster of factory chimneys across the river – and, plainly suspecting that I had been playing truant, what I had learned at school that afternoon. I said that we had first done dovetail joints (I had recovered my woodwork apron safely from its privet hedge depository) and after that we had learned all about the Corn Exchange and did she know there was still a corn market held there? My mother gave me one of the old-fashioned looks that meant she wasn't sure whether to believe me or not, but did not pursue the matter.

8 Architecture was a word I had yet to encounter, and so I had no idea that I had an interest in the subject. What I did know was that buildings, their shape and proportions and fabric and style of adornment or lack of it, fascinated me. Although I suppose my love of the cobbled terraces and the dark satanic mills made me a traditionalist, I had great enthusiasm for the modern, Lewis's being a gleaming example.

It did not require any great knowledge of the passing show to be able to grasp from the contrast between the white Portland stone frontage of the Civic Hall and the soot-blackened Yorkshire stone of the Town Hall, or between the streamlined Middleton trams and the old bone-rattlers clanging along Hunslet Road like land-locked tramp steamers, that Leeds – and, insofar as I knew anything about it, the rest of the country all around – was in a state of transition.

Leeds was in many respects at that time of the mid-to-late Thirties a schizophrenic city, half of it with its clogs firmly planted in the Edwardian and Victorian past, the other half determinedly modernistic. We still had a lamplighter and a knocker-up in our street and there were still horsedrawn funerals (my father was the first in Middleton Park Grove to be seen off by motor – ironic, since he was the only one in the neighbourhood to own a horse); but the Tivoli Cinema with its rounded brick frontage and the tram shelter at the top of the street were, although neither I nor anyone else in Middleton had ever heard the expression, pure Bauhaus.

The roadway out of City Station alongside the new Queen's Hotel overlooking City Square was constructed of rubberised briquettes so that slumbering guests would not be disturbed by the sound of Silver Line taxis gliding in and out of the station; yet in Hunslet and Holbeck, when somebody was lying ill, the cobbles were still spread with stable straw to deaden the rumble of cart wheels.

Behind the lace curtains of our up-to-the-minute council residences, with their every modern convenience such as gas pokers and an indoor coal shed, you could find what looked like waxworks tableaux of Victorian domestic life, with old grandmothers dressed from head to toe in black presiding over stuffy parlours crammed with rocking chairs, horsehair chaise-longues, wax fruit in glass domes, copies of the Stag at Bay covering the rising damp, and the family Bible open at the Book of Psalms.

Bakelite wireless sets driven by accumulators — among my routine tasks was to take ours to be recharged at Morrison's Garage on the shopping parade, taking care not to let the acid splash my bare legs — blared out slick American-style comedy patter to an audience which in large part still spoke in a dialect that would have been barely comprehensible to anyone in the next postal district, let alone the next county. The *News of the World* each week printed half a page of sheet music for a populace still thumping away on its cottage pianos every Sunday afternoon; but the songs were no longer tasteful ballads but wireless and gramophone hits like "It's a Sin to Tell a Lie", "Nice Work If You Can Get It" and "Horsey, Horsey". While over her washtub and scrubbing board my mother was still singing her favourites from the old music-hall, "On Mother Kelly's Doorstep" and "The Little Shirt My Mother Made For Me", my sister subscribed to McGlennon's sixpenny song book which gave the words to all the latest tunes as recorded by the popular dance bands such as Jack Payne, Ambrose, and Carroll Gibbons and the Savoy Orpheans.

Even in the small world of childhood there was change in the air. There was high excitement when a new chocolate bar called Aero came on the market, consisting mainly of bubbles. Mars bars were another sensation. We all ran to the top of the street to see the first double-decker bus go by. Our old-fashioned penny comics like the *Joker*, the *Jester*, *Illustrated Chips* and *Funny Wonder*, printed on flimsy blue, green or pink paper, were giving way to the new coloured D.C. Thomson titles, the *Dandy* and the *Beano*, and later the *Magic*, with "Free inside — sugar bullets for you to eat". *Mickey Mouse Weekly*, the first photogravure paper for children, had a swop value of three conventional comics.

We could speak the local dialect effortlessly — "Sither" for "See thou", "Weer's ta bahn?" for "Where are you bound?" and so on, but we did so in a parodying way, aware that it was a different language from a different time; and while we had access to a rich anthology of street songs and snatches as later identified by the Opies in their *Lore and Language of Schoolchildren*, and would still repeat the saws and sayings used by our elders and betters, many of them quite baffling – "Not a pot washed and the house full of Chinamen" was one I could not fathom: another music-hall relic, probably – our repertoire was beginning to silt up with wireless and cinema catchphrases and jingles – "I thang yew", "You dirty rat!", "It's Monday night at seven, Oh can't you hear the chimes" etc. In the *Yorkshire Evening Post* wireless columns I read of the public surveillance potential of an invention called television which could see around corners, and pondered on the dire consequences of such a device falling into the hands of the Board Man.

So I was very conscious of living in a melting-pot, and every time I took out the white card from its hiding place between the pages of a book called *Fifty Years of Progress: the Story of Hemingway's Brewery*, which Uncle Herbert, who worked there, had introduced into the house upon hearing from his sister my mother that I was a big reader, I knew that my trip into Town was bound to yield some further example of the old giving way to the new.

One day, for example, I ventured into the newly completed booking hall of the City Station adjoining the Queen's Hotel and its rubber roadway, to find a breathtakingly spacious chamber straight out of Hollywood, its high, pastel-painted concrete arches hung with what I did not yet know were art deco lanterns, its walls lined with what I did not yet know was glazed terracotta, its floor carpeted with what I did not yet know were faience tiles, its back-lit advertising displays for permanent waves and the new Black Magic chocolates framed in bronze in the manner, and I did not yet know this either, of the display cabinets in the lobbies of New York skyscrapers. (Monstrously, and unforgivably, it is now a British Rail car park.) But beyond the trellis gates of this elegant thirties hall were chuffing, cinder-scattering steam trains; and below it were the Dark Arches, the Dickensian labyrinth of brick catacombs on which the station was built, and under whose viaduct spans gushes the converging waters of the River Aire, the Leeds and Liverpool Canal and the Aire and Calder Navigation.

There was Leeds modern and Leeds ancient; and when, the booking hall having been admired and inspected, I retraced my steps past the passengers' private carpeted corridor into the Queen's

Hotel, and the adjoining flower shop and Parfumerie Continental and the News Theatre on the corner, it was to Leeds ancient I returned as I found myself back in the brooding presence of the Black and blackened Prince, his attendant nymphs and, now that I had the leisure to inspect them, the statues of Joseph Priestley, discoverer of oxygen but also, more importantly, a minister of Mill Hill Chapel across the street; Dr Hook, Vicar of Leeds 1837 – 59; John Harrison who founded the Grammar School; and James Watt of steam-kettle fame, who like the Black Prince seemed from his inscription to have no local connection. Back to the past. But the Majestic news scanner's electric-light headlines – GERMAN TROOPS MARCH INTO SUDETENLAND – spelled out the uneasy future to those who understood what they meant.

There was no statue in City Square to the Rev Charles Jenkinson, Vicar of Holbeck and a councillor, but there might well have been had he not been still alive and active, for while he was known to his political enemies as "Red Ruin", his ambitious slum clearance programme had made him a local hero (though not necessarily with the slum dwellers themselves). My interest in him was that he was the instigator of Quarry Hill Flats, another wonder of the world. Leeds modern again: the biggest housing development in Europe, made of ferro-concrete and as up to date as Lewis's. Architect: R.A.H. Livett ARIBA.

Quarry Hill, not yet finished, was always in the columns of the *Yorkshire Evening Post* for one reason or another – its revolutionary rubbish chutes would do away with dustbins; it would have its own laundry and ironing rooms; the Great Curve of Karl Marx House, with a frontage of half a mile, was now completed – and I wanted to see it all. Which I did, proceeding through Kirkgate Market to what was still officially called Leeds Central Omnibus Station, newly built together with a reinforced concrete air-raid shelter, and subjecting the Great Curve opposite to a good long stare. Then I wandered across the road into the development through one of its whalebone-arched gateways, and had a self-conducted grand tour. I approved of Quarry Hill and wanted to live there. How jolly to live two minutes' walk from the Market, five minutes from Lewis's and the Paramount Cinema, ten minutes from City Square! Despite its huge size – twenty-three acres – the Great Curve somehow gave the estate a human scale. Nor did it feel in the least remote, possibly because of its proximity to Town and the clanging trams; also, to my satisfaction, it had a homely gas works in the middle.

I had no way of knowing that I was gazing at one of the few mass housing developments that could have worked, but for some quite stupid structural flaws. Quarry Hill has long been pulled down after years of going to seed. It seems incredible now that there was a time when what after all was no more than a block of council flats would be proudly pointed out to relatives visiting from out of town; along with Lewis's, City Station and the Civic Hall, Quarry Hill was a Leeds landmark to be shown off – and if your aged aunt would not come to view these modern marvels in person you could send her tinted picture postcards of them.

As for my own unguided city tours: from the start my informal architectural field studies always embraced a few pleasing shopfronts. Many was the detour I took to gaze at the frontages of Boots, Cash Dispensing Chemists, Montague Burton the Tailor of Taste, or W.H. Smith & Son, Booksellers, Librarians, Newsagents, Stationers, simply because it gave me an inner glow to look at them. I had no idea what it was that pleased me about them – that Smith's with its fumed oak, pictorial tiles, chaste fascia lettering and newsboy hanging sign, was designed on Arts and Crafts principles, or that Boots and Burton's were classic examples of the use of decorated clerestory glazing: it was to be many years before I rationalised from books what as a boy I simply sensed.

The presence of some other shops on my itinerary was down less to good taste than to gusto. The Horse Meat Shop in the stew of tumbledown premises at the side of the Market was always a draw, principally because it took very little imagination to visualise the unappetising purplish joints and lumps of yellow fat in the window as horse, and partly because its frontage was painted in a vivid red, like blood; I liked to hear my mother tell me, as she often did, that it had to be painted this colour by law, to distinguish it from ordinary butchers' shops.

The herbalist's shop in Vicar Lane, with row upon row of little saucers containing powdered ginger, bee salve, prune and senna mixture, licorice root, cinnamon, dragon's blood (was it real dragon's blood?), was also good for a stare. So was the Murder Shop whose window display of scissors and kitchen knives I imagined in my confused way to be murder weapons. There was a secondhand bookshop at the bottom of Kirkgate where I could actually finger the old books in the nothing-over-sixpence trough outside, but it was to be some years before I would dare venture inside. Back to the modern: the Polyfoto studio on Boar Lane was a much talked about recent arrival to Leeds: the latest high-speed camera snapped twenty-four pictures of you and you selected those you wanted enlarged to the postcard or cabinet size from a specimen sheet. Examples of these multi-snap sheets were in the window and I would pause to count up in how many wasted exposures the subject was blinking.

The pork shops were always an attraction, and I would feast my eyes on their marble slabs of pies and pasties and polonies, not out of hunger but simply because these gastronomic displays were visually pleasing — particularly the bisected veal, ham and egg pies in Redman's in the County Arcade, which always left me puzzling how they got a whole hard-boiled egg into the middle of a meat pie. It was while I was figuring this out one day — they would cook an ordinary oblong pie, I reasoned, then scoop out an egg-shaped quantity of meat, then wedge the egg into the aperture, then seal the pie up again with some kind of edible glue — that I thought I spotted the Board Man keeping an eye on me from across the Arcade. It was not him at all, I saw at once, just someone waiting for his wife to come out of the corset shop; but it did set me wondering how I should explain things had the Board Man been following me and seen that while I had given barely a glance to the toy shop up the Arcade with its Meccano suspension bridge in the window, here I was staring at pork pies and previous to that at the Horse Meat Shop and the Murder Shop, and then Montague Burton the Tailor of Taste (not only did I admire Burton's decorated clerestory glazing but I was beginning to hanker after a Burton's suit).

It was, as I could readily acknowledge in moments of insight, weird behaviour for a boy of eight or nine. I suppose I was a weird child all round.

9 The wonder is that I never came to any harm in the course of my wanderings. It never swam into my head that I might. Streetwise I may have become to some extent, but I was still as sexually naïve as most children of my age. Child molesters were as remote a threat as Bluebeard. Occasionally in school assembly the headmaster would utter an obscure warning against strangers who might offer us sweets, but beyond thinking that chance would be a fine thing we never gave this improbable prospect any further contemplation, or if we did it stopped short at the sweet-offering stranger carrying us off in a sack — what his motive could be we had none of us the faintest idea. My mother, too, would sometimes, and to her own embarrassment, feel obliged to advise me to keep out of public lavatories but to go behind the bushes instead. I thought she was talking about hygiene.

No doubt somewhere in the length and breadth of Leeds sex reared its ugly head but not to my knowledge, and the subject was kept out of the papers, or anyway dressed in euphemisms that took it way above my head (this was when a body found cut up into small pieces could be described as "not interfered with"). Homosexuality was unknown — not only to a sexually witless child such as myself but, I would conjecture, to most of the adult population, at any rate of Middleton: certain men were known to be good to their mothers, and that was as far as it went.

There were some peculiar characters about, true — Silly Alan, as he was known, who went about in a school cap and was said to have been shell-shocked in the Great War; and Barmy Ginger who wore a yellow raincoat at all times of year and rode about on a bicycle making quacking noises: such as they were harmlessly at loose in the community long before the concept of being returned to the community was thought of, but beyond warning us euphemistically never to "go anywhere" with them or their like, our parents were

61

unconcerned. More serious cases were carted off to what was still called the lunatic asylum, at a place out on the edge of the moors called Menston. I always thought Menston merited a stare, but I had no idea where it was and could not persuade any of my elders to tell me — not because they thought my curiosity about the care of the insane in any way bizarre, but because adults simply did not answer questions put to them by children: if I asked my mother who was the man she was just talking to at the door, she would reply cryptically, "Him on the Quaker Oat box."

Some odd characters were to be found in Town also; but these were "characters" in inverted commas, well-known local personalities, part of the passing show — every town had its company of street eccentrics at that time. Our star "character" was Woodbine Lizzie, a grimy-faced lady tramp who wore a tram conductor's cap, hobnailed boots and three or four overcoats including an army greatcoat, who used to stand outside a public house called the Whip, aggressively demanding Woodbines from all who passed by. Of course there were stories that Woodbine Lizzie was high-born, the illegitimate daughter of a duke and so on; in fact she had been a mother with six children living out in Pudsey, where the crows fly backwards (to keep the soot out of their eyes); something had snapped and she had become what would nowadays be called a bag lady. Her bedroom was a park bench on Woodhouse Moor, the cinder-paved inner north Leeds equivalent of Hunslet Moor. Having heard of Woodbine Lizzie almost since birth — she was more famous even than the royal personage, a gibbering lunatic, who local legend had it was locked in a garret in Harewood House, just outside Leeds — I judged her worth a stare. Catching me at it, she streamed tobacco juice in my direction.

Our supporting, second-billing "character" was the deformed shoe black who was always to be seen outside Trinity Church in Boar Lane. His useless legs were tucked away behind his back, giving the impression of a man with no legs at all, and he propelled himself about on a small bogie, a rough cart on pram wheels, clutching well-worn wooden blocks to push himself along. Naturally he had his own mythology too: it was widely believed that when he got home to Hunslet each evening he would straighten up, put the bogie under his arm and walk into his house like any normal person. Seeking clues to this supposed imposture I gave him one of my longest stares until he told me to go away.

Other than the tram conductor, and the odd Market stallholder if I had any money to buy anything, the Trinity Church shoe black was the only person in Town who had so far spoken to me. These were completely solitary explorations of mine and I never sought company. I had no need to: I was an immensely self-contained child, and such conversational nourishment as I needed to sustain me took place inside my head. But I must have been noticed: a pale-faced, staring, wandering boy must have stood out among this teeming Township of adults and their infants. Yet no one ever asked me what I was about, not even those who were recognisably – and reassuringly, so long as they kept their distance – official personages such as tramways inspectors, commissionaires, railway porters and the like, not to mention policemen.

I did once become aware that a stranger was taking an interest in me. This was in City Square, where there were then public lavatories. Down in the Gents' I noticed that a man in a belted mackintosh and soft-brimmed hat, which made him look altogether too much like a detective for my peace of mind, had his eye on me as he slowly lit a cigarette while loitering under the "No Loitering" sign. I climbed the steps up into the Square as casually as I could and went to stare at one of the nymphs. There was a legend that at midnight the torch-bearing young hussies came down off their plinths and danced, and while it was still broad daylight and I did not expect any hint of terpsichorean activity, I was always on the lookout for some sign that the nymphs had changed their posture since my last visit. Convinced that Eve, the particular bronze lady I had under scrutiny, had switched her weight from one foot to the other, I was giving her a good long stare when I saw that the stranger had followed me up out of the lavatories and was having a good long stare at me. As he began to saunter towards me I felt a frisson of panic; but then, noticing, I think, that the City Square newsvendor was giving him a good long stare in turn, he changed his mind and walked quickly away. Not a detective after all. For the benefit of the newsvendor, who could himself have been a detective and master of disguise, I looked earnestly at my white card as if checking an address and marched decisively off in the opposite direction.

The Dark Arches, not two minutes from City Square, were genuinely dangerous – there had been more than one murder down there, and muggings, to use a then non-existent term, without number. So naturally I wanted to go and have a look at them. What I did not know at the time was that the Dark Arches were notoriously the haunt of sex deviants of every kind.

Even today, when the area has been gentrified into the north's answer to Camden Lock, the vaulted tunnels still have a sinister air. Then, when they were practically pitch dark, the only light seeping in from the culverts below my feet through which coursed the seething waters, they were positively frightening. Was there anybody lurking in the shadows? I couldn't be sure, but halfway through the dank vaults I did hear echoing footsteps other than my own – unless they were my own re-echoing. By starting to count up to eighteen million – the number of bricks used in the Dark Arches' construction, so I had heard or read – I managed to keep at bay the certain knowledge that there were black rats scuffling and sniffling around my ankles. I got through somehow, and somehow got through unscathed, and never went there again.

The river which flowed under the Dark Arches, on the other hand, unwisely became one of my haunts. I had lately become acquainted with the stories of W.W. Jacobs – adult books, but I had been allowed to commandeer all the family's library tickets in consideration of an undertaking to bring back my brother Kenneth a Crime Club novel and my sister Stella a romance ("Not an *I* book," she would stipulate, which ruled out *Jane Eyre*) whenever I changed my books, and so I had the run of the grown-up library. One evening, selecting a third-person novel by Naomi Jacob to whose work my sister had taken a fancy, I espied a row of books by W.W. Jacobs and out of curiosity took one out. Most of my reading was inspired by this kind of serendipity: I discovered Evelyn Waugh's row of works by looking among the W's to see if there was yet any writer called Waterhouse.

Jacobs's village tales I didn't much care for, being too countrified by half for me; *The Monkey's Paw* and suchlike macabre stories I enjoyed; but most of all I relished the night watchman's yarns of the rogues and vagabonds aboard the bobbing tramp steamers and barges around the East India Docks. This dockland sounded right up my street and I resolved to go there one day.

But then I was delighted to discover, upon venturing off Leeds Bridge and along the river walk one afternoon, that we had a dockland of our own in Leeds. I spent many hours absorbing it, either on my white card voyages or as representative of the Middleton Hiking Club. There was a constant traffic of boats and barges in and out of the timber yards, coal wharves and olive oil and wool sheds below Warehouse Hill; the sun glittered on a thousand warehouse windows and once I heard funeral hymns being sung in the tiny riverside mission church. I found it all incredibly romantic, as any boy would. I wandered then through dark alleys and found the quieter waters of the Aire and Calder Navigation and pottered about around the locks and canal basins. Here it could be very quiet, and when the sun went in I could feel a sudden chill, but having no previous experience of premonition I did not know I was scenting danger. But, as in the Dark Arches, my guardian angel was watching over me and I came to no harm.

My one real moment of peril, when it did come, was in the very centre of Town, and not even in one of the twisting gas-lit alleys behind the city streets, but in busy Briggate itself, outside Lewis's. I had just emerged from the store and was wondering what to do next, whether to go down and look at the Horse Meat Shop or at another interesting shop I had found which sold false limbs, when a very kind gentleman, small of stature and wearing a grubby raincoat — that is all I can remember about his appearance — came up to me and explained that since it was his birthday he would like to give me a shilling.

I thanked him very much: I had been warned against taking sweets from strangers but no one had said anything about shillings, and it was an enormous sum. With a shilling I could buy a milkshake at the White Rose milk bar across the street and still have eightpence over, perhaps for a soft ice-cream and a chocolate eclair at Lewis's soda fountain. I had always wanted a chocolate eclair of my own.

But the kind gentleman had other plans. He would furthermore like, this being his birthday, to take me to the pictures. I didn't particularly want to go to the pictures — with all this money in my possession there were picture houses around Middleton I could go to, and in my own free time rather than in precious white card time — but having accepted his shilling it seemed churlish to refuse. Clutching the coin in one hand and placing the other trustingly in his, I allowed myself to be led over not to the Paramount super-cinema opposite, whose Wurlitzer organ I wouldn't have minded seeing rise out of the floorboards, but to the rather fly-blown Tower Picture House a little way up Briggate, noted for its cheap prices.

Of the performance I can remember nothing save that the main film was Gary Cooper in *The Adventures of Marco Polo*, that the cinema was nearly empty at this early hour, and that the kind gentleman for reasons of his own wanted to rest his hand lightly on my knee, which I found slightly embarrassing. But he had not offered me sweets; I was rather surprised that no sweets were forthcoming, since it was his birthday and he was pushing the boat out.

When we came out of the cinema I thought it was high time I was making tracks for home, but I didn't quite know how to detach myself from the kind gentleman's company. Confessing an interest in old buildings and firmly gripping my left hand while I with my right hand firmly gripped my shilling, he led me across Briggate to the church of St John the Evangelist opposite.

I still had no sense of danger: my only concern was that the kind gentleman didn't seem to know when he had outstayed his welcome and would be difficult to shake off. He pushed open the wooden gates of the churchyard. Although it would still be some months before war was declared, public shelters and static water tanks were appearing all over Leeds, and there was a brick shelter among the gravestones of St John's.

The kind gentleman seemed as interested in air raid shelters as he was in old buildings — more so, indeed. He said he had always wondered what they were like inside and asked if I had ever been in one. Although I wasn't going to let on, I had, as a matter of fact, once made it my business to inspect one of the shelters down at Quarry Hill Flats. It was dark and smelled of cat pee. The kind gentleman's grip had transferred itself from my hand to my wrist and had tightened; as he reiterated that he would like to see inside the air raid shelter I realised at last that he was not such a kind gentleman after all and that he was prepared to drag me into the shelter if necessary.

Although we were but feet from the teeming pavement of Briggate, the entrance to the blank-walled air raid shelter was round the back, out of sight of passers-by. Alarm bells rang inside my head and with a mighty effort I tugged myself free of the not so kind gentleman's grasp and tore out of the churchyard and across Briggate, narrowly missing being sliced in two by an approaching tram. I ran all the way down the Lower Headrow and threw myself headlong through the swinging doors of the Vicar Lane end of the Market. Here I felt among friends. I dodged through the length of the Market, zigzagging around the stalls in case I was being followed, and came out at the far end near the Corn Exchange, where, barely giving my Bovril sign a glance, I hurried to the sanctity of the No. 12 tram stop.

All this time I was clutching my shilling, which I now felt to be contaminated money. Although at the very last second I had managed to extricate myself from some unimaginable fate, I regarded myself, in an obscure way, as tainted, and was anxious to wipe my predatory benefactor and his gift from my mind. I considered giving it to my mother with the explanation that I had found it in the street; but then I thought it would taint her too. The church collection box was rejected for the same reason. I debated whether to present the money to Woodbine Lizzie on my next trip to Town but decided that the gesture would draw too much attention to myself. In the end the shilling went into the funds of the Middleton Hiking Club and was frittered away on sweets and lemonade within the week. I had no more alarming adventures. I was now streetwise.

10 All these excursions had to be paid for, naturally, and it was not every day that strangers were handing out shillings on the street.

One source of revenue was the handleless teacup in the chocolate-brown cupboard by the hearth, half filled with worn Victorian pennies for the gas meter. (There was a theory, based on what scientific evidence I have no idea, that the thinner the penny the more gas you got for your money, the belief being that thick coins caused the dials to go round faster.) Provided the Plimsoll line of pennies was not too low, and being ever careful not to carry the pitcher to the well too often, I could rely on perhaps twopence or threepence a fortnight from the gas money, enough for a return tram ride into Town plus light refreshments at Granelli's sarsaparilla stall at the entrance to Kirkgate Market, or for a sustaining bag of chips on the Middleton Hiking Club's continuing explorations into the interior of Hunslet.

Another source was my income, legitimate and otherwise, from my first ever employment, as a choirboy with the Church of the Holy Cross, aka the Holy Hoss (Horse). Having learned, at the age of eight, that the Holy Hoss choir paid the astounding rate of ninepence a quarter to its juvenile members, I auditioned with a rendering, in my bell-clear treble, of "There is a green hill far away, without a city wall", a rendering so well received that I was later emboldened to offer it as my contribution to the 23rd SE Leeds Wolf Cubs' Christmas concert, when I was mortified to be told it was not suitable.

My ninepence a quarter was augmented by the tithe I regularly extracted, with the aid of the bread knife, from the church funds collection box that was issued to all choir members to rattle in the faces of their relatives and acquaintances. Given that the box was in the shape of the Holy Cross itself and that its predominant colour was an awesomely ecclesiastical purple, I was keenly aware as I prised out my illicit share of the takings that I was committing a mortal sin. Consequently each act of theft was always accompanied by a prayer, when I would set out to convince God that He must regard these twopences and threepences as a loan, and that He would be getting His money back with interest one of these fine days. My failure to donate the kind gentleman's shilling to the church probably scotched that particular piece of special pleading. But even had it been put to me that in helping to finance my trips into Town in this way I was paving my path to Hell, I should have settled for the Bovril sign and the Arcade tableaux vivant and the Majestic news scanner and the trams squashing spilled blood oranges to pulp as they rocked past the back of the Market, and let my chance of any future, further heaven go.

Another and far more audacious criminal activity, which would have led me straight through the gates of Shadwell Reformatory had it gone wrong, was the lucrative Yorkshire Penny Bank Forgery (twenty-odd years later to be turned to even greater profit as the basis of a short story).

The Yorkshire Penny Bank — now the Yorkshire Bank and no longer even Yorkshire-owned — was the people's bank, with reassuringly Corinthian-columned branches in even the poorest suburbs. Several times I had jumped up and down outside the tall windows of its headquarters building in Town, just to catch a glimpse of its mahogany-lined, commissionaire-protected interior. I felt I had a personal interest in the institution, for it was known to every child as our very own school bank, its management having hatched out a scheme whereby every Monday morning all the teachers in all the schools in Leeds turned themselves into unpaid bank clerks for half an hour while they collected our threepences and sixpences and entered them in the blue, linen-covered miniature paying-in books issued by the Bank. While no one ever said it was compulsory to have a Yorkshire Penny Bank account from the age of about eight onwards, no one ever said it wasn't, and some faint social stigma attached to those who did not come to school on Monday mornings clutching a threepenny or sixpenny bit wrapped in a scrap of newspaper.

Having seen a good deal of Leeds by now I was developing a hankering to have a look at Bradford. Bradford was regarded as pretty well our twin city, certainly our rival city. Plum-coloured

Bradford Corporation buses went from City Square, and Bradford LNER trains from the misnamed Central Station well out of the city centre. It was also well known that you could travel to Bradford all the way by tram, changing at a distant Leeds terminus and crossing a no-man's-land of cinders to the Bradford border.

Bradford was accessible. I had not costed such an ambitious excursion but I reckoned that it would be realistic to capitalise the venture at a shilling. My weekly contribution to the Yorkshire Penny Bank was threepence. I could be in Bradford within a month.

The money would have to be repaid some time, somehow, of course. While my mother was not in the habit of inspecting my bank book week by week, she was bound to check it sooner or later, upon which – I had my story already worked out – I should explain that the teacher had been too busy to mark it up lately, but that every penny was accounted for in his register whenever she wished to draw our savings out. This she would undoubtedly wish to do at once. There would be a shilling to find.

This was an impossibly large sum to conjure out of thin air, and short of out-and-out theft, for which I had had little appetite ever since the gates of Shadwell had clanged upon an ashen-faced classmate after he had been found stealing from the teachers' common room, my only hope was that the day of reckoning would coincide with the three-monthly payout from the Holy Cross choir, which I could augment with coppers saved by forgetting to pay in my school milk money, or, when despatched to the fish and chip shop for five twopenny pieces and sixpennorth, buying only fourpennorth of chips in the hope that no one would notice (they always did). The sensible thing would have been to wait until I had the Holy Cross stipend in my hand before embarking on the Bradford adventure; but I was too impatient to cross that cinder-patch frontier.

In the event I was never to get to Bradford, or at least not at that stage in my exploring career. On the first Monday morning upon having hatched my plan I duly withheld the Yorkshire Penny Bank's threepence, telling the teacher without a blink that my mother could not afford it this week – a common excuse for every kind of non-payment, and one which was always accepted without comment except, semi-sotto voce, from the snickering plimsolled have-nots in the back row. My explanation was rendered more convincing by the circumstance that my account was currently empty, my life savings of half a crown or so having been withdrawn the previous week to

71

pay for some household necessity or other. Thus I should have raised a quarter of my required capital. Alas, the threepenny bit did not survive the week; like the kind gentleman's shilling it was squandered on aniseed balls and licorice allsorts. Despite my assurances to myself that this was a one-off indulgence and that next Monday the savings programme would begin in earnest, the following week's threepence went the same way – and the next week's, and the next.

By now, the Bradford adventure indefinitely shelved, I had begun to regard the Yorkshire Penny Bank contributions as part of my income. I had unleashed a voracious appetite for sweetmeats that had to be fed. One week I invested in a foot-long bar of everlasting toffee that so much lived up to its name that I could not finish it even by dawdling the long way home from school. I was obliged to bury it in the hole I was digging to Australia. Much later, when my brothers requisitioned the hole as part of the foundations for the Anderson air-raid shelter that we and every other family were by now erecting, I felt as Christie must have done when the police came to dig up the floorboards of No. 10 Rillington Place. But the remains of my bar of everlasting toffee were never unearthed; or if they were, nobody disclosed the fact.

By the time the inevitable day came round when my mother took it into her head to examine my bank book, it was all of one and sixpence in the red. The expected scene took place – what a way to run a school bank etc. I had all my answers ready, even for the contingency that my mother might decide to go down to the school in person and sort the matter out (teacher off ill). Happily this nightmare scenario did not arise, but as expected I was ordered to close down my Yorkshire Penny Bank account instantly. I had until Monday to find one and six.

But how? My Holy Cross quarterly ninepence, always erratic, had yet to materialise. The gas money was low. I had but one possible source of quick revenue, and that was the 23rd SE Leeds Wolf Cub pack's impending trip to Belle Vue Zoo, Manchester, for which intended participants had been paying in threepence a week for some weeks past. There was two shillings in the kitty so far – one and six plus sixpence over.

An interview with Baloo was called for – a matter for some apprehension. Baloo, a lady so heavily moustached that she was almost a Kipling lookalike, was the assistant cub mistress who attended to administrative matters such as this. She was believed to be in love with Akela, a remote figure approachable only by those of the rank of sixer and above. Whatever Baloo's feelings for Akela, there was certainly no love lost between Baloo and me. Baloo it had been who had scotched my notion of singing "There is a green hill far away" at the Christmas concert. Then, when I had concocted a little magazine called the *Wolf Cub Weekly* and painstakingly made six copies of it with their pages neatly stitched together with needle and thread, she had confiscated the entire issue on the grounds that my illustrated article on knot-tying might be − not was, might be − misleading. I hated Baloo and I believe she hated me for the odd creature I was, but she had to be faced.

On cub night, Friday, therefore, I approached Baloo and put it to her that after all I would not be going on the Belle Vue trip, since it clashed with a projected family outing to Bridlington, so please could I have my money back. Baloo, knowing full well that we did not possess the means to get collectively past the end of the street, was deeply suspicious, and asked, cunningly it seemed to me, if I would like her to go and see my mother and talk it over. Equally cunning, I intimated that it was not my mother but my Uncle Edward she ought to be talking to, since it was in his car that we would be going to Bridlington, and in his caravan that we would be spending the weekend. This supplementary piece of misinformation seemed to convince Baloo and after Taps she handed over a florin in a clean white envelope.

A forged withdrawal from the Yorkshire Penny Bank would require red ink. Luckily there was for some reason a supply in the house, otherwise I should have had to sink my surplus sixpence in the purchase of a bottle. As it was, it went into a quarter-pound of Dairy Box chocolates, then new on the market, which I had seen in the window of the Tivoli Chocolate Cabin and coveted. They took even longer to eat than everlasting toffee, and I couldn't finish them. Sooner than bury them in my hole to Australia I took the remaining two or three caramel cups and nut clusters home with me and told my mother that our teacher had come to school with an enormous box of chocolates and handed them round. She was even more suspicious than Baloo had been, but I was able to mollify her with the production of one and sixpence in cash and a Yorkshire Penny Bank book in which, during her absence at the shops over the weekend, I had forged, with a fair imitation of my teacher's scrawled initials, the blue ink entry of six sums of threepence paid over in successive weeks, and the red ink entry of one shilling and sixpence withdrawn, the transaction being neatly ruled off with a double red line. Should my mother wish to re-open the Yorkshire Penny Bank account at some future date — I doubted that she would, and she never did — then I would tear the bank book into shreds and declare it lost.

I was not out of the wood yet, although it was some consolation that the wood was more garlanded with confectionery than the one frequented by Hansel and Gretel. I thought it prudent not to mention to my mother that I had opted out of the Belle Vue Zoo venture and so threepences continued to be provided towards the trip over the next four weeks, when the fund was supposed to be maximised at three shillings. These threepences, needless to say, went on sweets. I was by now sated on slab toffee and all-day suckers — this was a time when threepence would buy you thirty chocolate caramels or six sherbet dabs — and I almost longed for the day when the endless supply of threepenny bits would dry up.

When it did, I had a problem. I had not thought too deeply about what I proposed to do about that fateful Saturday when the 23rd SE Leeds pack would be roaming around Belle Vue — secretly I hoped that the outing would be rained off, or that three shillings would fall out of the sky and I should be able to go on it after all. I now bitterly regretted having frittered all that money away — I didn't particularly want to see the zoo, but I did want to see Manchester.

The black letter day dawned. I had thought of feigning illness but rejected the idea in case my mother demanded her money back. There was nothing for it but to go through the motions. Accordingly I rose at six and was in my uniform, neckerchief straight and green garter tabs in position, by half past, and with a packed lunch and a packed tea inside my rolled-up mackintosh. My last fear was that my mother would insist on accompanying me to the Holy Cross scout hut from which the coach — a Sammy Ledgard one, of course — was to depart. But she didn't. She gave me twopence to spend on myself, counselled me to go to the lavatory before embarking on the return journey, and waved me on my way.

With twopence I could get to Town and back and have a penny for a glass of sarsaparilla in the Market. But in my uniform I felt too conspicuous: I would be a marked boy. For the same reason I rejected the streets of Hunslet. I headed, instead, for the park. If questioned, I would explain that the rest of the pack were roaming about in the rhododendrons playing hide and seek. The park was not even open at that hour and I had a considerable amount of trudging up and down to do before a uniformed ranger finally appeared and unlocked the gates. I filled in some of the time wandering down to the old parish church of St Mary's where my father was buried, and staring at his grave for a while.

It was the longest day. I walked several times around the boating lake, skimmed stones across it until my arm ached, played on the swings until the melancholy creak of their chains induced tears of self-pity, traipsed aimlessly through the Murder Woods, set off to crawl through my storm drain but found it silted with mud, went and looked at the colliery and the coal railway, and then ate my lunch of potted meat sandwiches and seed cake. It could not yet have been nine o'clock. I resumed my meanderings, spent my twopence on chocolate macaroons in the park café, visited the drinking fountain for the tenth time, carved my initials in the old men's shelter with a piece of broken bottle, ate my packed tea, trudged back into the Murder Woods and had a lie down.

When I woke up it was pitch dark. There was a lot of rustling going on among the ferns and I was quite frightened. I hurried out of the park, fearful that the gates would be locked, but they were still open. I had no idea what time it was — the only nearby clock was on the tower of St Mary's but it would be far too dark to see it. So far as I knew it got dark at this time of year around nine o'clock — I could not say for certain for I had developed a minor neurosis which compelled me to close my eyes at seven p.m. promptly and not open them again until morning, otherwise I should sleep in and be late for school. I kept to this regime so rigidly that I would not open my eyes even to get up and go to the lavatory, and one day when my brother Dennis went on a school trip to Filey and came home late at night with a souvenir cardboard telescope, I refused to open my eyes to look at it but sat up in bed and felt it like a blind man, and put it to a blind eye like Nelson.

My mother was in the scullery when I got home, washing clothes and straining her eyes in the gloom to save electricity. It meant that she did not notice the filthy state I was in. She gave me a slice of bread and dripping and a mug of cocoa and allowed me to prattle on about the animals I claimed to have seen. I had mugged them up in Arthur Mee's *Children's Encyclopedia* at school so my account of the chimps' tea party and the elephants squirting water over one another was pretty convincing, or so I thought. My mother showed no signs of disbelief and my only worry was that it was long past my curfew and I should be late for church in the morning.

The next day the conversation in the Holy Cross vestry was exlusively and excitedly about Saturday's total eclipse of the sun, which had plunged our little world into darkness at around lunchtime. It could not possibly have been later than one in the afternoon when I got home from my fictitious journey across the Pennines. Yet my mother never asked me, then or ever, how I could have got to Manchester and back in so short a time, nor did she ever question my colourful account of a day at the zoo.

I have often wondered how much my mother secretly knew about my bizarre goings-on – the white card truancies, the wanderings around Hunslet, the petty thefts from the gas money, the childish figures in my bank book. She regarded me, I know, as a strange, mutant child – she was at the same time proud of me but, I believe, a little frightened of me. She seemed to have blind faith in my ability to do whatever I set out to do – she bought me that manuscript paper from Banks's music arcade when I was set upon becoming a composer, notebook and pencils when I decided I wanted to be a writer, a battered old volume of the plays of J.M. Barrie, which I still have, when I showed an interest in the theatre. Once, because she had heard me mention the magazine *Punch*, she bought me a bundle of back numbers, circa 1920, from Stringer's bookstall in Kirkgate Market – a periodical that would have been as comprehensible to her as *Pravda*. Another time, having heard me trying to speak French from some phrases in a public school story I was reading, she came home with a secondhand copy of Daudet's *Lettres de mon Moulin*. When, a few years on, my own stories and articles began to get published, she never showed the slightest surprise nor made any comment, although when I got to Fleet Street I did hear that she had remarked to someone that it was a pity my father wasn't alive, as he would have liked to have seen how her cuckoo in the nest had risen in the world.

The Yorkshire Penny Bank forgery marked the end of my criminal career, for shortly afterwards I gained a regular income of two shillings a week as a paper boy, contrary to the provisions of the Children and Young Persons Act of 1933 which required me to be two years older before I could legitimately hoist the *Yorkshire Evening Post*'s hessian satchel across my shoulder. My first round was the evening one, when I lived in hopes of being summoned to run through the streets shouting "Special! Murder! Special!" The call never came; but in due course I was awarded a second round, and then a morning round. In the fullness of time I had five newspaper rounds: two morning, two evening and one Sunday. In addition, I was assigned the task of collecting the paper money in my spare time. By now, I was earning twelve and sixpence a week.

A perk of my newspaper rounds was that I got to read my fill of comics and magazines. I had noticed that while most of the weekly papers came out on Tuesday or Wednesday, their publication date was always given as the Saturday. I therefore saw no harm in delaying delivery by a day or two until I had read them; my own house being on one of my rounds I made it a habit to drop in with a pile of literature which I would squat under a sofa cushion to read at my leisure. Thus I had access to the expensive twopenny comics like *Tiger Tim's Weekly* and *Playbox*, as well as to the D.C. Thomson "Big Five" – the *Hotspur*, the *Wizard*, the *Rover*, *Adventure* and the *Skipper*; and popular magazines such as *Answers*, *Titbits* and *John Bull* (for which, twenty years later, I was to write a moonlighting weekly column under a pseudonym). To my regret there was no call on our estate for the *Strand* magazine, price one shilling, which I had seen on W.H. Smith's railway bookstall and which was currently running the Eggs, Beans and Crumpets stories by P.G. Wodehouse; but we did have one customer for the twopenny journal *John O' London's Weekly* which I read avidly before passing it on to its rightful owner, a lonesome-looking, owlish figure who was said to be very good to his mother. That a literary weekly crammed with articles on the likes of Hardy, Victor Hugo, Shaw, Wells, Arnold Bennett, could be successfully targeted at the working classes, or anyway at a night school audience of aspiring clerks and office boys, now seems incredible. My illicit reading of *John O'London's* taught me a good deal about books and their authors; and in due course I subscribed to it myself.

But I was still at an age when my favourite reading was the comics, and of all the papers at my disposal – the *Butterfly*, *Chips*, *Comic Cuts*, *Crackers*, *Funny Wonder*, the *Jester*, the *Joker*, *Jingles*, *Larks*, the *Sparkler*, *Tip-Top*, the *Dandy*, the *Beano* – my favourite was the black-and-white *Film Fun*, with Laurel and Hardy on the front and back covers. Just as I had accepted that the priceless pair, as they were billed, came regularly to Leeds to act behind the magnifying-glass screens of the Tivoli, the Crescent and the Rex, running or catching the tram from one cinema engagement to the next, so did I entirely accept the *Film Fun* artists' proposition that they and all the rest of the paper's characters – Old Mother Riley, George Formby, Harold Lloyd, Wheeler and Woolsey – lived in the equivalent of Hunslet terraces, ever threatened by top-hatted rapacious landlords, their only access to wealth being the occasional feed at the Hotel de Posh as a reward for catching a striped-jerseyed burglar, or a charabanc visit to Shrimpton-on-Sea. I think I was ten before I gave up hopes of bumping into Laurel and Hardy or Frank Randle outside the Joseph Street baths.

My newspaper rounds not only provided me with a considerable income, even after I had donated three-fifths of it to the hard-pressed family coffers, but they gave me a taste for earning money. It was a lark.

On Saturday mornings, equipped with a soapbox on pram wheels which my brothers had knocked up for me, I would station myself outside the Thrift Stores and volunteer to transport old ladies' groceries home for them (this was when a stone of flour was still a regular part of the grocery order), for which my reward was usually twopence, or, in the case of the Little Sisters of the Poor who were most generous, threepence. Another Saturday morning activity was to hop on an errand boy's bike and cycle down to the Walls factory to restock the fridge for the newsagent who employed me as a paper boy; this would add another sixpence to my earnings. Then on Saturday afternoons I would often go golf-caddying for a shilling, a back-breaking chore in the days before golf carts. In due course I secured a regular Saturday afternoon job, in tandem with my friend Eric Bright – a three-and-sixpence-a-week contract to clean out a cobbler's shop, which involved clambering around the innards of a leather-grinding machine, from which I would emerge covered from head to foot in leather dust and stinking of hide like a cobbler's water baby. Eric went to work for the shop full time after leaving school, and subsequently inherited the business which he runs to this day. He is welcome to it.

Cleaning windows was another sideline – ground floor flats only, since I had no ladder – as was my firewood round: a bucket of raw wood chips for twopence, ransacked from council building sites and chopped with the lethal family hatchet over a brick. All in all, I was earning almost as much as I was to make in my first job after leaving school a few years later. While these activities did limit the outings of the Middleton Hiking Club except in the holidays, my expeditions into Town were carried off in some style, and I was no stranger to the soda fountain at Lewis's.

11 At some very early point in my life, possibly on the occasion of his death in 1932, although I would have been only three years old, I saw a picture of Edgar Wallace in the paper which was to have the most profound influence on my future.

It was of Wallace wearing the peaked cap of a Reuter's war correspondent when covering the Boer War. Shortly afterwards, on what must have been one of my first journeys into Town with my mother, I observed that the two newsvendors standing under the Bovril sign opposite the Corn Exchange also wore peaked caps, one emblazoned with the legend Y.E. POST, the other Y.E. NEWS. These, I reasoned, would be newspaper reporters like Edgar Wallace. Wearing their peaked caps and carrying their spiral notebooks, they would set off in the morning to find out all the news that was going. This they would write up, and the papers would print what they had written. The reporters would then don their hessian satchels and set off with quires of newspapers fresh off the presses, which they would sell opposite the Corn Exchange and other strategic points. This seemed to me an altogether agreeable way of earning a living, and from that day forward I never seriously contemplated spending my working life in any other fashion.

My resolve to follow Edgar Wallace's footsteps was considerably strengthened at the age of nine when Margaret Lane published her colourful biography of Wallace. Having learned about this from the pages of *John O' London's*, I promptly borrowed the book from the public library on one of my brothers' tickets and devoured it at a single sitting, crouching over the fire with my knees mottling bright red. I have re-read it once a year or so ever since. Wallace's romantic career – from street urchin to soldier poet, war correspondent, prolific journalist and novelist, dramatist, racehorse owner, Hollywood scriptwriter – was so crammed with adventure that the idea of pursuing any other course, even though he died with liabilities of £140,000, seemed unthinkable.

The other great influence on me was the theatre, but despite the example of Edgar Wallace who had six West End plays on in two years, this did not immediately strike me with the same thunderclap enthusiasm as my passion for journalism.

Like every other child in the north I was taken annually to the pantomime, although not usually until around April when the seats were cheaper (it was not unknown for the Leeds pantos to run on into the summer), and always to the Theatre Royal where the cut-price seats were cheaper than the Grand. We would perch up in the balcony, which raked so steeply that I went through the evening clutching my wooden arm-rests for fear of being pitched down into the stalls. I did not become a pantomime addict. While I enjoyed the transformation scenes and Kirby's Sensational Flying Ballet, I found the straight scenes leaden and the knockabout stuff involving bailiffs and dames inferior to what I could get from Old Mother Riley and Co. at the pictures. The audience participation spots ("He's behind you!") were a good excuse for indulging in juvenile hysteria, but in truth I was more impressed by the occasion than the event — being taken into Town in the evening when the trams and the streets were all lit up, queuing under a lamp-twinkling frosted glass canopy before the doors were open, the real live "augmented" orchestra playing the National Anthem before the performance instead of after it like the cinemas, the pungent stench of oranges that gradually permeated the whole theatre, the safety curtain — "For thine especial safety" — in the interval, and the lantern slide advertisements for Melbourne Ales, Sparkling Phosferrade and the King Charles First restaurant ("opposite circle entrance").

The panto apart, my first visit to the theatre was to the Leeds Moss Empire, when out of the proceeds of an afternoon's golf-caddying I treated my mother to a seat in the gods to watch the *Billy Cotton Band Show*, a favourite of hers on the wireless. I cannot remember who else was on the bill but they would have been mainly radio personalities of the order of Stainless Stephen whose gimmick, indeed his entire act, was to speak the punctuation marks in his patter; or Nosmo King who took his name from the No Smoking sign in a railway carriage and specialised in maudlin monologues; or Revnell and West who dressed up as schoolgirls; or any of a dozen comedians and comediennes whose faces I had hitherto seen only in the pages of the *Radio Fun* comic. It was interesting to identify them in the flesh, but while it was a red-letter evening I cannot claim to have yet been hooked on the theatre, which I regarded as very much an occasional divertissement like Belle Vue Zoo or Hunslet Feast, and not something that would become a part of the fabric of my life.

My conversion came about in a convoluted way. A fondness for the Red Circle school stories in borrowed copies of the *Hotspur* (Billy Bunter, Greyfriars and the *Magnet* were unheard of on our side of Leeds) had led me to start taking public school yarns out of the public library — among them, selected only because it was a big thick book, *Mike* by P.G. Wodehouse, which I recognised as being far superior to any of the stuff in that genre I had so far come across. *Mike* of course introduces Psmith, the very first of Wodehouse's gallery of comic characters. Browsing in the adult library, I subsequently came across, with my usual serendipity, a couple more Psmith stories — *Psmith in the City* and *Psmith Journalist*. These were enough to start me on a course of reading everything Wodehouse had published, and before long I was his disciple, able to quote long passages of his work years before I knew how to pronounce his name properly, and writing stories in what I believed to be an exact imitation of the Master's style.

One Saturday I read in the "Stage and Screen" notes in the *Yorkshire Evening Post* that a play adapted by my hero from the Hungarian of Ferenc Molnar, and starring Clive Brook, would be coming to the Grand Theatre the forthcoming week. It was *The Play's The Thing*, a touring revival, I imagine. I had never heard of Molnar nor of Clive Brook either but I would have walked to Bradford to see P.G. Wodehouse's name on a theatre programme, such was the extent of my fan-worship. Accordingly, the following Saturday I played truant from my stint at the cobbler's shop and took myself off to the matinee performance of *The Play's The Thing*. This was on my own: although my mother enjoyed the occasional play on the radio, I did not think Wodehouse's adaptation of a writer from a far-off country of which we knew little would be quite her cup of tea.

While I found the Grand an intimidating institution, a gilded palace in comparison with the rather down-at-heel Theatre Royal, and bristling with strange varnished signboards indicating *loges* and *fauteuils*, it was a great adventure; but on this occasion, as the afternoon wore on, even the thrill of being at the theatre by myself could not deflect from the excitement of what was going on down there on the stage. The play was indeed the thing. I was grabbed.

I cannot at this distance recall a single thing about the plot, the cast or the set. What I do remember, vividly, is the Act II curtain, which was an eye-opener. The characters start to argue about how they would end the act if life were a play. One of them delivers his idea of a curtain line and the curtain begins to come down — only for it to be halted by another, who has a far better ending. As the argument continues, so the curtain yo-yos up and down until, to roars of applause and laughter, they find an ending to Act II to suit all tastes. I found the device more theatrically breathtaking even than the transformation scene in *Cinderella* (and indeed was so impressed by its audacity that fifty years later I stole it for the ending of my play *Bookends* starring Michael Hordern and Dinsdale Landen). In those few anarchistic moments I had learned that the dramatist has manipulative powers equal to those of any wizard, and from then on the theatre had me in thrall. I went as often as the string of odd jobs that provided me with the means for theatregoing permitted. The Theatre Royal was the home of a thriving weekly rep company, Francis Laidler's Court Players, where a seat cost all of fourpence, so that as well as the post- or pre-West End touring productions at the Grand I saw a fair selection of the standard Thirties repertoire together with a certain amount of junk theatre in the way of bad detective plays and sub-Rattigan light comedies. I lapped it all up uncritically.

But life was not all the bright lights of the theatre and the Bovril sign. While I would sneak off to Town or into the bowels of Hunslet at every opportunity, like every boy of my age I spent the greater part of my spare time either at home or in the near vicinity, especially in winter when the nights were dark. Although I played my quota of street games I preferred to be indoors, where I could indulge my twin obsessions with journalism and the theatre.

Almost from the moment I learned to read and write I was making up little magazines, hand-printed on any scrap of paper I could find or on cheap scribbling blocks foraged from the Market by my mother, in purple ink which I manufactured by extracting the lead from indelible pencils and grinding it up into powder.

Most of these publications, like the *Wolf Cub Weekly* banned by Baloo, ran for only one issue — and at least one, the *Middleton Evening Argus*, not even that, since I could not find any news to put in it; but where readership surveys indicated a favourable response (the readership usually consisted solely of my mother), then some of my efforts might flourish for six or seven numbers. One such was *Ronnie Rabbit's Weekly*, intended as a direct rival to *Mickey Mouse Weekly* and featuring the adventures of Ronnie Rabbit, Percy Pig, Freddy Frog and any other alliterative creatures I found easy to draw and colour in with crayons. Another long-runner was the *Flag*, a monthly short story magazine in imitation of the *Strand*. Most of my publications were derivative: *Scotland Yard Weekly* (one issue) was a slavish copy of my brother Kenneth's favourite *Detective Weekly* starring Sexton Blake (mine starred one Inspector Steele); the *Film Fan* owed much to *Film Fun* — so much, indeed, that its contents consisted entirely of glued-up pictures snipped out of that paper.

But my most ambitious journalistic venture was the *Daily Treasure*, published six days a week for the enlightenment and entertainment of my friend Eric Bright, and put through his letter-box each morning along with his father's *Daily Herald*. The *Daily Treasure* consisted of pages torn out of an exercise book and folded across to make usually eight pages — ten on Friday, six on Saturday, twelve for the Bumper Xmas Number. It contained a serial story, a strip cartoon, a puzzle page, a jokes page (courtesy of the Merry and Bright column in the *Joker*), and several other features including a readers' letters corner which I had to make up myself in the absence of any contribution from my only reader. As if this were not enough, the back page of the first Saturday's edition, for no other reason than that I had run out of editorial copy and my newspaper round beckoned, rashly promised the launching of the *Sunday Treasure*. Resisting the temptation to add an *Evening Treasure* to the stable, I managed to keep up this prodigal feat of journalism for a good month before the *Daily Treasure* languished into a mere four pages filled with easy-to-compile maze puzzles, finally suspending publication with the announcement: "GREAT NEWS. From tomorrow the *Daily Treasure* amalgamates with the *Sunday Treasure* — bigger and better than ever! Order your copy now!" The *Sunday Treasure* lasted another two issues before following its former companion into oblivion.

At this time my favourite possessions were a toy Simplex typewriter on which I picked out short stories (very short stories, since the tiny little machine's keys were activated by a dial system, like a telephone, and it took about half an hour to compose a sentence); a John Bull printing set from whose rubber type I made up the billheads of the Middleton Printing Works (props: the *Daily Treasure*, *Ronnie Rabbit's Weekly*, the *Flag* &c. &c.); and a length of draught excluder attached to a Tate and Lyle sugar carton which was my wireless station, Radio Middleton, broadcasting comb and tissue paper and mouth organ recitals, occasional harp zither concerts, news bulletins culled from the *Yorkshire Evening Post*, and variety performances in silly voices (script again courtesy of the *Joker*'s Merry and Bright column). But one morning while eating my breakfast of Dalton's corn flakes — a local brand which we favoured as being cheaper than Kellogg's — I saw on the side of the packet a coloured illustration of a magical model theatre, free to anyone sending in eight packet tops plus a few stamps for postage and packing. I had to have it.

I already had a model theatre of sorts, which I had constructed myself out of an orange box. Part of my required reading at the time was a book which I kept out on more or less permanent loan from the public library, called *Let's Do A Play*. Fascinating and useful though this volume was in its advice, it did rather call for a double drawing room divided by folding doors behind which one could set up one's stage, besides presuming the existence of a dressing-up chest and a large repertory company of cousins and friends. Lacking all these components I tried to organise alfresco productions in the local Clerk of Works' sapling plantation, somewhat on the lines of the Regent's Park Open Air Theatre, with a grass hillock for a stage. Unfortunately I had difficulty in recruiting acting talent for the little plays I wrote and was soon reduced to using home-made hand-puppets with papier-mâché heads and rag costumes, after the manner of Punch and Judy. I gave performances out on the pavement, charging buttons for admission (buttons, abstracted from parental workboxes or in desperation ripped from one's own clothing, were the accepted currency for all street activities demanding payment, a humble trouser button being worth one unit, a mother-of-pearl hexagonal from a lady's coat representing six). Attendances were low.

But now came the Dalton's Corn Flakes Theatre. Eight packets to collect: not only were their torn-off tops to be saved up but, it seemed, the packets themselves would be required for the framework of the theatre — four boxes nestling horizontally for the stage, twin towers of two vertical boxes atop one another for either side of the proscenium. Eight boxes in all. It was a lot of corn flakes. Eating double my fill of them every morning, and sometimes for tea as well, did not make them go fast enough. Impatiently I took to filling my pockets with corn flakes each morning, scattering them behind me on my way to school or flinging them by the handful into privet hedges. Once I tipped half a packet into the hole I was digging to Australia.

At length the eight packets were accumulated and the packet tops sent off with the requisite stamps. After a nerve-racking wait of days that seemed like weeks, a large flat package eventually arrived by parcel post. Unlike most "sensational offers" then as now, my free gift was not a disappointment. In fact it was an enchantment. Fashioned on the lines of a Pollock's toy theatre, it consisted of a highly coloured pasteboard proscenium arch and orchestra pit; two sets of pasteboard gilt and red plush boxes or *loges* as I knew they were called; a deep blue pasteboard curtain with realistic wrinkles; a stage covering and three sets of wings; two pasteboard backcloths, one a castle interior, the other a castle exterior, together with some bits of cut-out scenery; and several cut-out characters. All this had to be constructed, with the aid of glue and much pushing of tab A through slot B, around the assembly of cornflakes boxes. The result was impressive. It was good and solid and it really did look like a proper theatre. I christened it the Grand and got down at once to preparing posters for my opening production with the aid of my John Bull printing set.

My wonderful theatre, I soon found, was capable of improvement. The accompanying scripts, which to my disgust were in rhyming couplets, were for *Cinderella* and *Aladdin and his Wonderful Lamp*. They made no provision for the low comedians and novelty acts I had seen fleshing out the Theatre Royal pantos, and after a couple of performances, one in front of my mother and the other in the presence of the cat, I proceeded to remedy this deficiency by cutting figures out of Donald McGill comic postcards and mounting them on strips of cardboard so that, like Cinderella and her cronies, they could be pushed on and off the stage. I then set about rewriting the scripts, interpolating comic dialogue which as usual owed much to the *Joker*'s Merry and Bright column. I then turned my attention to the scenery which was too skimpy for my satisfaction; I proceeded to augment it with scenes of my own construction, including three-dimensional furniture made out of matchboxes, plus some special effects such as a trap-door cut into the stage through which a demon king might emerge when required, and a Christmas tree fairy who could fly across the stage invisibly suspended on cotton in fair simulation of Kirby's Sensational Flying Ballet. Finally, I got my brothers to help me set up proper footlights − a string of torch bulbs concealed behind a strip of cocoa tin, and connected to a bicycle lamp battery.

While the Middleton Grand Theatre was to remain my most cherished toy until I put childish things behind me, the pantomime as an art form quickly palled and I began to mount more or less original productions of my own devising, including a melodrama based on some penny dreadful yarn I had read in one of the comics, which featured not only a realistic snow effect but, anticipating *Miss Saigon* by half a century, a cardboard autogiro which landed on the stage after circling the flies. I also, pandering to a street audience of reluctant button-payers who were not overly impressed by the legitimate theatre, introduced a season of variety shows after the fashion of the *Billy Cotton Band Show* and featuring Donald McGill characters whom I pedantically insisted on endowing with proper names such as McDonald & Fraser ("Scots Wae Hae!") and Bobby Lupin ("Here to Amuse You") so that they would look the more authentic in the John Bull-printed programme. These performances, needless to say, were favourably reviewed in whatever publication I happened to be editing at the time.

So a supposedly deprived childhood drifted blissfully by. Looking back I can see that a good deal of it − the white card trips to Town, the urban rambles of the Middleton Hiking Club, the hours spent making up little magazines or playing with my toy theatre − was pure escapism. But it was an escape into realism, not away from it: I wanted to be in this real world of smokestacks and department stores and printing works and newspapers and theatres and wireless stations. All along, I was rehearsing for what I was determined would be the shape of my adulthood.

TWO

Billy Liar

'I did nothing but walk around town for an hour and a half, watching Saturday evening begin to happen and the slow queues forming outside the Odeon and the Gaumont. The people walked about as though they were really going somewhere. I stood for a quarter of an hour at a time, watching them get off the buses and disperse themselves about the streets. I was amazed and intrigued that they should all be content to be nobody but themselves.'

– BILLY LIAR, 1959

1 When I was ten and a half my mother, after first asking if I
would like to see where we might soon be going to live, took
me so far into the outskirts of the city that the suspicion
arose in my mind, as the landscape grew more remote and grass-
dominated, that this was another Mickey Mouse ruse and I was
about to be delivered up to Shadwell Reformatory.

It was a dual tram ride: the familiar No. 12 Lance-corporal into
Town and then the unfamiliar, foreign-looking No. 20 – for each
area had its own style or class of tram, models readily identified by
tramway buffs as the Chamberlain, the Beeston Air-Brake, the
Brush-bodied Horsfield and so on – whose roller indicator
pronounced that it was going to a place I had never heard of, Halton.

Setting out from Kirkgate Market we trundled past Quarry Hill
Flats, beyond Beckett Street and St James's Hospital, and so up the
York Road, which seemed interminable. Fortunately the tram,
whatever make it might have been, was not one of the old sick-
making bone-rattlers. Rows of terraces, so much cleaner on this side
of the city that their brickwork might have been scrubbed like the
donkey-stoned steps, gave way to modern, single-storey clothing
factories – single-storey because land was cheaper out here, and it
was more efficient to have all the work processes on one level – and
pockets of "bought houses" interspersed with mock-Tudor
shopping parades and the odd luxury cinema; then an alarming vista
of fields and what I suspected could be even meadows before we
passed under a railway bridge and alighted at a modern pub, almost
a roadhouse had I known anything about such things, called the
Wykebeck Arms.

This was strange territory indeed. Ahead of us was a dismal
scrubland, through which had been cut a long, straight, unmade
road. A good half mile ahead of us, shimmering in the summer haze,
was a brand-new housing estate, Halton Moor. Shadwell, I reflected,

as we plodded along the caked mud path towards it, would have been an improvement. We were at the end of the Earth.

The estate was so new that it smelled of raw wood, paint and putty. Not yet of tarmac: there was no tarmac. The earth road and dust pavements, and the wooden-framed rooftops of houses waiting to be tiled, reminded me of a Wild West town as seen at the Tivoli – or perhaps I was romanticising, from a wish that I was in Main Street, Dead Man's Gulch, rather than Cartmell Drive, Halton Moor estate. (All the streets and crescents and the drives wide enough to herd cattle down were named after Lake District beauty spots – Kendal Drive, Ingleton Drive, Ullswater Crescent, Windermere Crescent – with the aim, no doubt, of persuading us that we were somewhere else.) As my mother led me up the dried mud path of No. 105 and let us in through the violently red front door – its redness reminded me of a surfeit of raspberry lollipops I had endured during my period of Yorkshire Penny Bank affluence – I tried to come to terms with my new address, putting it in as favourable a light as possible.

It was, to begin with, a proper house and not a flat masquerading as a house. The architectural style was R.A.H. Livett ARIBA in his Dutch period – white pebbledash with overhanging red-tiled eaves, so that the bedroom windows peeped out of the roof. I rather approved of that. There were more of these bedrooms, furthermore, than at Middleton – practically one each (we were being moved because of overcrowding). I wasn't sure I approved of that – being squashed three in a bed with two of my brothers, while it had led to many a midnight demarcation dispute, had been a cosy arrangement. Stairs were a novelty and I looked forward to sliding down the banister like Just William. The back garden boasted a brick air-raid shelter and that, once we had got some bits of furniture and a storm lamp in, could double as the clubhouse of the Halton Moor (late Middleton) Hiking Club and the offices and factory of the Halton Moor Printing Works.

But the house, as even my mother had to concede – and she was quite taken with such mod cons as the galvanised stove that didn't need blackleading and the indoor coal shed – was "at the back of beyond". If the planners had got Middleton wrong they had got Halton Moor even more wrong. It was half a mile to anywhere anyone wanted to go: half a mile to the tram stop, half a mile to the shops, half a mile to school which was in fact on an older,

Middleton-vintage estate across the wasteland. The fish and chip shop was so far away that the five pieces and sixpennorth were cold before we got them home. There was no public library, no church, no scout hut, no park, no cinema. How would I get to Hunslet? How would I get to Town?

We moved in — "flitted", as the vernacular had it. With three wage-packets coming in our circumstances had much improved by now and I was awarded my own bed. In place of the oven-hot house brick wrapped in an old woollie that had been my bed-warmer, I now had a proper hot-water bottle. I missed my brick. To my surprise, I even missed Middleton, and took to wandering around the neighbouring estate, Osmondthorpe, because of its resemblance to what was already beginning to seem, in retrospect and in contrast to the harsh open space of Halton Moor, a mellow, human-scale estate. But most of all I missed Hunslet, particularly since I had no idea how to get there from here.

The Halton Moor Hiking Club drew a blank. Exploring what was left of the original Halton Moor — the tract of pointless grass that our little settlement of Dutch houses overlooked — I found that a wandering stream — the Wyke Beck, after which the Wykebeck Arms was named — ran through it. It was an unappetising beck, scummy with waste from the TB hospital a couple of miles upstream and sometimes bobbing with hideous, misshapen bladders which youths who knew the facts of life swore were human foetuses but which I believe were the bloated carcases of stillborn water rats. But it was fast-flowing and, at about four feet wide, quite navigable for anyone with a small craft. Almost certainly, I reasoned, with hazy recollection of something I had read about waters and their tributaries, it must lead either down into the canal or the river. I had lately been reading *Tom Sawyer*: my immediate resolve was to build a raft and sail it into Town, mooring at Leeds Bridge.

That evening, on a scrounged sheet of greaseproof paper, I drew up an elaborate blueprint. It was an ambitious raft: it would have a mast and a sail, a rudder, a cosy shelter aft with a roof, and a handsome supplies box with rope handles and my initials burned into it in pokerwork which would serve also as a seat. The craft would be called the *Spirit of Loidis* (I had also been reading about the exploits of Lindbergh: and we had learned at school that Loidis was the olden-days name for Leeds).

First I had to get my materials together. Of prime importance was the raft itself, which ideally should have been constructed of logs trussed together with rope. Although there were more than enough trees about I had no access to a proper saw, and the voice of reality told me that the task of chopping them down was beyond me. The next best thing would have to be a ready-made substitute. The Halton Moor estate at the time was one great building site and there was wood about in plenty, most of it unguarded (very handy for anyone with a new firewood round to build up). I knew where there was a supply of unpainted front doors, stacked under a tarpaulin like Middleton Park deckchairs. They were on the side of the unmade road very near to a convenient loop in the beck, and it was with no great difficulty that I managed to dislodge one and drag it down through the scrub to a stretch of cracked mud below the bank of the beck which I intended to serve as my boatyard.

While I appreciated that I had yet to find my mast and sail and all the other accoutrements necessary for the *Spirit of Loidis*'s maiden voyage, I saw no harm in launching my council house front door at once and taking her for an experimental sail. Accordingly I pushed it into the beck, climbed gingerly aboard, and with the aid of an overhanging branch cast off. My front door raft at once took on water through the keyhole and promptly sank, leaving me standing up to my knees in the middle of the Wyke Beck as a dead rat floated gently by.

I was puzzled and disappointed. If I knew anything about elementary physics it was that wood does not sink; yet sunk my raft was and sunk it remained, in the fullness of time silting over with mud until it was all but invisible on the bed of the murky beck. Thus ended the first and last voyage of the *Spirit of Loidis*. It was as well. Subsequently I learned that had I managed to negotiate the weir a little way downstream, the Wyke Beck did indeed flow into the Aire and Calder Navigation – but only after it had become, for a spell, the main effluent channel of the Skelton Grange sewage works.

My bacon was saved by the declaration of war, which came soon after the move to Halton Moor. The morning of 3 September 1939 found me sitting on the garden gate with no particular place to go. Mr Chamberlain's tired voice floated out from a dozen open windows: ". . . No such undertaking has been received . . ." The implications were blindingly clear: I should have access to my brother Kenneth's bicycle.

Kenneth was (and remains) a cycling freak. He had accumulated three machines over the years: his lightweight racing model with the cane-spoke wheels, which he kept in his bedroom and greased with Vaseline; his touring bike on which he was (and is) in the habit of going to Wales and back, which was kept either in the hallway or leaning up against the sideboard; and his everyday working bike, which was usually left out by the back door or, if wet, in the scullery. The word conscription had been in my vocabulary for some time: Kenneth's call-up, I knew, was imminent (the other two brothers would follow him into active service in due course). There was no point in asking his permission to ride either his racing bike or his touring bike, both of which in any case would be smothered in Vaseline and immobilised for the duration. But he would not mind my borrowing his workaday machine. At least I assumed he wouldn't. He had gone for a soldier before I ever had the chance to ask.

The immediate consequence of the outbreak of war, then, was the disbandment of the Halton Moor Hiking Club and the formation of the Halton Moor Cycling Club. I immediately pedalled forth in search of Hunslet. A pall of sulphurous smoke – smog, as it came to be known – hovering in the far distance beyond a cluster of cooling towers told me that that was as likely a direction as any. (I had yet to acquire a map of Leeds. Probably it never crossed my otherwise enquiring mind that there was such a thing. Maps were what you found in school atlases, and they were of oceans, deserts and mountain ranges rather than of Sweet Street, Meadow Lane and Pepper Road.)

The Halton Moor Cycling Club's inaugural spin began unpromisingly, taking me off the by now tarmacadamed boring streets of the estate to bumpy tracks leading first to the sewage works, where I should have ended up on the *Spirit of Loidis* had the voyage down the Wyke Beck ever got underway; and then even more dismayingly to a farmyard complete with animals. Doubling back on my tracks, however, and keeping the cloud of smog firmly in view, I eventually established that I had taken a simple wrong turning. By wheeling right at the end of Cartmell Drive instead of pushing straight on through the self-evidently rural lanes I found myself bowling along a good firm lane of crushed cinders known as Black Road, which led, through a gate proclaiming PRIVATE ROAD, into a good firm lane of packed red sand known equally appropriately as Red Road. And this in turn, via a couple of twists and turns, led me to a familiar-sounding thoroughfare called Easy Road, which either

Ur-memory or the change in the texture of the surrounding buildings from smallholding stone to factory brick persuaded me that I was in the proximity of Hunslet.

So it proved. Easy Road, to my delight, led me into South Accommodation Road, which took me across the river Aire and into Hunslet Road to the right and Low Road to the left. I was home.

2 As for the war itself, apart from some initial frissons at the possibility of the Germans invading Leeds and using the Little Sisters of the Poor as human clappers for the parish church bells, it was for a ten-year-old a huge adventure.

The expeditions into Town offered fresh excitements, starting with the tram ride. All the tram windows were covered with thick protective netting against bomb blast or shrapnel, with little diamond-shaped apertures so the passengers could see where they were. If I was lucky I might board a tram stripped of its advertisements and painted khaki, as if about to join a great invasion armada of trams that would sail across the Channel and rock from Ostend to Berlin. The fact was that there was a national paint shortage and the corporation had run out of its livery blue.

Town on a war footing had to be re-explored to the full. The entrances to Kirkgate Market were reduced to narrow slits in a barricade of sandbags, while the glass roof was painted black in accordance with the Air Raid Precautions regulations, as were the roofs and domes of all the arcades. No paint shortage there. The windows of all the shops were draped in netting like the trams, except for one or two go-ahead establishments such as Lewis's and Montague Burton the Tailor of Taste, whose windows were protected by a patent contraption of cross-diagonal taut wires that would prevent their shattering – a principle I did not entirely trust. To enter a shop you had to claw your way through swathes of blackout material, and the effect, if you were stepping out of the dusk into a brightly lit Woolworth's or Marks and Spencer, was of entering an Aladdin's cave.

Air raid shelters like the one in the churchyard of St John the Evangelist had dotted the city for some time. They were now augmented by huge static water tanks, like free-standing swimming pools, which were erected in the middle of the Headrow and the other main thoroughfares for the benefit of firefighters with their stirrup pumps. Hastily built brick air raid wardens' posts and first-aid stations appeared in all the public squares, there were fire boats on the river painted grey like submarines, and concrete pillboxes with machine-gun slits guarding such strategic points as Leeds Bridge, the marshalling yards and, more importantly to my mind, the back of Kirkgate Market. It was comforting to think that if the enemy wanted to take Game Row he would have to go round to the front entrance.

My Bovril sign was extinguished for the duration, as were all the other lights in Town. It was the first time I had ever seen it unlit and I gave its naked light bulbs a long and melancholy stare. Although I had never yet set foot in a theatre by daylight, when the sun streaming through the open exit doors shows up the tattiness of the moth-eaten red plush and the peeling caryatids, that was the effect: the Bovril sign was reduced to a structure of girders and nuts and bolts and a tangle of wires, like a signal gantry over the railway lines.

Hunslet, too, had to be rediscovered. With my gas-mask case bobbing against my hip I prowled the area noting that the incidence of sandbags and static water tanks was much higher even than in Town. The reason of course was the high concentration of factories and mills in Hunslet, most of which had gone over to war work. Factory walls were now topped with coiled barbed wire, and the tall gates of some of them were guarded, to my great satisfaction, by rifle-bearing soldiers in sentry boxes. The Halton Moor Cycling Club, noting these developments, militarised itself into the 1st Mobile Cadet Corps and regularly patrolled Hunslet in search of spies and unexploded bombs.

In fact, much to my disappointment, not a single enemy bomber had yet come anywhere near Leeds, although I listened hopefully each night for their ominous drone, and searchlights sweeping the sky picked out the barrage balloon that protected the Skelton Grange cooling towers like a stationary *Graf Zeppelin*. The searchlight unit was on Hunslet Moor and the 1st Mobile Cadet Corps had been along and given it a good stare.

At home, there was the novelty of ration books, blackout blinds on the windows, the bucket of water at the ready to put out incendiary bombs, Churchill and Lord Haw-Haw on the wireless, and officious neighbours in the regalia of air raid wardens patrolling the streets shouting, "Put that light out!"

My comic papers were doing their bit, or some of them were: all the characters in *Film Fun*, with the understandable exception of Old Mother Riley, enlisted as privates in the British army the moment war was declared – even Abbott and Costello, Harold Lloyd and Joe E. Brown who were American citizens. From the nature of their lowly duties, Laurel and Hardy appeared to be in the Pioneer Corps, which squared with the humble working-class dwellings behind the gasworks from which they had been mobilised. The inhabitants of *Radio Fun*, on the other hand, excepting only Jack Warner who was a soldier already by virtue of appearing in the wireless show *Garrison Theatre*, remained non-combatants to a man, the Western Brothers even flouting wartime austerity by continuing to wear top hats and tails.

Needless to say, the publications of the Halton Moor Printing Works were fervently patriotic. The *Flag* magazine was resuscitated, its front cover featuring, in full crayon colour, the flags of all the Allies. For the first time the *Flag* carried advertising, in the shape of government exhortations to lend to defend the right to be free and not to be a squanderbug, which I clipped out of the newspapers. Until now I had always resisted printing advertising matter: although it would have made my magazines look more authentic and reduced the number of editorial pages that had to be slogged out, I resented the idea of giving free space to the likes of De Reske Minors cigarettes and Chilprufe Vests.

My mother sanguinely saw three of her sons off to war and informed me, in a rare sentimental moment, that I was the man of the house now – a post that seemed entirely honorary, since in common with all northern mothers she took even the heaviest household chores upon herself, accepted personal responsibility for locking up and winding the clock, and slept with her handbag under her pillow. Her own war effort was to enlist as the street National Savings collector. When my various preoccupations permitted, I would accompany her on her rounds, and when I was twelve I was to write a short humorous account of some of the odd customers we encountered. This I copied out in the neat purple lettering I employed in my magazines and sent it off to the *National Savings News*. They published it – my first-ever professional appearance in print – but without fee.

The subject of evacuation came up. I was ambivalent about the scheme. On the one hand it was a lark. You were billeted on complete strangers who by all accounts were benevolent auntie and uncle figures who gave you their sweet ration and other treats. On the other, you would be living in the country. Several boys of my acquaintance were evacuated to a tolerably large Dales village called Pateley Bridge. Their mothers, after visiting them at weekends, reported that they were as brown as nuts. I did not like the sound of this at all. I had been as brown as a nut myself once, and that was during my sojourn at Silverdale Poor Children's Holiday Camp. It was when I heard that Silverdale itself was to become an evacuee reception centre that I firmly vetoed the whole idea. My mother seemed relieved. She liked having me about the house, even though she sometimes complained about the interminable squeaky voices on Radio Halton Moor, which was now on a war footing and broadcasting nightly.

The most significant event of the "phoney war", as this uneasy period of nothing very much happening was known, was yet to come. This was the momentous announcement by the headmaster in assembly one Friday morning that the school would be closed until further notice.

I could not believe my luck. I had not yet dared try on the white card trick at my new school — the card was by now grubby and dog-eared, and I very much doubted that it would deceive my teachers who seemed altogether smarter than the Middleton bunch. The school closure, which was occasioned by the need to find training camp space for battalions of conscripts, meant that for the foreseeable future I could roam around Town as I pleased without fear of the Board Man's heavy hand on my shoulder as I sipped my glass of sarsaparilla while watching the passing show in Kirkgate Market.

I quickly developed a routine. Each morning after delivering my newspapers and perhaps cleaning a few windows or selling a bucket or two of firewood, I would go and stare through the railings at the squads of soldiers drilling in the playground and digging trenches in the playing fields. Since I had always been hopeless at games this sight afforded me a great deal of quiet satisfaction. I would then either set off into Town or on one of the excursions of the Halton Moor Cycling Club.

I did not invariably cycle over to Hunslet, in fact I set about thoroughly investigating the east side of Leeds where our new estate was situated. My most notable discovery, in the course of trying to locate the Barnbow munitions factory where my mother had worked in the First World War and subjecting it to one of my stares, was that of a splendid custom-built public library, the Percival Leigh branch, in a residential district of "bought houses" known as Crossgates. I was so taken by it that I quite lost interest in the nearby munitions plant. Middleton library, while I had been greatly attached to it, I could now see was a poor affair by comparison – it was in fact the school assembly hall converted into a public library in the evenings by sliding back the series of panels which concealed the shelves of books. Osmondthorpe library, such as it was, was also housed in the school. There had apparently been plans to build a proper library on the Halton Moor estate, but these had been scotched by the war. But the Percival Leigh branch – whoever he may have been – was all a library should be. It was an airy, elegant, single-storey Thirties structure of red brick, with many windows, and cork-tiled floors. Its wide steps were used as a gathering place by girls in green blazers from a nearby private school, giving it to my mind the air of the college campus in the Andy Hardy movies. The girls were a sight more clean and wholesome than any I had so far encountered in my life and I fell in love indiscriminately if platonically with all of them.

But I was even more in love with the Percival Leigh branch itself. Besides a well-stocked adult library and an entirely separate children's library where, had one still considered oneself a child, one could sit at modern light wood tables and browse, it had a reference library containing the *Encyclopedia Britannica* – a work I had often read about but never set eyes on. To my delight and astonishment there was also a big reading room with rack upon rack of all the latest publications, most of which I had never heard of – not only *Punch* and *John O' London's Weekly* but the *Times Literary Supplement*, the *Quiver*, *Sea Breezes*, the *Wheatsheaf* (journal of the Co-operative Wholesale Society), *Britannia and Eve*, the *Illustrated London News*, the *New Statesman & Nation*, all of which became regular required reading. I was to spend very many happy hours in that reading room.

I also decided to patronise the lending library proper in future, since it was so much more superior to the one housed in Osmondthorpe Council School. Reasoning – wrongly, as it happened – that I should not be able to use my Osmondthorpe branch tickets in Crossgates, I set about applying for two sets of tickets for this wonderful library – one for the children's section, the other for the adult. Again wrongly, I was of the impression that one could only belong to a particular branch library if one lived in that particular district: accordingly, I deemed it prudent to give a false address − 82 Templemeads Way, Crossgates. In the belief − this one probably well founded − that they kept a central membership record, I thought I had better use a false name too, and so I registered myself on the application form as one Trevor Austin. That was for the juvenile tickets. For the adult ones I raised my father from the dead and rechristened him Ernest Arthur Austin, trade or profession bank clerk (a touch of snobbery creeping in here, I fear, under the influence of the girls in green blazers. At least I did not make him a bank manager). With E.A. Austin's signature adorning both forms, in my case as parent or guardian, I had no trouble at all in acquiring my tickets. The pleasures of the Percival Leigh branch were mine for the taking.

This harmless deception was, however, to have an unfortunate sequel. When I was around fifteen, I began to "go out", as the expression was, with an attractive assistant at the Percival Leigh branch, a former green blazer-wearer named Doreen. By fast-forwarding my age to sixteen I was by now a member of the adult library in my own right, if not under my own name. Doreen, stamping my books while we engaged in the tongue-tied conversational rituals of teenage courtship, naturally took the view that my name was Trevor Austin. There was nothing I could do to disabuse her of this idea even if I had wanted to, which I did not particularly − Trevor Austin I considered a dashing, Crossgates sort of name, and in any case to confess all would mean also confessing that I lived on a council estate (more snobbery − Doreen was the first girl I had ever taken out who lived in a "bought house").

All went swimmingly until one evening when we were travelling by tram to the Shaftesbury Cinema halfway between Crossgates and Town, the film at the local Regal being not to our taste. As we stood on the platform waiting to alight when the tram drew up at our stop, the conductor asked if we had paid our fares. We had not. This was not criminal intent but standard practice: you parted with your tram fare only if directly asked for it. When challenged as we were now, it was usual to come clean. Doreen, however, for some reason took it into her head to claim recklessly that we had indeed paid − since we were going Dutch she probably had plans for the copper or two she hoped to save by this deception.

The conductor said in that case he would trouble us for our tickets. By way of lending Doreen immoral support I said we had thrown them away. The conductor said in that case he would trouble us for our names and addresses. Doreen said her name was Janet Smith and that she lived at some fictitious address in a densely populated area known as Burmantofts. I said my name was Trevor Austin of 82 Templemeads Way, Crossgates. The conductor said we would hear more of the matter and we got off the tram.

Doreen was alarmingly upset. How could I be so stupid as to volunteer my real name and address? The police would now trace her through me and she would get into awful trouble, not only for evading her fare but for giving a false name and address. The case would bring shame upon her parents and even if she wasn't put away − I tried to reassure her that Shadwell Reformatory didn't admit girls but she would not be comforted − she would certainly get the sack. Doreen then began to weep copiously and there was nothing for it but to put her on the next tram home, counselling her to be careful to pay her fare. Not wishing to waste the evening, I went to the pictures alone.

It seemed time to bury Trevor Austin. It would be embarrassing to go on meeting Doreen, and since by now I had access to the Central Lending Library in Town, under the name of Michael Fox, 79 Karl Marx House, Quarry Hill Flats, it seemed prudent to bid a fond farewell to the Percival Leigh branch library. It remains the repository of some of the pleasantest and most fruitful memories of my late childhood and early youth. When I last revisited it the reading room was a branch of the social services and the reference library had become a police post.

The no-school idyll ended as abruptly as it had begun. The soldiers marched away and a proclamation by Geo Guest was hung on the school gates, rather in the manner of the pronouncements that from time to time appeared on the gates of Armley Jail after an execution (I once went and stared at one), to the effect that our interrupted education was to be resumed. We had been left to roam the streets for three months or so. For me, this period was an education in itself. I had read much of the *Encyclopedia Britannica*, become acquainted with a fascinating fat volume called *Bartlett's Book of Popular Quotations* (and begun to compile my own − *Waterhouse's Dictionary of Everyday Quotations*), and become a regular reader of the *Lady, Horse and Hound*, the *Methodist*

Times and the *Stage*, among other journals.

The return to school marked the end of the phoney war. I had begun to despair of Leeds ever being bombed but eventually the air raid sirens wailed at last, and not in vain. As exclusively reported in the Special (and only) Edition of the *Halton Moor Gazette* (more orthodox newspapers were subject to censorship restrictions), incendiary bombs followed by high-explosive bombs rained down on the city one unexpected moonlit evening, causing satisfactory conflagrations along a far spectrum of the horizon ranging, so it was to be confirmed by eye-witnesses to the damage, from Quarry Hill Flats and Marsh Lane goods yard to Low Road, Holbeck, my spiritual home. By standing out in the front gardens instead of repairing to the shelters as recommended, Halton Moor had a grandstand view of the fires, the flares, the enemy bombers caught in the criss-crossing searchlights, and the noisy pyrotechnics of the anti-aircraft guns.

At the earliest opportunity over the weekend I rode out to Hunslet in my capacity as war correspondent (alas, I had no peaked cap) of the *Halton Moor Gazette*. Many of the familiar terraces of Holbeck and Hunslet had "copped it" as the saying went, and the hosepipes of the auxiliary fire tenders snaked all over the cobbled roads around the great engineering works. The impressive Holbeck railway viaduct, a favourite artifact, to my relief mingled with regret for the histrionic potential of such a tragedy, had not come down in a spectacular heap like a toppled pile of building bricks, but the factories all around had had their roofs blasted off. It needed a solid two or three hours' staring to do justice to the damage. Later I journeyed into Town and inspected the shattered glass roof of Kirkgate Market, the shrapnel wounds to the stone lions guarding the Town Hall, the fire-bombed umbrella shop in Schofield's Arcade and other points of interest. The City Museum, with its dinosaur skeleton and mangy Bengal tiger, had sustained a direct high-explosive hit, and on the pavement outside I picked up a splinter of what might or might not have been bone that might or might not have belonged to the dinosaur. This I added to the fragments of shrapnel I had been collecting during the course of my observations. In the absence of my brother Dennis at the front I had converted his bedroom into a Halton Moor War Museum, and my finds went to flesh out the display of army greatcoat buttons, cap badges, sleeve flashes, German propaganda leaflet and my father's Mons Star which formed the basis of the collection.

There were about half a dozen more raids on Leeds but nothing again so spectacular, and deprived of a proper Blitz and nights spent in a deep shelter singing "Run, Rabbit, Run", my interest in the war began to pall. Austerity and the blackout became a bore. I began to pine for the city lights, for the flag-bedecked illuminated trams which had plied Briggate and City Square on special occasions such as the Silver Jubilee and the Coronation; for the electric news scanner over the Majestic Cinema; for the red neon; for sunbeams streaming in through the glass roof of the Market and bouncing off the prismatic surfaces of pyramids of pineapples (what were pineapples?); and above all for my brightly twinkling Bovril sign.

3 It was always taken as read, not least by me, that I was the brightest boy in the school. It therefore came as a considerable shock when I failed the entrance examination for Cockburn High School, south Leeds's answer to the grammar school on the other side of the tracks.

It has to be said I was in good company. Richard Hoggart has recorded that he too failed the Cockburn exam; but in his case his headmaster canvassed the great Geo Guest who wisely interceded and had a place found for him. My friend Willis Hall failed too, but poor as his parents were they managed to scrape together the money to send him on a fee-paying basis. In fact between us we know so many successful Leeds men who muffed that exam that we once toyed with the idea of having a Failed Cockburn tie made. As for me, my own headmaster would not appear to have been on interventionist terms with Geo Guest, and any idea of my mother paying the fees was out of the question.

Doubtless the fact of having been deprived by the exigencies of war of three months or so of formal schooling had an effect on my performance; nevertheless I was mortified. It had never crossed my mind for a second that I should not pass with flying colours, and I had set my heart on wearing a school cap and carrying a leather satchel containing a Latin primer and an apple. Besides, Cockburn was on the very edge of Hunslet, just past the Pavilion picture house and across from Hunslet Moor. Had I not flunked that exam I should have taken a tram every day for the rest of my schooldays to Kirkgate Market and then changed to the No. 25 bone-rattler into the heart of Hunslet and crunched across the Moor, satchel swinging. What more, short of my mother moving her temporarily depleted family into a terrace house off Low Road, could I possibly ask of life?

I had taken Cockburn to my heart at first sight when I had gone there to sit the entrance exam, somewhere around my eleventh birthday. It was an Edwardian building four or five storeys high, set in half an acre of uncompromising tarmac surrounded by walled railings, and not a blade of grass in sight. Inside, there were clattering stone steps, high grime-stained windows, bottle green and livid orange tiles, dark wood, downward-sloping desks with lids to hide behind such as you saw in the illustrations by H.M. Brock in public school stories; all this and the heady smell of cabbage wafting up from the basement. It was all that a school should be and in marked contrast to Middleton and Osmondthorpe, replicas of one another, which were single-storey modern buildings with too many French windows for their own good, grouped around playing fields big enough to land Spitfires on. Too airy by half.

There was nothing for it but to make the best of a bad job. Leaving school at fourteen would, after all, be more in the Edgar Wallace mould than indulging myself in a secondary education. And it wasn't as if I were not enjoying my elementary schooldays.

I liked everything about school except, at the top of the list, physical training which I abhorred and in due course managed to be excused by waving my white card about and pointing out my displaced rib; cricket which I was also excused after sustaining a permanently damaged tendon caused by a muffed catch; football, where I was so hopeless that I was quickly reduced to linesman; and woodwork and metalwork, in the course of each period of which I usually drew blood, at the end of term producing hideous malformations of dovetailed pine and bevelled copper purporting to be bookends, ashtrays or serviette rings. Swimming I was able to endure only because, while we were at Middleton, the nearest baths were a noisy tram ride away in Hunslet. While the shivering experience of undressing and dressing on wet, slimy duckboards was not to my taste, I liked the echoing white-tiled institutional feel of the place, and the post-swim option of either a cup of steaming Ovaltine or Bovril. (While frankly I preferred the taste of Ovaltine, I stayed loyal to Bovril.) At Osmondthorpe, there were no swimming baths near at hand and so we did not swim.

For the rest, while I would never have volunteered for elementary science, technical drawing, nature study or arithmetic, I could tolerate them as school subjects and was reasonably proficient at all of them. Where I came into my own, however, was in English, geography, history and scripture – all interlinked subjects to my mind, since they each required the writing of an essay or "composition" in tests or exams. If I had not been top in all these subjects at the end of term, I should have wanted to know the reason why.

But my favourite period by far was the last hour of Friday afternoon, when the whole school was allowed to read quietly while the teachers marked up their registers. You were allowed to bring reading matter of your choice from home, barring only comics, comic annuals and, following a test case, bound volumes of the *Vivid War Weekly*. This set me something of a poser, since apart from the *Vivid War Weekly*, Daudet's *Lettres de mon Moulin* in the original French, the plays of J.M. Barrie and *Fifty Years of Progress: the Story of Hemingway's Brewery*, the only remaining books in the house were a big fat volume of household hints that had been given away by the *Daily Herald* and a book of *True Tales of Horror* which I had read many times, particularly the account of a man-eating orchid in South America. Fortunately, there was a brisk swopping service in operation on these literary Fridays, and my book of horror stories was much in demand. Thus I had the bartering power to keep me ploughing contentedly through volumes of *Chums*, the *Scout Annual*, *Boy's Own Annual*, *Fifty Famous Murders* and suchlike improving reading.

Lessons aside, while both Middleton and Osmondthorpe were roughish schools where the teachers took care to arm themselves with unauthorised weapons such as T-squares, chair legs and cricket stumps, the atmosphere was congenial enough. But I was not much of a one for joining in. On the whole, with my dislike of team spirit and organised activities of any kind, my policy was one of studied non-co-operation; in consequence I was never made a prefect or even a milk monitor.

On only one occasion did I display any qualities of leadership. I had always enjoyed morning and afternoon breaks, when the playground was a seething forum of news and rumour, such as that the newly established Richard Shops were giving away pairs of silk stockings for every 100 − or was it 500? − tram tickets with their advertisement printed on the back (sisters would pay good money for them); or that the paradoxical miracle of white chocolate had been invented; or that so-and-so, hitherto believed to be in the TB sanitorium, was in reality in Shadwell Reformatory. But the playground was also the stronghold of shaven-headed, clog-flaunting school bullies, whose idea of fun was to stamp on the feet of lesser privileged plimsoll-wearers. It was I who dealt with this unpleasant situation.

In my last term at Middleton I had been reading a school story by, I think, one Michael Poole, in which the denizens of Study Ten form a secret society called the Cranks, the main object of which is that if any member of the society finds himself being bullied by the cads of the Remove, all he has to do is shout "Crank! Crank! Crank!" and hundreds of boys will come running to his rescue. Without much faith in my own ability to evoke anything like such a response, I started my own Cranks society, more as a lark than anything. The thing captured the imagination of my classmates and soon caught on like wildfire. Only a few days after its formation, as I was walking home from school, I saw a small boy in tears at having his arm twisted by one of the bullet-headed clog-wearers. There were a few schoolmates near at hand. I cried "Crank! Crank! Crank!" and to my astonishment not only they but just about every boy in the school came tearing to the scene from all directions, like the urchins in the Ealing comedy *Hue and Cry*. As the bully took to his heels, pursued by the whooping, terrifying mob, I stood amazed, flattered and awe-stricken at the Pandora's box of mass hysteria I had unlocked. The organisation was proscribed by the headmaster the very next day.

My teachers were a mixed bunch, so far as I was concerned. Those in charge of sport or handicrafts despised me as a milksop. Others thought I was too clever by half. One or two, who were not themselves all that bright, were wary of me. Two teachers, both at Osmondthorpe, went out of their way to help me.

The first, whose name I have shamefully forgotten, encouraged me to draw cartoons, a modest peripheral talent I had brought to the art class from the pages of the *Daily Treasure* and *Ronnie Rabbit's Weekly*. He went to the trouble of putting my efforts together in a book and placing it in the school library, where for all I know it remains to this day.

The other, Clifford Exley, taught me English. That he did this spectacularly well (another, later, pupil of his was the writer Jack Higgins) could have been in some degree due to his not being a regular English teacher. His subject was science, but since most of the staff had been called up for national service, those who remained because they were medically unfit had to become educational jacks-of-all-trades. Mr Exley approached English as he approached science — as an adventure, a voyage of discovery. He had a talent for enthusing even the dullest of the dullards amongst us. None of us appreciated, as pupils never do, that he was a superb teacher – to be frank, most of us thought he was a soft touch. For instance, when he was supposed to be teaching us elementary algebra he spent most of the lesson reading us that classic essay of Stephen Leacock's, where A, B and C are always laying wagers that one can fill a cistern faster than the others – but B has a leaky bucket and C's cistern has a hole in it. In the end C dies of exhaustion and A and B have to bury him. A can dig twice as fast as B who has a broken spade . . . Not only did we find all this hilarious, but with many a nudge and snigger we congratulated ourselves on having got out of a whole boring lesson. Little did we realise that we had been learning algebra. In addition, I had been acquiring a taste for Stephen Leacock – one of the many writers to whom Mr Exley introduced me, including Conan Doyle, Jack London, Kipling, Arnold Bennett . . . His usual ploy was to toss a book on my desk with the throwaway remark, "You might find this worth a glance some time."

Because of his grey hair, shapeless tweedy jackets and flannel bags, and his faintly eccentric disposition – I was once quite shocked to come across him eating a pork pie in the street – for many years I looked back on Mr Exley as an elderly, Mr Chips figure. It was only quite recently that I learned he must have been in his mid-thirties when he was teaching me. But he had the wisdom of a Mr Chips. It was entirely down to him, as I also subsequently learned, that one day in 1941, when I was thirteen, I found myself in an Osmondthorpe Council School classroom in a mildly bemused state of mind as I sat an unusually stiff series of test papers on English, elementary maths and geography. While exams seemed to come round fortnightly at Osmondthorpe, it was quite out of the ordinary to face this minor ordeal, as it was to some but never to me who welcomed the chance to shine, with a motley crew of boys from other forms. I conjectured that the idea was perhaps to settle which stream we should all be moving into next term (this was when school classes were still categorised – or stigmatised – A, B or C according to academic performance). I thought no more about it and got on with my work, taking no particular pains over it but in due course learning that I had won a special place award at Leeds College of Commerce.

The trick was in the casualness of it all. Had I been told in advance that I was to take the College of Commerce scholarship exam, or if I had had to report at a quarter to nine on an execution-grey morning to the College itself, and to sit at a strange desk in a strange classroom with a strangely clanking radiator, as I had had to do for the Cockburn High School fiasco two years earlier, I should undoubtedly have failed that examination too. With what consequences, I have no idea. School-leavers of fourteen went into the clothing factories or foundries. But then Alan Sillitoe went from elementary school into the Raleigh bicycle factory and a few years later he had written *Saturday Night and Sunday Morning*.

My cup ran over. The College of Commerce was in the middle of Town. Daily, after all, I would be taking that tram as far as Kirkgate Market, thence to meander along Vicar Lane, or through the Market itself if I so pleased, to school. The world, or anyway Town which to me came to the same thing, was now my oyster.

There was more. I received a letter personally from Geo Guest himself. "I have pleasure in informing you that you have been successful in gaining a Special Place at the College of Commerce, Woodhouse Lane, Leeds. The Scholarship is awarded for two years, and the award will cover the whole of the tuition fees and carry an allowance of £7/10/0d. The Education Committee reserve the right to revise the value of the award at the end of the school year, having regard to your family circumstances at that time. I am, Yours faithfully, Geo Guest, Director of Education."

Then there was a letter to my mother from Dr Austin, Principal, Leeds College of Commerce, on crested notepaper with the College's Latin motto, *Fortiter, Fideliter, Feliciter*. A real academic doctor, like Dr Arnold in *Tom Brown's Schooldays*! ". . . I congratulate you on your son's success. I am enclosing a permit for the School Cap, which may be obtained at Messrs Rawcliffe, Duncan Street, Leeds."

I knew Rawcliffe's, the school outfitters, with its display of college and high school uniforms. I had given its windows a stare many a time. I knew that the College of Commerce cap was segmented navy blue and maroon, like a jockey's, and that the blazer was all maroon, like a Butlin redcoat's. I knew too that I would never get the blazer – my seven pounds ten a year allowance was barely enough to pay for my keep when I should have been about to start earning a wage packet, never mind blazers. I didn't care. I would swagger off to the tram stop each morning with my satchel bouncing against my bum and the School Cap on my head and the clog-wearers' cries of

"College cad!" ringing in my ears, and every day I should be in Town.

While I had never played my white card at Osmondthorpe I had suffered from Town withdrawal symptoms after the unexpected freedom of three months off school, and I had taken to playing truant regularly with the explanation that I had to have an X-ray at the General Infirmary for my dislodged rib. Many years later at some school reunion I asked one of the staff, an old friend of Mr Exley's, whether my old mentor had ever suspected that I was playing hookey. He laughed. "Suspected? He knew all along – you were seen going into the Central Library!" Then why did he never say anything? "He didn't want to cramp your style."

4 The College of Commerce, Woodhouse Lane, Leeds, proved not to be in Woodhouse Lane at all, the premises having been requisitioned by the wartime Ministry of Food. Instead the College was relocated at what had formerly been Darley Street Elementary School. Why the Ministry of Food couldn't have been housed in Darley Street was never explained. Nor did I ever learn what became of the school's former pupils. Perhaps they were given an indefinite holiday, like Osmondthorpe when the army moved in.

I found the arrangement perfectly agreeable. The school was an Edwardian or late-Victorian pile of the same model as Cockburn High School – all tiles and tarmac. The street itself was a cul-de-sac off North Street, an extension of Briggate and only three or four minutes' walk from Lewis's. This I found most convenient. It was a run-down neighbourhood of shabby terrrace houses, seedy corner shops, small clothing workshops where hunchbacked tailors sat cross-legged in the windows to get the available light, and a dusty little patch of grass and shrubbery known uneuphemistically, indeed officially, as the Jews' Park.

Far more interestingly, it proved to be a red light district. We were apprised of this fact in our first assembly by Dr Austin's deputy, who in a speech of consummate and cryptic delicacy warned newcomers to the school against having any truck with persons loitering in the street, however amiably disposed they might seem. It had to be explained to me by more worldly boys what he was driving at. I had never consciously set eyes on a prostitute, although it was by now part of my secret general knowledge that such creatures as "woars" as they were known in the Leeds vernacular did exist and were recognisable by the bangles around their ankles. From now on, when out and about in the murky environs of the College of Commerce, I would keep a sharp lookout for ladies sporting ankle bangles or other manifestations of their trade such as a fur stole or an over-abundance of lipstick, and treat suspects to a good long speculative stare. In reality most of them were probably pocket hands and trouser machinists from the clothing factories, waiting to meet their boyfriends.

Nor was this the only manifestation of my newly awakened interest in the opposite sex. I knew, because obviously I had hurried along to stare at the place the moment I heard about my scholarship, that Leeds College of Commerce was co-educational, and I had been keenly looking forward to sizing up the maroon-blazered equivalents of the pretty girls in their green blazers loitering on the steps of the Percival Leigh branch library. What I had not been prepared for was that girls would account for a good half of the College of Commerce's new intake, most of them quite fetching, and that we would sit in mixed classes.

The pairing-off process began at once. Three or four of the boys in my form were blond young Adonises who carried steel mirrors and pocket combs and had creases in their flannels, and they quickly commandeered, or were commandeered by, the three or four most comely girls. This was the signal for the rest of us similarly to seize partners. Only the boldest spirits made a direct approach: the convention at the callow age of thirteen was to despatch an emissary to test the water. Should he report back that the girl nominated for attention was prepared to entertain overtures, then if in funds you would invite her to the pictures, or if not then for a walk round the Jews' Park after school. Having prudently kept on my morning and Sunday paper rounds plus my various Saturday chores, I was still reasonably affluent, and the girl of my choice lived on my side of town within walking distance of the Shaftesbury Cinema in York Road, which had those double seats in the back rows known as "love seats". She was a raven-haired beauty called Heather, with full, generous lips and what even I could recognise was a good figure, and I could not believe my luck. We became engaged to be married on her fourteenth birthday during the *Gaumont British News* and were to remain in this state of innocent bliss until pitched out into the cold world at the end of our two-year course.

My emissary (and I his) was a lad I had known slightly at Osmondthorpe called Ray Hill. We were the only two in our year to have made it to the College of Commerce — in fact it emerged that most of our fellow-examinees were being tested for the College of

116

Technology, where their skills at fashioning bookends and copper ashtrays in woodwork and metalwork classes would be channelled into jobs that would give them a future as engineers and draughtsmen in the great foundries and locomotive and printing works of Hunslet. For our part, we were to be trained as clerks. Ray and I, in our scornful mutual rejection of so dreary a scenario – he was to become a teacher, jazz clarinettist and subsequently a lecturer in drama – were quick to establish ourselves as the best of friends, and have remained so all our lives.

Despite the distraction of Heather at the adjoining desk, I quickly settled into the College of Commerce routine. The lessons were novel and interesting: economic history instead of boring kings and queens, commercial geography instead of rivers and mountain ranges, business economics instead of John having twelve oranges and Mary three, and shorthand and typewriting in place of finger-lacerating handicrafts. I could not have enough of either of these latter activities. We were taught touch typing, a tin shield screening the keys from view so that one had to synchronise one's fingers to a representation of the QWERTY keyboard as displayed in the exercise manual. We typed our exercises rhythmically, accompanied by a selection of military two-steps on a tinny old gramophone, to which show-offs would get up and dance when our typing instructress went out of the room, which she did frequently since the wartime shortage of teachers obliged her to take two classes simultaneously. She also taught us shorthand: this I loved from the start and quickly mastered the intriguing grammalogue repertoire of hooks and whorls and curves, all reminiscent of the extravagant hieroglyphics with which I had covered the staves of my Banks's Music Arcade manuscript paper so long ago now. Billets-doux in near-impeccable Pitman were soon passing to and fro between Heather and me.

The atmosphere of the place was delightfully informal after the constraints of a council school. At break-time you were not turned out of doors regardless of the weather but could loaf around in form room or assembly hall chattering or catching up on homework. At lunchtime, after you had eaten your sandwiches (exotic ration-stretching concoctions of dried currants and raisins, grated carrot and cocoa powder, inspired by the government's Food Facts hints in the newspapers) in the basement refectory – there were no school dinners available – you were expected to remain on the premises and

117

certainly not to go into Town, perhaps because of the good Dr Austin's fears about the ankle-bangled street-corner influences we had been warned against (it did cross our minds to wonder, the subject of the North Street "woars" being a recurring topic of conversation, why the College had agreed to move into a red light district in the first place); but the rule was widely ignored.

Ray Hill and I therefore regularly gulped down our sandwiches or even ate them on the hoof in our hurry to get into Lewis's or over to the Market; or, increasingly, to such intriguing venues as the rubber goods shop on Leeds Bridge with its baffling but provocative display of faded booklets with titles like *What Every Single Man Should Know* and *Talks to the About-to-be-Wed*; and to the City Varieties, a theatre then of low repute, where we would feast our eyes on the display case of star-spangled photo-stills of scantily dressed showgirls appearing in such daring revues as *Strip, Strip Hooray* and *Nudes of the World*. This distinct widening of my Leeds horizons was under Ray's influence. While I suppose my age of innocence would have been drawing to a close anyway, he was certainly instrumental in hurrying it along.

More innocently, if no less foolhardily had we been spotted by anyone in authority, we became habitués of the city's only amusement arcade in a dingy street near the Corn Exchange, where we would try to win cigarettes – then in chronic short supply like practically everything else – from the penny-in-the-slot mechanical crane. Like most boys in Leeds I had been smoking whenever the opportunity arose from the age of about eight, usually the odd cadged Woodbine or dog-ends picked up at tram stops. Now that I was in long trousers I regarded smoking, along with going about with Heather, reading much-passed-around copies of a racy magazine called *Razzle*, and staying out till what my mother indulgently called "all hours", as part of my emancipation. With my new-found freedom, the allure of Town was stronger than ever: it now promised illicit joys of which I had so far had only a glimmer, and I wanted to be on hand when the time for sampling them came around.

While I had left Hunslet and the Halton Moor Cycling Club somewhat in the lurch by now, I would still continue my explorations of Town whenever the opportunity presented itself, now often with Ray who shared my insatiable curiosity about facets of Leeds not previously encountered. Ray was something of an artist and so we would sometimes amble around the Art Gallery, giving any portrayals of naked or near-naked females a particularly attentive stare; we were also to be first in the queue when a travelling exhibition of Picasso and Matisse came to Lewis's, loftily distancing ourselves from the ribald comments of those − the majority, it seemed − who had come to scoff. Ray was interested in poster work and would happily travel great distances across the city to study the latest handiwork of some admired commercial artist. I was equally happy to accompany him, and through him learned to recognise individual styles. One lunchtime, having discovered in the course of my travels that Hemingway's Brewery, of *Fifty Years of Progress* fame, had a spanking new advertisement hoarding of quite impressive design, I insisted on taking Ray by tram to stare at it, and to the bemusement of passers-by blindfolding him with my handkerchief as we neared the spot so that the head-on impact of this splendid work of art should not be spoiled for him. The consequence of this aesthetic pilgrimage was that we were fifteen minutes late back for the afternoon typing class. We were sent to Dr Austin's deputy who questioned us keenly if obliquely, plainly not believing the account we gave of our movements and probably suspecting that we had been lured into a house of ill-fame. No such luck. Though solemnly warned that we must not venture beyond the school gates without permission in future, after a decent interval we cautiously resumed our lunchtime rambles, but taking care to steer clear of such pits of iniquity as the City Varieties, the rubber goods shop, the amusement arcade, and − a recent acquisition − what passed at the time for a smutty bookshop, stocking pin-up magazines, Hank Janson paperbacks, *Razzle*, and a saucy local publication entitled *A Basinful of Fun*. But siren-like, they were beckoning.

It does need to be said about the *Basinful of Fun* that my interest in its mildly risqué contents was not exclusively lascivious but also vocational. As a published, if not paid, contributor to the *National Savings News*, I had for some months been looking fruitlessly for another market undemanding enough to take my standard of work of the time. *A Basinful of Fun*, a compilation of feeble short-short stories and feebler jokes, seemed right up my street: I had a whole cupboard drawerful of feeble material at home. Furthermore, the editorial announcement in each issue of the *BOF* could not have been more encouraging: "The Editor invites contributions of Jokes, Bright and Breezy Articles, or Sketches. All material accepted is paid for at the Highest Rates on Publication. Address your contribution

119

to: Editorial Department, A Basinful of Fun, Stafford Street, Leeds 10.''

Having raided the pages of the *Flag* and other Halton Moor Printing Works titles, I assembled a batch of my work at once. Realising from the postal address that the *BOF* must be in Hunslet, I then set off to hand in my submissions and at the same time have a good long stare at the editorial offices. With any luck, I might catch a glimpse of the editor himself, sitting with his waistcoat unbuttoned at a roll-top desk and chuckling over the galley proofs of his next issue – perhaps, with even more luck, including one or more of my own effusions, although I was bound to concede that since I was still clutching them in my hand this was more than unlikely. After asking directions I was happy to discover – an encouraging portent – that Stafford Street was but a short step from Low Road. I looked around for the Editorial Department of *A Basinful of Fun*, which in my mind's eye I had occupying a building of the size and grandeur of Alf Cooke's Printing Works. There were no commercial premises of any kind in the street, which was an ordinary cobbled terrace hung with lines of washing. The offices of the *Basinful of Fun* were undistinguished by so much as a brass plate or even a bakelite one. The editorial sanctum could only have been either a net-curtained front room or the spare bedroom. Putting disappointment behind me – after all, had not Edgar Wallace produced a racing sheet from a garret over a barber's shop in an alley off Fleet Street? – I emboldened myself to rattle the letter-box. There was no reply, and so I posted my contributions through it, never to set eyes on them again.

My two years at the College of Commerce ticked pleasantly by. Academically the competition was tougher than at my elementary schools, while the laxity of discipline provided more opportunities for fooling around, a combination which at the end of my second term was to result in my coming a humiliating fourteenth out of twenty-seven in English. This was after I had skimped an essay and comprehension test in my eagerness to complete a surreptitiously hand-printed samizdat magazine entitled, in Gothic lettering inspired by the masthead of the *Yorkshire Evening Post*, the *Prostitute*, a supposedly satirical review of the activities of the ladies of North Street and their imagined connection with thinly disguised members of the staff and some of my fellow-students, both male and female (though not, of course, including Heather). This disgraceful production, for which I should surely have been expelled had it fallen into the hands of Dr Austin, was to be the last in a line of hitherto wholesome publications that had stretched all the way from *Ronnie Rabbit's Weekly* via the *Flag* to the *Daily Treasure*. It was a lamentable end to the Halton Moor Printing Works.

In one subject, however, I consistently excelled, and that was commerce itself, which might have been tailor-made for me. Since the business of the College was to turn out succeeding waves of the city's office fodder, doubtless in the hope that we should all imperceptibly rise over the decades to become bank managers and chief accountants (as indeed most of us did), it had evidently been decided that we might as well know something about the trade and commerce of Leeds itself. To this end, rather than dealing in concepts so remote that they were near-abstract, such as the volume of New Zealand's wool exports, we were talking about the actual arrival of actual bales of wool on actual barges on the River Aire and the Leeds and Liverpool Canal, and their progress through the named mills of Leeds such as the Perseverance or the Albion to the named clothing factories of Leeds like John Barran's who invented the ready-made tailoring industry or Montague Burton the Tailor of Taste, to known retail outlets like Marks and Spencer who had got their start in Kirkgate Market, or the Mutual Clothing Club. It was like a non-alcoholic version of *Fifty Years of Progress: the Story of Hemingway's Brewery*; and while our commerce teacher was no Mr Exley, commercial Leeds came vividly to life for me in these lessons.

We also did commercial history, and this embraced the expansion of Victorian Leeds when it was throwing up public buildings with such vigour and confidence – Cuthbert Broderick was only twenty-nine when he designed the Town Hall, and only a few years older when he built the Corn Exchange – that I rather pined to have been a part of it all, to have attended improving classes at the Leeds Mechanics' Institute and public meetings at the Coliseum and *conversazione* at the Leeds Philosophical and Literary Society, to have risen in the world to rub shoulders with the clothing barons and philanthropists at the Leeds Club and the Leeds Stock Exchange, to have had my account at Beckett's Bank and bought my cravats and linen at the Pygmalion, to have bathed at the Oriental Baths and worshipped at the Ebenezer Chapel and to have read my *Leeds Mercury* in the newsroom of the Leeds Church Institute and borrowed three-decker novels from the Leeds Library and taken my luncheon at the Great Northern Station Hotel. They must have been heady days and the effect of hearing about them was to make one itch to get out and take one's place in the commercial life of Leeds. Perhaps that was the idea.

5   Another favourite period in my College of Commerce days
    was sports afternoon, Friday. This was because, after
    putting in one or two tentative appearances when my
services were never called upon, I ceased to attend it. Nobody seemed
to notice, let alone mind. In the admirable absence of playing fields
of our own, games – cricket or rugger for the boys, hockey or
basketball for the girls, according to season – were held in Beckett
Park, near the Headingley Cricket Ground. You were supposed to
make your way there under your own steam, but the convention
seemed to be that if you hadn't actually been picked for a game –
and after the initial trial scrums, I never was – you were not obliged
to turn up unless you wanted to watch or take part in a scratch
kickabout. I for one had other fish to fry.

There was at that time a small chain of weekly newspapers in
Leeds which rather grandiosely called itself the Leeds Guardian
Series, comprising the *Armley and Wortley News* covering south
Leeds, the *North Leeds News* covering north of the river, and the
Leeds Guardian itself covering the central area in between. They
were dull little papers, the equivalent of today's free sheets, devoting
their editorial columns largely, indeed almost exclusively, to blurred
group photographs and long lists of the names of those present at
various functions ranging from weddings and funerals to whist
drives and sales of work. I had been bile-green with envy to learn that
a boy in another form at the College of Commerce, who went by the
exotic-sounding name of Connor Walsh, had a Saturday job
working as a part-time reporter for the Guardian Series. Covering
bring-and-buy sales and Women's Institute bunfights might not have
been exciting but it was a much better way of spending a Saturday
than scraping out the innards of a leather-grinding machine, and so I
sought out Walsh's company.

Alas, the Guardian's Saturday shift was over-subscribed, being abundantly supplied by a seething Fagin's mob of schoolboys hurtling about the city on their bicycles, feverishly picking up news snippets from parish halls and other centres of local intelligence, for which they were paid at the rate of about half a crown a column. However, I was granted an interview with the editor himself, the first editor I had ever met, a Mr Glover I think his name was. I was a little put out to find him wearing a leather apron — it seemed that as well as being the editor, Mr Glover was also the compositor, advertisement manager and chief reporter. The aproned editor was encouraging. While he could not offer me any work he was willing to consider for publication any items that I might bring in off my own bat. He gave me some valuable advice. "Remember," counselled Mr Glover, "that names make news." He meant that names sell local newspapers.

Enlisting the support of the Halton Moor Cycling Club, and armed with a list of contacts culled from church hall notice-boards, I began at once to devote my College of Commerce sports afternoons to pedalling furiously from vicar to vicar and social secretary to social secretary, filling my notebook with the names of marrow show prizewinners, dancing class medallists, best iced cake awards, and the like. Thus, as often as not, I was able to scoop the Guardian's authorised representative who came plodding behind me on the Saturday. It didn't matter to Mr Glover. He would give me half a crown and set my sheaf of news-making names in closely packed type.

In my last term at Darley Street, our commerce teacher transmogrified himself into our careers teacher and began to talk about jobs. It was assumed that most of the boys would go into banks and insurance companies or the council rates department, while the girls would become junior secretaries in the building societies and solicitors' offices. I had different ideas. My shorthand was verbatim, I was by now, after the initial shock, consistently top in English, and I had had some reporting experience. I went to Mr Glover and asked if he could see his way to taking me on full time. I was gratified to be offered a job there and then. I took this to be in recognition of my initiative in getting my Friday afternoon scoops, but he would probably have given the post to a horse had it accepted the terms. These were ten shillings a week.

I knew before even broaching it with my mother that it was out of the question. With the war droning on and three breadwinners at the front, she had been looking forward to my bringing home a proper wage packet. An extra thirty shillings a week coming in, the going rate for a fifteen-year-old clerk with shorthand and typing certificates, would make a great deal of difference. Even with the selfishness of youth, I could see her point. Her clothes were shabby – so were mine, come to that – the cheap oilcloth under the clip rugs was threadbare, and she was tired of counting the pennies. The clip rugs themselves had seen better days. I could remember, as a child, sitting by the fireside clipping strips from a carrier bag of old cloth remnants, which my mother would fashion into a rug by pricking them through a hessian backing. Now, in the modernistic Forties, she had been developing an insane desire for a proper factory-made half-moon hearthrug as seen in the Littlewood's catalogue. A proper rug demanded a proper job.

I ruled out Lloyd's Bank in Park Row, where Ray Hill and a few other classmates had taken themselves. I similarly resisted the temptation to follow Heather into the Leeds Permanent Building Society. In both these institutions you toiled in large open-plan offices under the beaky gaze of stoop-shouldered senior clerks. I knew precisely what I wanted: a small family establishment where the office was divided by frosted-glass partitions, preferably in one of the Victorian rabbit-warren chambers with which Leeds was then well endowed, where I should have access to a typewriter, and where I should be left in charge of the office during my employers' lunch hour. If I could not be a reporter then I would be a freelance journalist, writing articles and short stories under cover of the day ledger and typing them up on the firm's trusty Remington.

Consulting the list of available vacancies at the College of Commerce, I found what promised to be the ideal situation, although our careers teacher thought it an eccentric first choice. This was with the firm of J.T. Buckton & Sons, the Leeds Funeral Furnishers, whose motto was "We Never Sleep" (to which the sniggering rejoinder from everyone who heard it was "Maybe not, but the customers do"). Why an undertaker felt obliged to offer a twenty-four-hour service (all it meant was that the telephone was switched through to one of the partners' homes at night, so that the bereaved could ring up at three in the morning if they so wished) I never properly understood. The small office was in a converted shop at No. 18 New Station Street, a turning off Boar Lane between a Finlay's tobacco kiosk where I should ingratiate myself with the

125

motherly type who ran it and thus be favoured with under-the-counter cigarettes, and a famous pen shop where I had had many a stare at the intricate fans of nibs in the window and whose advertising placard I knew by heart: "They come as a boon and a blessing to men, the Pickwick, the Owl and the Waverley Pen." It was so near City Station that the windows rattled as the trains pulled out — the perfect address from my point of view.

The office was divided, as required, into cubicles and cubby-holes, and in one of the cubby-holes reposed the required trusty Remington. I was interviewed, or rather auditioned, by one of the two partners, Mr Palmer, a tall, schoolmasterly individual, reedy of voice and reedy in appearance, with a stiff collar a size too big for him to accommodate a prominent Adam's apple, who dictated a not too difficult letter which I took down in shorthand, and then directed me to transcribe it on to the typewriter. The subject-matter of the letter, concerning the sale of a suburban bungalow, seemed a curious choice for an undertaker, unless J.T. Buckton & Sons had a sideline in selling off the estates of the deceased. All became clear when I rolled a sheet of the firm's headed paper into the machine. As well as being funeral furnishers and incidentally a car hire service, which made sense when they had a fleet of limousines to maintain, they were also in business as auctioneers, surveyors and valuers, and estate agents. The explanation for all this diversity was that Mr Palmer, the estate agent, had married into the family of Mr Buckton, the undertaker — or perhaps Mr Buckton had married into his. At any rate they found it convenient to pool their resources and share an office. From my point of view it meant that my duties, however onerous, would at least be invigorated by the spice of variety.

In fact my duties — for my shorthand and typing having passed muster, I was appointed without further ado — proved remarkably light and extremely congenial. My first task of the day was to take down the heavy window shutters, which, in the first flush of working for a living, made me feel romantically like Kipps. Then I had to go across the street to the Craven Dairies cake shop and café with a filing tray of mugs for our early morning coffee. There were eight of these, the office being absurdly overstaffed. Besides Mr Palmer and Mr Buckton there was Mr Stead the cashier, Mr Pepper the rent collector, and four clerks including myself. Mr Palmer was out and about a good deal doing his surveying and valuing, while Mr Buckton — a dapper rubicund, bustling figure who was known as Mr

126

Percy to distinguish him from his extremely aged uncle Mr Willie who sometimes pottered into the office – was for ever hurrying off like the White Rabbit with the words "Get me next at the Infirmary" or "Get me next at the Old People's Home", where it was assumed he hustled for business for the undertaking side. Mr Pepper, a saturnine-looking fellow much given to singing snatches of obscure low music-hall ditties such as "My old woman Marie Anne, scraped out me ears with a corned beef can", would gulp down his morning coffee, seize his rent register and disappear for the day, not returning until around five o'clock to cash up. This would leave the office in the possession of the four clerks and Mr Stead, an amiable soul who sat over his ledgers smoking his pipe and when the chattering got out of hand would look over his glasses and say, "You all remind me of that phrase 'generally speaking'."

I was put in charge of the postage book. This suited me perfectly, for much of Buckton's correspondence was with other firms in Town, and it was the partners' policy that any letters within the Leeds 1 postal district had to be delivered by hand to save postage. From the start, then, I enjoyed a carefree forty-five minutes or so each morning wandering around Town. My daily post round, furthermore, got me into buildings I had only dared stare at before – a rare chance to gape into the magnificent interiors of the Gothic banks and assurance companies with their mosaic floors and marble pillars and brass grilles and mahogany fittings and Venetian windows, not so very long before they were all brought tumbling down by the developers; and at the domed university library, as splendid as the British Museum Reading Room, and which I got a peep at while delivering a letter to an improbably appointed Professor of Leather with whom Mr Palmer had some business; and, by contrast, the stunningly modernistic lobby of the Queen's Hotel, where I ventured down into the men's lavatory to see what it was like, and was so impressed that I abandoned the smelly City Square Gents' and in future – so long as I was clutching a bundle of letters as my passport – always made use of the Queen's.

There were other regular errands from which there seemed no pressing need to hurry back: collecting inscribed coffin plates from the engraving firm of Ingall, Parsons, Clive and Co. in Basinghall Street, or placing death notices and property column small ads with the *Yorkshire Evening Post* and *Yorkshire Evening News* – I never crossed their thresholds without reminding myself that I was walking into a real live newspaper office; and while of course I never got beyond the advertising counter, there was always an interesting display of news pictures to look at. Then, the car hire wing of Buckton's being in the habit of booking out limousines just when they were needed for funerals, I was quite often required to run along to the cab rank at the side of the Majestic Cinema and requisition a couple of taxis. This, by and by, gave me privileged access to the Quebec Street Taxi Shelter, a ramshackle wooden structure going back to the horse-cab days, built for the cabbies by sympathetic Quakers as a place to have a warm and a cup of tea. It was also used extensively for games of penny brag, which perhaps the Quakers did not have in mind. Losing all my money to the taxi drivers made me feel immensely grown-up. And they never charged me for the tea.

Another source of dalliance was the basement Gambit Café in Park Row, a real find – an Edwardian survival where all the tables were marked out as chessboards and not only rheumy-eyed old men but keen young clerks and middle-aged bookkeepers played out their tournaments over a cup of coffee and a Marie Louise biscuit, and the waitresses went about on tiptoe. Office staff, in the absence of canteens or dispensing machines, were then commonly allowed leave from their desks for a fifteen-minute morning and afternoon break, usually extended to half an hour or so, when they were entitled to relax in the café or teashop of their choice. I imagine the privilege extended to me too, but I was never in the office long enough to exercise it. The Gambit Café, long ago demolished of course, became a regular haunt. Although I did not myself play chess it was a fascinating game to watch, and the players even more so – perhaps I did not yet recognise that many of them were ever so self-consciously "characters". Heavily under the influence of P.G. Wodehouse, I planned a series of tales with a chess club background in emulation of his Oldest Member golf stories. Since I did not know the first thing about the game the project fortunately never got under way.

Back at the office, life went at a leisurely pace. A good deal of Craven Dairies coffee was drunk and such work as there was to do was performed against a background of chit-chat and badinage. My little cubby-hole was tucked away at the end of the still extant shop counter, and there I spent much of my time none too surreptitiously scribbling away at my sub-Wodehouse stories set in Mayfair, wherever that might have been (the notion of using an undertaker's

128

parlour as a setting did not cross my seething mind). Occasionally these endeavours would be interrupted by Mr Palmer who was in the habit of dictating long letters on the subject of property tax and death duties to the *Yorkshire Post* (like me, he never got to see his efforts in print); or by the even more occasional tinkling of the shop bell when I would have to turn away some hopeful looking for a flat to let or assume a suitably sombre expression for someone wishing to arrange a funeral. With so much freedom to come and go during working hours, I rarely went out in my lunch hour but spent the time typing up my stories, invariably sustaining myself with two toasted teacakes from the Craven Dairies. (I subsequently calculated that in my service with Buckton's I consumed some 1,400 toasted teacakes.)

When I had nothing to type up and fresh inspiration flagged I would sometimes potter around in the basement stockroom where I took a morbid interest in the stacked cardboard boxes of shrouds, coffin plates and coffin handles in a range of qualities to suit every pocket. (The actual coffins, or caskets as they were known in the trade, were carpentered in one of the many back-street workshops of Hunslet.)

It was while mooning about in this manner that I discovered something of an incendiarist streak in myself. There was rather unwisely stored among the cotton shrouds and cardboard boxes a can of petrol for the emergency use of the limousines. I had heard that petrol was highly combustible but had never wholly believed it, since I knew what an age it took to set fire to the small quantity of brandy my mother allowed on the Christmas pudding, and what a dismal flicker it finally produced. I decided to put the theory to the test. I poured a few drops of petrol into the stone sink next to the lavatory and tossed in a lighted match. It blazed merrily. During subsequent lunchtimes I developed the experiment further. There was a tin wash-bowl in the sink. I found that by uptipping the bowl, pouring a little petrol beneath it and then throwing in a match, there would be a small explosion and the bowl would most satisfactorily jump a few inches into the air. In easy stages I increased the dose until the wash-bowl was shooting up ceilingwards like a flying saucer, and the sink was a blazing inferno in miniature. Fortunately for me − for if a leaping tongue of flame had ever touched the nearby stack of shroud boxes the whole office would have gone up and I with it − the petrol-can began to feel alarmingly light and I thought I had better desist.

That did not, however, quite put an end to my arsonist tendencies. One day I was sent on some errand to the firm's garages up in the university district, opposite the Leeds Maternity Home. Here there was a petrol pump to service the hearse and limousines. Recently there had been a delivery to the pump and a few feet away from it was a shallow pool of petrol where the tanker driver had allowed a good couple of gallons to escape. I was smoking a cigarette and wondered idly whether I could get as spectacular an effect from this pool of petrol as I had been getting from the more contained basement sink. Without further thought I stupidly threw in my cigarette end and stood well back.

If there were flames I could not see them, for instantly a black, impenetrable cloud began to rise from the ground. It went on rising and expanding at an alarming rate, its acrid billows fanning ever outward. A light breeze carried the black smoke, as thick as any smog, through the open windows of the maternity home, which was instantly evacuated. As bewildered hordes of pregnant women in their nightdresses and nurses clutching armfuls of mewling babies streamed out into the forecourt, two or three of Buckton's drivers, carrying buckets of sand intended to extinguish incendiary bombs, dealt efficiently with the conflagration. One of them asked if I had been smoking. I denied doing anything so half-witted, and blamed a passer-by. Again I had been lucky: had the pool of petrol been connected by the merest trickle to the pump and its underground reservoir of hundreds of gallons, it would have been not a tin basin but a hearse and six limousines that had flown sky-high. That episode concluded my experiments.

After I had been with Buckton's about a year, the senior clerk who had been Mr Pepper's assistant, collecting stray rents from outlying districts two or three afternoons a week, was called up into the army and I was appointed in his place. Mr Pepper took me across to the Craven Dairies for coffee and Kunzle cakes and, so to speak, marked my card. The rent rounds I had been assigned were all a long bus ride away and, he intimated with a wink, you could wait a long time for some of these buses. If by any chance I did happen to get back into Town much before five, there was little point in giving anyone the impression that the job could be done in a couple of hours, now was there? Better while away the time at the News Theatre or take myself off for afternoon tea somewhere — not Jacomelli's, because that was where Mr Percy took his afternoon tea. I got the message, and I would certainly not be the one to let Mr Pepper down. With another wink, this time a lascivious one, he gave me one further piece of advice. When I got to a certain street, I might find a certain tenant quite obviously wearing nothing but a dressing-gown. If I was nice to her and didn't press her for the arrears, she might be nice to me and give me one of her home-made baps. Mr Pepper cackled wickedly. I got that message too.

My rounds were all in isolated mining villages on the outskirts of Leeds, each consisting of no more than a dozen to fifteen calls — mostly the estates of ladies of a certain age who had been left a clump of cottages or even a street or two by their fathers, like Mrs Codelyn in Arnold Bennett's *The Card*. Most of the properties were near-slums and the war-controlled rents, half a crown a week or three and sixpence at most, barely worth collecting. The certain lady in the certain street, on my first day as a rent collector, when I rapped on her door with beating heart and called "Rent please!" in a near-falsetto voice, proved to be a toothless old crone — Mr Pepper had been pulling my leg. Or had he? For the grimy rag on her back was undoubtedly a dressing-gown, and wrinkled skin was visible through the tatters. I took the rent money and fled.

But Mr Pepper was certainly right about one thing. My rents collected, I could comfortably have made it to Town by three o'clock. My predecessor, like the senior rent collector himself, had never got back to the office before five at the earliest. I wondered how Mr Pepper spent his afternoons.

As I stood at the corporation bus stop, tossing up in my mind between the News Theatre and a stroll round Kirkgate Market followed by a visit to the White Rose milk bar, I saw an unfamiliar Yorkshire Woollen District double-decker coming the other way. It was going to Bradford. On impulse, I ran across the road and flagged it down. It had been a long time since my burning desire to go and have a look at Bradford had culminated in the Yorkshire Penny Bank forgery, but I had made it at last.

Thus began a new series of expeditions and explorations to places that had hitherto only been names in the newspapers or on the fronts of buses — Bradford, Dewsbury, Wakefield, Halifax, Heckmondwike . . . each with its covered market (Bradford's was impertinently called Kirkgate; even more impertinently, it has long since been pulled down and replaced by the Kirkgate Shopping Centre), each with its Town Hall and municipal offices and chapels

131

and tabernacles, each with its arcades and accompanying carillons, each with its tram-cars or anyway trolley buses, each with its theatres and cinemas and pork shops and Pen Corners and Montague Burton the Tailor of Taste and department stores, each with its statues of aldermen and benefactors, yet all so different from Leeds.

I liked the smaller mill towns, nestling under the moors so that from the top of the unfamiliar bus before the steep descent you had a bird's-eye view of the whole community from its cradle to the grave – schools, chapels, shops, office buildings, factories, meeting halls, pubs, hospitals, all crammed together in one compact hollow, the crowded mill chimneys poking upwards like the sticks in a saucer of cocktail snacks, and the graveyards edging slowly up the hillsides.

Wakefield, the West Riding's county seat, I cared for less – too clean and orderly by far, and too much like a southern market town – not that I had ever set foot in a southern market town – for my liking. As for Bradford, on the other hand, if at first sight it seemed superficially a replica of Leeds I soon saw otherwise: not only was its Lewis's called Brown Muff's, its Grand Theatre the Alhambra and its *Evening Post* the *Telegraph & Argus*, but the buildings were blacker, their stone stonier and sturdier, the accents broader, the very air tangier from the city's closer proximity to the Pennines; and the people were more confident, cockier even, conscious that if Leeds was the city of a thousand trades then Bradford was the city of one, and that one was wool. Woolopolis.

I took to Bradford and went there often, as happy to be wandering its streets and squares as those of my home city. I was, so I was discovering, cosmopolitanly promiscuous. I belonged anywhere, so long as it was big enough and bustling enough and brash enough, and sported a Bovril sign picked out in electric light bulbs.

6 As to where I went after I had put up Buckton's shutters, my last duty of the day, that would depend. It was rarely straight home to Halton Moor.

If I had a girl in tow we might go to the pictures — nearly always one of the local houses, half the price of the super- and not-so-super-cinemas in Town. The trick was to find a girlfriend who lived on your own side of the city; otherwise, after the prolonged goodnights by the garden gate or, if she lived in one of the back-to-backs, within the communal midden, you would find yourself tramping miles homeward from the catchment area of some God-forsaken Electra or fleapit Picturedrome where the tramlines ended.

There was, happily, no shortage of cinemas on my side of town. As my friend Gerald Kaufman reminds me in the entertaining Leeds chapters of his book *My Life in the Silver Screen*, the best volume of film-going memoirs ever written by a politician, there were then fifty-five cinemas in Leeds, and while there was none within walking distance of Halton Moor — or not the distance anyone would trouble to walk without the incentive of a girl waiting at the other end — there were a good dozen within fairly easy reach, all changing their programmes twice a week, and ranging in quality from the first suburban super-cinema in Leeds, the Regal at Crossgates, to the nearby Ritz as it laughingly called itself, which was little more than a corrugated-iron-roofed brick shack within rattling distance of the railway.

My routine on these occasions was to have a modest high tea in Town and then meet the girl at about half past seven on the steps of the appointed picture house. This was not meanness but economy: with the few shillings my mother allowed me back out of my wages, plus the earnings from my Sunday newspaper rounds which I still had the sense to keep going, plus the odd coppers my creative bookkeeping methods managed to squeeze out of Buckton's petty

133

cash for my rent-collecting expenses (I had found that one ninepenny bus ride only cost sixpence if I got off a couple of stops early and walked an extra third of a mile), I had little more in my pockets now than when I had been a schoolboy entrepreneur; and my expenses were heavier. Besides, it was received wisdom that girls always liked to go home and change before they went out for the evening – and anyway, they were in with a good chance of being treated to a fish and chip supper after the speeded-up, scratchy notes of the National Anthem had emptied all but the patriotic one-and-nines where the patrons still stood to attention. For just about every cinema was ringed by fish and chip saloons, and their siren, batter-and-vinegar tang and the tempting sight of them, even in the blackout – some of them little art deco gems with enamelled sunburst cooking ranges; others, the older ones, with their leaded windows and stained-glass galleons, looking like miniature naval memorial chapels; and all of them with seagoing pubby names, the Argosy, the Neptune, the Golden Hind, the Lighthouse, the Mariner – was irresistible.

And besides again, I was enjoying exploring the cafés and restaurants of Leeds on my own – a novel experience, for of course I had never dared cross the daunting threshold of any of these premises on my white card perambulations or even in my College of Commerce days, although I had often stared at some of their more prepossessing exteriors.

Even though it was wartime it was still possible to eat in some style in Leeds, or in any provincial city. While the days had long gone, to my great regret, when one could dine at the Grand Restaurant in Boar Lane to the strains of the Imperial Viennese Orchestra, or in the onyx and marble splendour of the King Edward in its heyday when it was described as the handsomest grill room in the kingdom and by the then Lord Mayor as the finest building he had ever seen in his life, there was still the Kardomah where I could sit on a leatherette banquette with my back against the oak veneer wainscoting and be served a Welsh rarebit by a properly uniformed waitress. Or I could enjoy cinammon toast – a hitherto unknown delicacy which I knew I had to experience the instant I saw it on the menu – in the elegant surroundings of Betty's Café, an establishment which continues to this day in Harrogate, Ilkley and York but whose Leeds branch closed in the 1970s over Betty's inability to provide sufficient emergency exits to the satisfaction of the city council, for all that the only fire risk was that the toasted afternoon teacakes might be slightly overdone for the blue-rinse ladies of Roundhay and Moortown.

Down in Lower Briggate on the roof of what was now a bicycle shop I had long ago espied, and stared at, the faded, painted sign "Cocoa House", a relic of those Victorian and Edwardian days when the city had more cocoa houses than it now has kebab houses. We were now about two-thirds between that epoch and the fast food era, when the popular café was still all the go, very much in the mould of the Lyons Corner Houses. While we did not have a Lyons Corner House — we had two Lyons teashops, full of muttering old-age pensioners and newsvendors cashing up their takings — we did have Jacomelli's and we did have Powolny's and we did have Hagenbach's, and all the department stores had their "high class" (their expression) cafés, including Marshall and Snelgrove's who, in the after-whiff of the lunchtime haddock special, put on the occasional fashion show — Ray Hill and I took afternoon tea there once in the hope that slim-hipped mannequins would be modelling peach-coloured underwear. They were not.

If, at the time, some of these establishments were too pricey for my purse, I was glad to know that they were there and I did not envy the businessmen who sat down to their five-shilling (the wartime maximum price) dinners in oak-panelled ease. With my *Yorkshire Evening Post* propped up against an electro-plated teapot, and a fishcake (3d) on my plate, I whiled away many a happy hour in Joe Lyons.

And so to my rendezvous: seven thirty at the Regal or the Ritz or the Hillcrest or the Shaftesbury or the Star or the Harehills or the Regent. Like everybody else in Leeds — everybody in the country — I had been an inveterate cinemagoer since I could walk, cutting my milk teeth at the children's "Saturday rush" and graduating to the grand double feature plus full supporting programme (news, cartoon and "interest" — anything from *The March of Time* to a *Pete Smith Speciality*) at around the age of seven. If the big picture had an "A" certificate, requiring children to be accompanied by an adult, you simply hung around the box-office pleading, "Take us in, mister!" until some grown-up patron obliged. Unless you were a real film buff like the young Gerald Kaufman, who, as obsessed with cinemas as I was with cities, would go as far afield as Bradford to track down the latest recommendation of his hero critic Richard Winnington, you would see pretty well anything that was going, so that even with a

135

preference for George Raft you would settle for Sonja Henie if necessary. So my cinemagoing being on the whole indiscriminate and uncritical, it did not matter to me in the least that by seven thirty when the usherette's torch guided us into, with any luck, the back row, the main feature would be half over. In those days programmes were continuous, an endless belt of cellulose nitrate, so anyone with any interest in how the film began would simply wait for it coming round again. What would now seem a bemusing way of seeing a film has never been better described than by Gerald Kaufman:

Then, at very long last, the lights dimmed again. The huge curtains swished open, revealing another curtain, this time satiny and frilled, which always startled by rising instead of parting. The screen, illuminated in colour, was revealed. The censor's certificate appeared. Then the lion roared or the searchlights flashed, or the WB shield challenged or the mountain encircled by stars loomed, or what appeared to be the Statue of Liberty shone her torch, or the World revolved or staccato radio signals sent their message, and the credit titles told me that I was at last to see the first part of what I had come to see.

Right from the beginning I recognised characters starting upon adventures whose outcome I already knew. I nodded with comprehension as some plot element which had puzzled me in its dénouement was made clear by its exposition. This act of deduction was not easy, for every few moments my concentration on the screen was interrupted first by the distracting beam of the usherette's torch and then by newcomers stumbling over my feet and impeding my view as they took their places, to be perplexed in their turn by what they saw . . .

By this system, when in 1944 we were afflicted with a passion for the scat songs of Danny Kaye, Ray Hill and I contrived to see his film *Up In Arms* four times in succession for the price of one at the Paramount on the corner of Briggate and the Headrow – at 12.35, 3.30, 6.15 and 9.15, sustaining ourselves with packed sandwiches during the long afternoon and evening.

But my experience when taking a girl to the pictures was that neither of us was particularly interested in the plot. The object of every youth in the auditorium was to insinuate his arm around the shoulders of his companion by the end of the trailer for next week's "forthcoming attraction"; the second and first features, with perhaps an ice-cream interval, were but the backdrop to his ongoing endeavours to perfect the art of French kissing as it was known, his free hand meanwhile setting off on as thorough an exploration of cleavage or stocking top as would be allowable. Opinion had it that factory girls from Montague Burton the Tailor of Taste were "easier" in this regard than office girls. That was not my experience: I found them equally resistant to whatever charms I supposed myself to have. When the sound of slapped wrists was ricocheting through the cinema to the distraction of Stewart Granger fans wishing to give *Fanny By Gaslight* their undivided attention, mine was not uncommonly the loudest.

Curiously, despite my fondness for the theatre, and the fact that a seat in the gods was a fraction of the price of the cheapest cinema seat, I never once invited a girl to the Theatre Royal or the Grand for as long as I lived in Leeds. Or perhaps not so curiously: I should have wanted to watch the play. There was also the problem of where to take them afterwards. Taking a girl to the pictures endowed one with the right to a minimum half an hour's dalliance in some blacked-out shop doorway or up a dark alley. An evening at the theatre would have culminated in nothing but a tram ride home, by which time it would be the moment for her to announce that she had to "go in", the gloom-inducing indication that the parentally imposed curfew hour had arrived. These curfews were rigidly imposed. When, over a two-year period, I was taking out Heather from the College of Commerce, we always said our goodnights in a telephone box at the top of her street. Nightly her father would pass within inches of us on his way home from the pub. Never did he show the slightest flicker of recognition of his daughter or the remotest concern over the white-faced young sex maniac who, his face twisted with lust fired by an intensity of purpose rather than an intensity of passion, had just hastily released her from his clutches. Heather's father knew that she would be home in precisely nine minutes, the moment her H. Samuel wristlet watch ticked up to the half hour.

There were other, and cheaper, venues than the pictures. There was what was euphemistically called going for a walk, which meant finding a secluded patch of grass and lying down on it. A favourite spot was Kirkstall Abbey on the River Aire, a celebrated beauty spot just down the road from the smoke-belching Kirkstall Forge, where suitors could conceal themselves among the ruins. Sunday afternoon in Roundhay Park was so popular an institution that come teatime, French-kiss-sated couples brushing leaves from their backs as they re-approached the magnificent gilt-tipped gates would find a whole fleet of a dozen or fifteen trams waiting to convey them back to Briggate.

My own preference for alfresco enjoyment of this sort was the corporation cemetery. One of my duties at Buckton's was to attend funerals and post myself in the church porch with a shorthand notebook in which to record, for the benefit of the deceased's loved ones, the names of all the mourners and which organisations they might be representing. This task I was only too happy to perform, since I could sell the list to the Leeds Guardian Series; it was also good for my ego to be mistaken for a proper reporter by the funeral party. Thus it was that I was acquainted with most of the cemeteries in Leeds, and their potential. It would not have been seemly to steer a girl towards the nearest cemetery on a Sunday afternoon, of course, for the paths between the headstones were busy with relatives changing the cut flowers; but on a dark evening, provided it was fine or anyway not actually raining, there was no better courting territory than among the polished granite vaults and marble broken columns and alabaster angels. Most girls thought it rather a lark, especially if the place was locked and we had to squeeze in through the railings (where these were mounted on a low wall they had mostly been taken away for scrap to help the war effort, and it was even easier to get in). At the convergence of the two wide boulevards that was the standard cemetery layout there would usually be a comfortable wooden shelter in the lee of the chapel of rest. It was a rare evening when it was already occupied, when it would become necessary to find a spot among the gravestones.

On balance I made considerably more progress in the cemetery than in the cinema, perhaps because my fumblings were not subject to the distraction of Alan Ladd.

Despite some modest successes in this area, what I was up against was that it was then extraordinarily difficult to lose one's virginity. The only contraceptive available was the half-crown packet of three bought from such furtive outlets as the rubber goods shop on Leeds Bridge; half a crown was a lot of money and most lads − with the exception of a few incurable optimists who carried a packet of Durex about with them for so long that their wallets became embossed with the circular ridge of its contents − did not care to make the investment until they were persuaded that they were going to get an adequate return. Consequently girls went in terror of becoming pregnant − as did boys of impregnating them, for there could only be one way to go upon learning that, in the misery-drenched words of Ingrid in Stan Barstow's *A Kind Of Loving*, "something that should have happened hasn't happened," and that was up the church aisle. Besides, convention very strongly laid down that respectable girls didn't do it until they were married, or at any rate properly engaged. I did contrive to become informally engaged on several occasions, but to no effect, possibly because no twelve-guinea ring from Dyson's of Time Ball Buildings ever changed hands.

The other route was to deliver oneself into the hands of the professionals. It was said that the minimum rate for the ladies of North Street was ten shillings, but that was for standing up against a greasy wall down a back alley, otherwise it was a pound. I demurred, and not only because I didn't know how to do it standing up (I didn't know how to do it lying down, come to that). We had all read by this time − a copy had circulated surreptitiously throughout the College of Commerce − a manual called *The Red Light*, with a picture of the stop-caution-go traffic lights on the cover, obtainable, by anyone with the unflagging nerve to go in and ask for it, from the rubber goods shop. As well as dealing with birth control, impotence, premature ejaculation, the periodic indisposition of women and so forth, it had a grisly section on venereal disease. While it was fairly specific, for its time, about the symptoms and possible effects, it was evasive on the subject of the cure; thus the wild stories circulating among the youth of the town about what they did to you in VD clinics with red-hot needles went unchecked. If that were not enough, the government − concerned more with its wartime manpower supplies than with the nation's health at large, I suspect − had mounted a fearsome campaign against VD that made today's AIDS onslaught look like a warning against tooth plaque. I particularly remember a poster of a couple of soldiers being enticed into the company of a streetwalker with the line, "Looking for a good time, boys?" or some such. The lady of the night was provocatively dressed and contoured, differing from the pin-ups in *Razzle* magazine only in the detail that instead of a pouting face she had a grinning skull. The assumption, or rather the presumption, was that gonorrhoea and syphilis were diseases passed on to men by women. While this was not one hundred per cent accepted – a strong school of thought had it that VD was introduced into the country by GIs, as the Great Plague was brought in by rats – nobody in my age group ever questioned that it was transmitted pretty well exclusively by prostitutes, or by women of loose morals if only one could find one, and that in the fullness of time it would make your nose drop off.

Like most of the population of Leeds I eventually lost my virginity on Ilkley Moor – in my case to a girl so well spoken that I thought there must be some mistake (I equated good diction with niceness, and it was well known that nice girls didn't do it – it took considerable persuasion to convince me that they sometimes did). Ilkley Moor was reached by a Sammy Ledgard bus and was distant enough from Leeds to persuade prospective lovers that they were practically abroad, where inhibitions are notoriously relaxed. Also the fare was so expensive – a shilling each way – that there was unspoken acceptance that the girl knew what she was letting herself in for. After the deed was done we trekked across the moor to a famous pub called Dick Hudson's – a familiar and almost compulsory pilgrimage for every visitor from Leeds – where, without my age being called into question, I bought us both a shandy. I had never tasted alcohol before, even in this diluted form, and I felt quite grown up. Two firsts in one day.

7   If there was no current girlfriend and Ray Hill was
    similarly unencumbered, we would as often as not meet up
    after work with a view to remedying the deficiency.
Usually we would assemble at the White Rose milk bar on Boar
Lane, in the hope of making the acquaintance of a couple of office
girls. Drawing a blank there, we would then try the Moo-cow milk
bar in Briggate. Failing any luck here either, we would roam the
Town centre in a search for talent, starting with the queues outside
the Paramount, Tower and Assembly Rooms cinemas just along
Briggate. Should we spot any likely candidates, we might insinuate
ourselves into the queue and engage them in conversation. This did
not happen often. We might then go and hang around outside the
College of Art where there were some quite attractive students who
might wish to paint us. This never happened at all.

Should we be feeling particularly desperate for female company,
we might even take ourselves out to Crossgates to see if there were
any recent additions among the green blazers on the steps of the
Percival Leigh branch library. One evening we encountered a set of
quite acceptable identical twins, Susan and Pearl, and persuaded
them to accompany us to the Regal across the road. In terms of
limited sexual progress, the outing could be counted a success. When
next we met this accommodating pair, by arrangement outside the
park gates, it was fairly obvious from their occasional fits of giggles
that Susan had elected to become Pearl and Pearl Susan. We didn't
mind the deception in the least – it added piquancy to the
relationship. This delightful comedy of errors continued throughout
most of one summer.

One evening at the White Rose milk bar Ray and I bumped into
our old College of Commerce colleague Walsh (he was one of those
individuals who are invariably addressed only by their surname, for
no known reason). Although Walsh was destined to become a

141

successful Fleet Street journalist, like me he had regretfully been obliged to turn down the *Leeds Guardian*'s offer of ten shillings a week and was working his way through a bewilderingly rapid series of office jobs, the thinking behind this apparent restlessness being that if you gave the management notice within your first fortnight, they would pay you off and let you go at once sooner than continue to train you for work you would not be doing, thus you would be getting a paid bonus of free time.

Once again I had cause to be envious of Walsh: on the excuse of having to stay up late playing the piano in a jazz group, he had managed to persuade his family to allow him to take his very own flat in Town. That this flat turned out to be the outside coal cellar of a crumbling old villa in the university area in no way diminished its desirability in my eyes. Snugly fitted out with a truckle bed, a primus stove, an old basket chair that Walsh had rescued from a compost heap, and stacked orange boxes to serve as bookshelves, it had all the bachelor cosiness, to me and no doubt to its occupant, of No. 18B Baker Street.

Walsh, with his glasses repaired with sticking plaster and a long yellow raincoat which he never ever removed, even while playing boogie-woogie on some battered old piano when it draped from his shoulders like the wings of a fruit bat, resembled a youthful Ukridge and was well on his way to becoming a bohemian. He had some interesting eccentrics among his friends. One was a formidably intelligent lad called Henry who could play chess blindfold, committing the moves to memory as they were transmitted to him. Unfortunately, Henry was to turn his unusual brain to cheque forgery and he finished up in Armley Jail. (There, remembering the Yorkshire Penny Bank forgery, but for the grace of God . . .) Another was Roy, a boy of restless but undirected intellect who was famous among his cronies for having stood up at a meeting of the Leeds Film Society and earnestly enquired of the visiting lecturer from London whether he would not agree that films made of celluloid were superior to those manufactured out of baked clay, owing to the greater flexibility of the former. Roy, possibly in the course of some teenage experiment, subsequently gassed himself. The jazz band to which he, Walsh and by now Ray Hill belonged played "When the Saints Go Marching In" over his grave, when I, who had had to get leave from an undertaker's to attend a funeral, was more moved than I cared to admit. But not so moved that I did not sell the story to the *Leeds Guardian*.

A third friend of Walsh's was Rick, now a highly respected Leeds solicitor, who while studying for his examinations was living a few doors from the coveted coal cellar in what I understood by the expression "rooms" – another enviable apartment. Rick had the first proper privately owned library I had ever set eyes on, one of his three rooms being devoted entirely to books in their hundred upon hundred, shelved on planks supported by house bricks, arranged not only around the walls but in four or five rows across the room like a public library. Rick was an intensely political animal, and his literary taste was almost exclusively political. He would lend out books by the armful; thus it was that I was introduced to the orange limp-cloth volumes of the Left Book Club, to Jack London's *The Iron Heel*, to Karl Marx, to H.G. Wells other than as the author of *Kipps* and *The Invisible Man*, to Shaw, to a writer known as George Orwell who had written *Down and Out in Paris and London* and *The Road to Wigan Pier* . . .

Then there was Will, older than any of us, a keen Esperantist and world peace fanatic and a great influence on Walsh who in his turn was a great influence on me. Chain-smoking OPs – that category, rather than brand, of cigarettes known as Other People's – and with his patched-up spectacles steamed up with enthusiasm, Walsh would harangue me, in Esperanto, about world peace by the hour. I drank deeply of this company.

On that chance encounter at the White Rose milk bar, however, our first interest in Walsh was that he was on his way to take part in a mixed doubles table tennis tournament at a church youth club in Hunslet. Mixed meant girls. With nothing else to do that evening, Ray Hill and I decided to accompany our friend and lend him our support.

We had never thought of youth clubs. Youth meant male, an impression dispiritingly confirmed by a single fleeting visit to the YMCA hut in Osmondthorpe, where the membership was uncompromisingly of our own sex only. But now we were about to be pitched into a world of mixed table tennis and mixed who knew what else? To Hunslet, then – where it had to be said that first impressions were disappointing, there being only two girls among a company of twelve, and both of them seemingly spoken for. But we acknowledged that Walsh had opened doors for us. And not only did we meet his beguiling friends Henry and Roy but Walsh introduced us to an equally interesting character named Willis Hall, a wiry, intense-looking youth of our own age who like Walsh and me had served his time selling columns of names – in his case, I learned, a sprinkling of them fictitious to eke out the space – to the *Leeds Guardian*. It had never crossed my mind to make names up and I was duly impressed. While this enterprising but taciturn fellow did not straight away admit to so flamboyant an ambition himself, I had it from Walsh that he had set his heart on becoming a writer or journalist or both, and had already made approaches to the *Basinful of Fun* and the *Yorkshire Evening News*. The *News*, in due course, was to take him on to its racing pages; meanwhile he was working in the Yorkshire Relish factory where by way of indoctrination the girls had smothered his private parts not in brown sauce as one might imagine, but in custard powder. We were to meet again, when he would admit to an addiction to vanilla flavouring.

New horizons having opened out for us, Ray Hill and I set about taking sightings of all the youth clubs in Leeds for female content. While there was a fair number of them, they all seemed to be attached to one or other religious denomination, to which members were supposed to owe allegiance and even occasionally to attend church or chapel. Thus, in the course of our researches, we became, in turn and sometimes simultaneously, members of the Baptist, Wesleyan, Congregational and Methodist persuasions, as well as returning to the bosom of the Church of England as and when expediency demanded. Only the doors of the Judean Club were closed to us.

Back in my white card days I had often stared at the Doric porticos and craggy frontages of some of these substantial places of worship and I was glad of the chance now to see the interiors – the youth club was usually down in the crypt – of such temples of non-conformity as the Brunswick Methodist Chapel with its box pews seating thousands, and the Oxford Place Wesleyan Chapel with its steep tiers of plain benches rising from an elegant circular balcony. But it was the attractiveness and availability of the female company rather than the architecture that won the day. Despite its being presided over by a Victorian throwback of a minister who believed modern ballroom dancing to be sinful (that was all right by me, since I couldn't dance), we settled eventually for the Belgrave Primitive Chapel (or if it was not, it certainly seemed it), just a few minutes' walk from Briggate and plentifully supplied with girls in blazers. To both Ray and me throughout the whole of our adolescence, a college blazer and white blouse was the last word in chic.

We settled down to a pleasant routine of Friday evening ping-pong, lantern lectures, mock parliaments and Camp coffee, the reward for which regime of clean living was to walk a selected girl home and see if you could make more progress this week than you had made last week. Sunday chapel was more or less compulsory if you wished to remain a member, and the Victorian throwback's hellfire sermons were interminable; but on these summer evenings there was always the tram ride out to Kirkstall Abbey afterwards with the promise of a white blouse yielding one more button. Admittedly, the promise may have been on the slender side but there was utterly nowhere else to go on Sunday anyway – we were still a good long way off the city referendum that was to permit the cinemas to open on the Sabbath, and all other places of entertainment and non-alcoholic refreshment were as firmly shuttered as if we had been living in Aberdeen.

Then, one golden week, the word began to percolate through the youth clubs and milk bars and office post-rooms of Leeds that an amazing new Sunday night youth club had just opened in the Priestley Hall of the Mill Hill Unitarian Chapel right on City Square, packed to the beams with girls (no doubt girls were hearing that it was packed to the beams with boys). Ray and I instantly became Unitarian converts, and on the following Sunday made haste to the Priestley Hall, named of course after the discoverer of oxygen and Mill Hill preacher whose statue out in City Square I had given many a meaningful stare in my white card era, perhaps unconsciously anticipating that he would be a useful contact one of these days. The place was thronged – not since morning assembly at the College of Commerce had I seen such a gathering of my own age group under one roof. It was only the second Sunday of the club's existence but that night – just in time for Ray and myself – the membership list closed at 250, the maximum allowed into the building. The following week there were hundreds of hopefuls queuing down the street to register their names on the waiting list – a scene that these days would only be replicated outside a commercial disco.

The Sunday Night Youth Club was the brainchild of Mill Hill's minister, the Rev Eric Price, one of the last of that lost breed of pipe-smoking, muscular Oxbridge Christians who used to organise East End lads' clubs back in the hungry Thirties. He had a talent for this sort of exercise such as I have only ever since come across in London club and restaurant entrepreneurs with the flair for magically transforming this or that establishment into the place of the moment. Without his apparently doing very much except puff away at his briar, the Priestley Hall became *the* place to be for the brighter teenagers (as they were yet to be called) of Leeds.

One of his secrets was his recognition that we were all children of the city, as attracted to the centre of things as moths to a candle. Another was his realisation that simply because you were placing a sizeable hall at youth's disposal you did not necessarily have to infest it with lantern slides and ping-pong – you could leave it to itself to become a seething indoor piazza where old friends would meet – Walsh and Willis Hall, I was happy to find, were among the earliest born-again Unitarians signing up with the Sunday Night Youth Club – and new friendships would be made. Besides this main meeting place the Priestley Hall was blessed with a goodly number of side rooms and in these, energetic and enthusiastic coteries quickly established little offspin clubs of their own – a music group, a discussion group, a philately group and so on, plus of course an Esperanto group and a world peace group. We were led to believe that we had started up these enterprises entirely on our own initiative. This was the third of the Rev Eric Price's great talents.

The hall had a proper stage with proper curtains, of the quality I could have done with when I was engrossed in the pages of *Let's Do A Play*. We did not do a play but we did several concert parties, of which I can remember little except that nothing could stop Ray Hill dressing up as a comic vicar and that girls used to come up to me and plead with me not to do my drunk act again. We also did our versions of various popular radio shows, the hit of the season being a spoof *Brains Trust* which Willis Hall and I knocked out together – the first of a series of collaborations which has so far continued, on and off, for close on fifty years.

The Club had not been going long when the Rev Price suggested – he never proposed, only put forward tentative ideas – that we might like to have our own magazine. I at once claimed the right to edit it, with Walsh, Ray and Willis as the editorial team. Fortunately no one seemed inclined to argue over this self-appointment, or I should have been most put out. The enterprising minister, who seemed to know everyone who was anyone in Leeds, went to his friend the general manager of the Yorkshire Conservative Newspaper Company, publishers of the *Yorkshire Post* and *Evening Post*, and persuaded him to print it for us. Having envisaged something run off on a jellygraph, I was most impressed and looked forward keenly to seeing the byline K.S. Waterhouse for only the second time in print (the S was for Spencer, my mother's maiden name: the style, of course, was in emulation of P.G. Wodehouse).

Ray Hill designed the cover. Walsh contributed an article on Esperanto and world peace. I contributed the short-short story that had failed to make the grade with *A Basinful of Fun*. Willis contributed his own *Basinful of Fun* rejections. By the time other members had handed in, or failed to hand in, their notes on various club activities (there was an especially lengthy report from the Esperanto group), there was still a page left over, and so I re-invented Michael Fox – one of my library ticket pseudonyms – who, a long way after the celebrated Cassandra of the *Daily Mirror*, whose waspish column I was one day to inherit, penned an attack on the editorial team for constituting a club within a club: "Whatever K.S. Waterhouse and his cronies may say to the contrary the Club is fast approaching the state where it is being governed by a clique . . ." This was a highly popular feature.

The magazine wasn't half bad as such efforts go, and whatever its deficiencies it did earn one distinction before it ran its course – it was the only youth club magazine I have ever come across to be threatened with a writ for libel.

It was just as I was about to put the Christmas number to bed that Walsh and Ray Hill came to me with the news that the club jazz band, from which they had jointly dropped out in disgust on the purist grounds that it was little more than a dance orchestra peddling Vera Lynn numbers, was demanding a fee of three shillings per performer to play at the Christmas social. While Ray and Walsh no doubt had an axe to grind, this was something for a frustrated journalist to make much of. Accordingly I cleared the Scrooge parody off the middle pages, and in a vitriolic article headed "SCANDAL!" trotted out Michael Fox to do his worst: "Let us expel these members from the club forthwith and make do with a comb and tissue paper . . ."

Unfortunately for me, the father of one of the traduced jazz musicians was a linotype operator on the *Yorkshire Post*, where a copy of the magazine fell into his hands before publication. He consulted the office lawyer who was at once on the telephone to Mill

Hill, warning that an action for libel could lie unless the offending issue was banned. To his great credit the Rev Eric Price did not take upon himself the role of censor as any other youth club leader in this situation would have done – he left it, or anyway gave a very good impression of leaving it, to my editorial discretion. My newly acquired sense of responsibility, naturally, went straight to my head and I agreed to suppress the Christmas number (I couldn't merely excise the offending pages, since in my excitement I had scrapped Ray Hill's standing cover and splashed the word WAR! across the front page in six-inch capitals). Sensing that everything after this would be anticlimax, I shortly afterwards handed over the editorial reins to others.

But Mill Hill remained a special place. Unlike most of the other youth clubs we had sampled, there was no pressure to attend its associated chapel, and I for one never did, for there was always some distraction in the Priestley Hall from early afternoon onwards. But a good number of members did start going to the Unitarian Chapel, out of curiosity or whatever motive – in those long-lost days it might even have been religion – and I was interested recently, upon glancing through a copy of the latest chapel newsletter someone had sent me, to see among the lists of stewards and flower-arrangers and so forth several well-remembered names from those effervescent days. But whether we finished up bona fide Unitarians or not, there cannot be any one of us who has forgotten Mill Hill or the excitement somehow generated by that pipe-puffing parson.

While there were girls in abundance at Mill Hill, the restless search for new talent went on unabated during the remainder of the week. Inspired by one of our fellow-members, a lad of Marxist bent who had given a talk on dialectical materialism, we tapped a new source of companionship – the political parties, beginning with the Young Communists, and progressing, when the only female young communist at the one meeting we tried proved to have a moustache, via the Labour League of Youth where we were similarly disappointed, to the Young Conservatives.

This was more promising. For one thing it gave me access to a handsome building I had often stared at – the Conservative Club on South Parade, next to the Bank of England. The Young Communists had been in a room over a shop and Labour in somebody's front room. For another, not only was there an excess of girls over boys but they were exclusively drawn from the blazer-wearing class. If there was a superfluity of tennis talk, Ray and I were well able to hold our own since we had played the odd game with the Crossgates twins on the municipal courts, using borrowed racquets. We were by now well versed, too, in those softened vowel sounds by which affected northerners try to pass themselves off as southerners, as in "Who's pat batter on the cashion?" The Young Conservatives made us most welcome, and on our very first – and, as it was to turn out, last – evening we were flattered to be invited by the very pretty secretary to attend the Club Flannel Dance the forthcoming Saturday. While we had no idea in what respect a Flannel Dance would differ from the Fifty Shilling Tailors Suit hops we had occasionally attended at Mill Hill, we keenly looked forward to it.

But there was a snag, an insuperable one. The very pretty secretary had no tickets about her very fetching person, and so she proposed to post them to us. And since I had snobbishly, if accurately, sensed that a council house address would not cut much ice with the Young Conservatives, I had resuscitated Trevor Austin of 82 Templemeads Way, Crossgates. Ray was my next door neighbour Nigel Fairfax. Any tickets sent to this completely fictitious thoroughfare would be returned to sender. I could, of course, have asked her to despatch the tickets to my workplace where I could have intercepted Trevor Austin's mail; but J.T. Buckton's the Leeds Undertakers (We Never Sleep) was hardly the most glamorous of office addresses, and in any case I had already told her that I was a reporter on the *Leeds Guardian* – not only to impress her but to corner any Young Conservative news item that might be going. The Flannel Dance would have been good for half a column and it was a shame I had to miss it.

But it did spur Ray and me on to do what we had been meaning to do for some time in our pursuit of the opposite sex, and that was to take dancing lessons.

It was customary at the time for offices to work on Saturday mornings, and a popular pursuit after a lunch of baked beans on toast at Woolworth's or Joe Lyons was to attend one of the several "studios of dance" which then flourished, all of them in upper rooms over shoe shops and dress shops, and all of them with names like the Yvette del Monte or the De Grey Firth School of Dancing. We enrolled at an establishment above the Co-op in Albion Street where, after a fashion, I learned to dance with a cane chair to the strains of Victor Sylvester records. Having grasped the rudiments of the waltz, the quickstep and the foxtrot we graduated to the various dance halls of Leeds which, from their revolving mirrored globes to their fretwork painted plywood music stands, were identical in all respects but one: at one class of dance hall you would be expected to enquire, "Excuse me, may I have this dance?", while at another you would ask, "Are you getting up?"; and the girls for their part would respond, "No thank you, I'm just waiting for my friend" in the former category, or "Go on home, your mother wants your boots for loaf tins" in the latter.

From the Capitol, the Mecca, the Majestic, the Astoria and the 101, we gradually transferred our Saturday evening affections to the Big Top, a draughty marquee on Woodhouse Moor erected by the council as an attraction to persuade the populace to spend its holidays at home in this time of austerity and seaside resorts swathed in barbed wire; and there we danced out the war. The blackout had become the dim-out, and the piles of sandbags round the entrances to the Market and elsewhere were being shifted away at last − rather to my regret, for ever since I had discovered girls it had been as if a friendly local authority had sent a works lorry down Lovers' Lane tipping out mattresses every few yards. Cautiously optimistic advertisements were beginning to appear in the *Yorkshire Evening Post*: "Forward to Victory and normal supplies of Bassett's Original Liquorice Allsorts." Then one day on my way past the Corn Exchange I saw a workman perched on a ladder above the Oyster Bar opposite; he was testing and replacing the electric light bulbs in the Bovril sign. And then I knew we had Hitler on the run.

8 Right from the very beginning of my meanderings I had always been conscious of, if not always intoxicated by, the smells of the city, from the heavy blend of malt and hops and horse manure wafting out from the breweries to the delicate breath of eucalyptus and zinc ointment from the patent medicine shops; from the stench of blood − and was it fear? − that enveloped the corporation abattoir to the scent of Lapsang, Orange Pekoe and Fine Darjeeling drifting in through Buckton's fanlight from Elgie & Co.'s tea warehouse two doors along (where, snug among the tea chests up in the rafters, I was a periodic member of the all-night firewatch against incendiary bombs − a lark, but it would have been a better lark had girls been allowed to firewatch too).

Kirkgate Market was oranges and pineapples and wet fish and spice cake; the glittering arcades were Brasso and Navy Mixture and Thornton's toffee; the pork shops were the Bisto fragrance escaping through the funnel supporting the crust of a meat and potato pie; and Lewis's was the sweet vanilla of the American soda fountain. But perhaps the most pervasive odour was that of stale beer and cigarette smoke from the dozens and dozens of city pubs − especially those tucked away up the alleys, where it had a tendency to be pungently tinged with urine.

As a wandering child, I had found this smell thoroughly obnoxious, and I had not been too keen on it as a wandering College of Commerce student either. Now that I was a little older, while I still found the stink of last night's beer repellent as I mooched about the town delivering Buckton's mail or generally time-wasting, I did notice that as the day wore on these pub smells, except from those of the lowest of low ale-houses, grew less disagreeable and indeed became downright inviting. This was, of course, after the carbolic had done its work and the pubs had opened up again and fresh pints were pulled and fresh plugs of twist lit up, and from behind frosted-glass windows engraved with Prince of Wales feathers and dandified words like LUNCHEON and FINE WINES there was a rising hum of chatter as the first wave of customers compared notes over their racing greens.

I had not until now been particularly intrigued by pubs, not even to stare at. The reverse, in fact: I had regarded them, if I thought of them at all, as places of debauchery, somewhere between the city's illegal but flourishing back-street betting shops which anticipated the Betting and Gaming Act by a good many years, and licensed brothels. This was before the idea of licensed brothels became itself intriguing. I suppose I was influenced by my mother who, probably in reaction to my father's excesses, was a strict teetotaller – apart from the thimbleful of non-igniting brandy over the Christmas pudding, her nearest brush with the demon drink was to be taken by one of my uncles to sit on a bench outside the famous Tommy Wass's with a glass of lemonade, and that only because the original Wass family had run their former farmhouse as a refreshment room serving teas to cricketers and tennis players, so it didn't really count as a pub at all in the drinking-den sense. And then, in my childhood, I had seen enough beer-drunks lurching around the streets of Middleton. I had a vivid recollection of trying, when on my way to the fish shop one Saturday, to help up a drink-sodden miner who was lying flat out on the pavement – I got him into a sitting position but then was forced by his dead weight to let him go, and he snapped back like a hinged box lid, his head crashing against the ground with such a thickening thud that it sent reverberations along the paving stones.

But suddenly I was interested in pubs – though more interested in what went on inside them, I have to say, than in the taste of beer. It was one more layer of city life that I wanted to explore. Fortunately for my sense of curiosity, Ray Hill was simultaneously beginning to awaken to the possibilities of alcohol as an element of social life. We resolved to explore them.

It would be a risky business, for while at sixteen we could probably pass for eighteen, especially since we were both attempting to grow moustaches, the wartime regulations required everyone to carry an identity card and our ages could easily be checked. Furthermore, although we had taken the Conservative Club in our stride we didn't quite know, didn't know at all in fact, how to disport ourselves in a taproom. The secret, we decided, was confidence, and what bred confidence was familiarity. Before, then, entering the pub of our choice, an obscure tavern on the wrong side of Leeds Bridge where no one would know us, we reviewed our studies of the signwriter's art as applied to breweries, recalling phrases useful to the novice pub customer. Our opening line rehearsed, and a toss of the shilling we proposed to spend on beer deciding who would utter it, we marched into the public bar with a fair display of swagger.

I had a confused impression of bevelled mirrors reflecting Victorian green tiles and dark wood and burnished copper, like the interior of a Hansel and Gretel house of marzipan, slab chocolate and glazed gingerbread. The landlord, built like the burly saloon bar-keep in all the westerns we'd seen, detached himself from conversation with the only other customer. Ray cleared his throat. "Could we have two sparkling dinner ales, please?" The customer guffawed. The landlord, with a weary shake of the head, spoke not a word but simply pointed to the door. We shuffled out.

It was not until my initiatory half of shandy at Dick Hudson's on the day I lost my virginity on Ilkley Moor that I was to enter a pub again, and then only peripherally, since Dick Hudson's featured a hatch where hikers with their muddy boots could be served without actually setting foot in the bar parlour. But thereafter, Ray meanwhile having similarly acquitted himself on both counts, we became, if not pub regulars, then fairly constant under-age irregulars.

By trial and error – the error sometimes compounded by an ignominious exit – we learned the grammar of drinking, beginning with the tongue-twister, "Two halves of half and half, please", a half and half being the popular tipple of the day, a mixture of mild and bitter. Then there was one's uncertainty over the multiplicity of socially graded rooms then common. We discovered that if we ventured into the public bar wearing collar and tie, there were strange looks from the overalled regulars – perilous for anyone trying to go unnoticed. If we went into the snug, the domain of gnarled old pensioners and ladies sipping stout, there were stranger ones. Should there be a waiter on duty (as there still was in some saloon bars, where you pressed a bell for service), we could deduce from glares and sniffs that those who bought their own drinks at the bar were not expected to sit down. In some taprooms it was regarded as effeminate to sit down at all, while in the bigger, street-corner tiled pubs peculiar to Leeds it was customary to leave the various comfortably appointed lounges and saloons to the womenfolk and drink out in the mosaic-paved corridor.

The nuances of drinking etiquette fascinated me – it was like being a volunteer in a Mass Observation survey. So, too, did pub architecture, for all that in most of the only licensed premises we dared venture into, usually insignificant little sawdust and spittoon houses well away from the city centre where we were unlikely to be spotted by neighbours out on the town, the decor seemed not so much to have seen better days as given up awaiting their arrival. But having seen pub interiors only in British black and white B movies until now, I was fascinated by their every dust-embedded detail.

But while relishing their cracked eau-de-Nil tiles, scuffed mahogany, blotched etched glass and wobbling cast-iron tables, I was well aware that Leeds could do better, that the city centre boasted gilded gin palaces and gleaming saloon bars to rival anything in the Wild West's roaring Nineties: for instance the historic Whitelock's First City Luncheon Bar, one of the few licensed premises I had ever condescended to stare at, since I had heard that it was frequented by newspaper reporters. While we demurred at crossing the burnished thresholds of these establishments, we did, at my insistence, once try to gain entry to the Wine Lodge (Albert Cowling, Licensee), a vast underground cavern the size and shape of the Albert Hall which featured a Wurlitzer organ among its attractions. But no one had acquainted us with Mr Cowling's personal licensing law, to the effect that no one was allowed down the steps under the age of twenty-one. To this end uniformed bouncers – commissionaires, as he preferred to call them – sporting magnificent plum-coloured uniforms with epaulettes like bath-brushes, stood on duty at the Wine Lodge's three entrances on the corner of City Square and Boar Lane. Turned away by each of these major-domos in turn, it was to be another three or four years before we plucked up the nerve to storm Albert Cowling's citadel again in earnest.

Not, had we been allowed in, that we should have given Mr Cowling a moment's trouble; for it was acceptance into the pub community that we craved, rather than access to alcohol of which, if only out of economic necessity, we drank as sparingly as possible, often making half a pint linger half an hour. That was our rule, but to every rule there is the exception that proves it: our exception was on Christmas Eve 1946 when, the pair of us being flush with a

154

modest annual wages bonus, we elected to make the great leap forward from beer to spirits.

To carry out this daring deed we thought we had better place ourselves, in case of accidents, outside the jurisdiction of the Leeds City Constabulary. On my recommendation, therefore, we took a train to Dewsbury, a town I had by now somewhat familiarised myself with in the course of my Buckton's rent run..We found a homely, back-street inn, crowded enough on this festive evening for two strange young faces to go unremarked. We bought halves and considered our serious drinking policy. Ray favoured whisky: I did not, I didn't like the smell of it. Brandy seemed too medicinal by far. Gin was an old biddy's tipple, as was port, and anyway port wasn't spirits — or was it? While we were dithering, a cheery soul barging past with the sausage-like fingers of both hands clutching two pints and two measures of dark rum called out, "Get a rum down you, lads — it's Christmas!" Now that I did like the smell of — like toffee. We ordered two rums at ninepence apiece.

There must have been a late-night licensing extension in the West Riding that Christmas Eve, for the next thing I could subsequently remember was a distant clock sounding an unearthly hour — two, was it, or three, or four? — as we sat in a deserted, unheated and unlighted train. Had we left Dewsbury yet? Ray was sound asleep. I peered through the grimy window at the forlorn, ill-lit platform, a scene straight out of *Brief Encounter*, a good portion of which I had recently seen in the back row of the Crossgates Ritz in company with a green blazer. The name of the station was spelled out in uncompromising iron lettering on a sturdy board. We were not in Dewsbury. We were not in Leeds. We were in Kingston upon Hull, on Humberside, sixty miles to the east of where we should have been and would have been had we got off the train at the right station.

Under the influence of who knew how many rums chased by who knew how much mild and bitter, we were neither of us in the least concerned. In that era there was still a train service of sorts over Christmas — with any luck, and subject to the availability of a Silver Line cab at Leeds Central Station, we could be back home and in bed before our mothers rose to commence their Christmas Day chores. Meanwhile, in the grey light of dawn, there was a new city to explore.

We stumbled out of the station. There was little of any consequence to see — Hull had been badly bombed during the war and all around us was still rubble and desolation. From the bowels of a boarded-up crater that had once been an office block or a public building came the drunken cries of revellers in an even worse state that we were. We retraced our staggering steps, just in time to catch what I suppose, had there been any milk deliveries on Christmas Day, would have been the milk train – fortunately for us, since the next skeleton service departure was not until around noon.

I got home, still swaying and by now feeling distinctly groggy with the aftertaste of rum welling up in my throat, at about seven in the morning. My teetotal but unperturbable mother, already up and raking out the grate, made no comment beyond a routinely rhetorical "What time do you call this?" Clutching the sideboard, which I was alarmed to find was dipping up and down like a rowing boat, I mumbled something about having fallen asleep in the fish shop. Realising, even in the state I was in, that this made no kind of sense, I felt it imperative to convince my mother that I was sober. For some reason I was persuaded that the way to set about this was to open the sideboard drawer nearest to me and replace therein the chain tie-pin I then affected. Unluckily, I pulled the drawer with such force that it shot clean off its runners and tipped its paraphernalia of rolled-up socks, crêpe bandages, bicycle clips and collar studs all over the floor. Announcing thickly, "Just looking for the Sunday papers," I lurched off to bed.

And there, apart from a brief and half-hearted attempt to participate in the family Christmas dinner, I was to remain for the next two days, rising only from time to time to retch up a thin stream of watery green bile. As with my fictitious trip to Belle Vue Zoo years earlier, my mother made no reference at all to my Christmas adventure, either then or later. Perhaps she didn't need to, for I was never to taste rum again – even today the very smell of it makes me feel ill. Nor have I ever again set foot in Hull, the only city I have ever visited that holds out no enchantment for me at all.

After a suitably subdued interval, Ray Hill and I resumed our drinking activities, within strictly prescribed limits yet growing ever bolder in our choice of venues as our moustaches showed signs of sprouting and we got closer and closer to the time when, excepting only Mr Albert Cowling's Wine Lodge, we might drink legally.

One landmark bar we did finally determine to infiltrate was that of the City Varieties music-hall, less because it was one of the oldest in Leeds than that we had been told it overlooked the dress circle, from which there was an excellent view of the stage on which naked ladies performed their tableaux vivants of Aphrodite Triumphing Over Psyche and the Temptation of Eve. We had this from our friend Walsh, who with his own eyes had seen the revue *We Never Clothed* or some such. He it was who broke the news that the celebrated striptease artiste Miss Phyllis Dixey was about to pay what was tantamount to a state visit to the City Varieties. Not to see Phyllis Dixey playing the City Varieties would have been like not seeing Sir Henry Irving at the old Leeds Hippodrome.

Accordingly, with Walsh as our pathfinder, we slunk up the wet cobbled alley that was then the old variety hall's main entrance, paid our few coppers at the box-office, climbed the scuffed steps, and without let or hindrance from the management entered the circle bar.

I was at once mesmerised, and wondered what on earth had kept me out of the Varieties for so long − my mother's disapproval of the place, I suppose. Reputedly the oldest theatre in the country, it had yet to be refurbished (as it subsequently was, lovingly, by its new owner Harry Joseph, a renovation that was to pave the way for Barney Colehan's long-running TV show, *The Good Old Days*, for which Leeds dressed up in Edwardian finery), and its moth-eaten plush and chipped gilt plasterwork were still agreeably shabby. A surprising feature, considering that its reputation for strip shows went back at least to 1910 when one Miss Pansy Montague was billed as "La Milo, wearing only a smilo", was the royal coat of arms over the proscenium arch. Legend had it, according to the knowledgeable Walsh, that Edward VII, as Prince of Wales, used to pay incognito visits to the theatre after shooting pheasant on the moors, and that he would watch the performance from behind the drawn curtains of what in a more respectable house would have been called the royal box.

The theatre bar was (and to this day remains) all that a theatre bar should be, its ceiling stained milk-chocolate brown with nicotine wafting back to the days of penny cheroots and cigar divans, and every square inch of wall taken up by old playbills and cracked photographs bearing the faded, extravagantly affectionate inscriptions of the likes of Charlie Chaplin (who came to the Varieties in a clog-dancing act called the Eight Lancashire Lads), Lily Langtry, Dan Leno, Marie Lloyd, and so on down to the moderns such as Robb Wilton, Max Miller and Wilson, Keppel and Betty.

Our original intention had been to go out into the circle only for

Phyllis Dixey, and spend the rest of the evening propping up the bar in masculine fashion. Walsh, however, was anxious to see a supporting act, the trumpet player Nat Gonella, for whom his uncle had once done some electrical work, a service which Walsh seemed to think brought Mr Gonella into the category of family friend. Thus it was, after the trumpeter had taken his bow and we were about to troop back into the bar, that we happened to catch the entry of the eccentric comedian with the collapsible legs who followed him, and were intrigued enough to linger.

His name was Max Wall; we had barely heard of him but were soon aware that we were in the presence of genius. A comedian who not only didn't tell straightforward jokes himself but mocked the jokes that lesser comedians told was an unusual turn indeed. He had not yet perfected Professor Wallofski but there was a good deal of foolery at the piano, plus the funny walks which, ignorant though we may have been of the ways of the old music-hall, we could recognise as referring back to some of the comics like Little Titch and Chaplin whose sepia likenesses guarded our barely touched halves of bitter back in the bar. Max Wall was so unconventional that we were dismayed when he signalled the end of his act by giving a cue to the orchestra and announcing, in the cloyingly patriotic manner of the times (we were still in the aftermath of war), "And now, ladies and gentlemen, I would ask you all to rise for a tribute to the lads in khaki and in blue." The audience shuffled awkwardly to its feet – and Max, standing to attention, broke into a rendering of "Yes, We Have No Bananas". It could have gone badly wrong and in fact his reception was ragged at best – but in three young would-be sophisticates leaning against the back rail of the dress circle, Max Wall had made slaves for life. Phyllis Dixey's second spot in the show – we had already seen her doing some nifty semaphore work with ostrich feathers in the first half – seemed tame by comparison, consisting as it did of a static series of famous paintings such as Gainsborough's *Blue Lady* as they might have appeared if posed for in the nude.

Miss Dixey's total contribution to the evening, indeed, might have proved tamely disappointing but for Walsh's wide theatrical connections. The uncle who had once done some electrical work for Nat Gonella proved also to have done some electrical work for the City Varieties itself, and was thus known to the stage doorkeeper. This gave us – or at any rate the enterprising Walsh, with Ray and I tagging in his wake — the entree to Mr Gonella's dressing room, the first theatre dressing room I had ever entered. Since I was less of a trumpet fan than Walsh or Ray it interested me far more than its occupant, and I gave its yellow-painted brick walls and chipped sink and mirrored dressing-table the keenest of stares.

Nat Gonella remembered, or affected to remember, Walsh, and while completing his change into street clothes was asking after the health of Walsh's uncle in the electrical line when there was a tap on his door and at its threshold appeared a vision I had only a few moments earlier seen totally naked except for the wisp of chiffon she clutched while standing in what looked like a large papier-mâché ashtray to depict Venus rising out of the sea. Miss Phyllis Dixey now wore an excessively sensible candlewick dressing-gown. What her errand was I had no idea: as in a trance I perceived that the obliging Mr Gonella was introducing his guests. ". . . And this is Keith." To which I added, automatically and unnecessarily, "Waterhouse."

The vision spoke. It might have spoken before but I had not been aware of it. "What a funny name," observed Venus.

It was to get worse. I searched for a reply — something witty, brief and sophisticated that would so etch into her mind that she would remember me for ever. "It's better than Nicholas Ridiculous," I heard myself saying, recalling the name of a character in a zany radio show of the time. But while I heard myself saying these words, Miss Dixey did not. My mouth having suddenly gone dry, all that actually came out of it was, "It's better than Nicholas." Miss Phyllis Dixey, I reflected upon reviewing the conversation in the course of a restless night, must have regarded this as the most pointless, goonish, stupid remark ever spoken by any human being since the first ape-man uttered the first grunt. She smiled vaguely and returned to her own dressing room. I did think of writing her a letter explaining that what I had meant to say when she had very kindly joked that I had a funny name was, "It's better than Nicholas Ridiculous," but I never got round to it.

At least I had met Phyllis Dixey as well as Nat Gonella, but I would rather have met Max Wall. (When I did eventually meet him nearly forty years on, it emerged that he was an even greater friend of the distinguished trumpeter than Walsh's electrician uncle, so it could just as easily have been Max Wall rather than Phyllis Dixey who tapped on Mr Gonella's dressing room door that evening. I expect I should have been equally tongue-tied.)

On balance, I believe Willis Hall had the better City Varieties dressing room encounter. Like me, he became a fan of the last master of Grand Guignol, Tod Slaughter, whose touring Victorian melodramas – *Maria Marten, or the Murder in the Red Barn*, and *Sweeney Todd, the Demon Barber of Fleet Street* – were to the Varieties' raucous audience what Donald Wolfitt's company was to the more upmarket Grand (for myself, I would as willingly queue for one as for the other). Willis was a confirmed autograph-hunting haunter of stage doors: he had Billy Cotton, he had Gracie Fields, he had Big Bill Campbell, he had Dante the magician, and one evening under the flickering lamplight of the cobbled alley outside the City Varieties stage door, he secured the sweeping signature of Mr Tod Slaughter.

Over-awed, as I should have been in his place, by the archetypal actor-manager in his spade hat and floor-length overcoat with the obligatory astrakhan collar, it was not until the great thespian had swept into the theatre that Willis realised he was still holding the expensive Waterman pen which Mr Slaughter had chosen to use instead of the proferred stub of pencil. Willis timorously pushed open the stage door, intending to hand the pen in to the stage door-keeper, only to find Tod Slaughter riffling through his mail. He glared at Willis – a tiresome fan who had already been dealt with. Then Willis produced the pen. The bushy eyebrows rose. The thick jowls quivered in surprised gratification. "Honestee," boomed the voice that had packed a thousand twice-nightly performances, "is thee best policee, laddie!" He then beckoned Willis into his dressing room, showed him the bloodstained apron he was about to don as the Demon Barber, plus the prop wooden razor with which he would dispose of his victims; and then, recognising a stage-struck lad when he saw one, presented him with a dozen or so stick-ends of theatrical make-up contained in an old cigar box. Willis's future was sealed.

The circle bar of the Varieties became a regular Saturday evening venue if we were not of a mood for the Hokey-cokey and the Palais Glide at the Big Top marquee. And when we were sated with strippers, comics, jugglers, unicyclists, xylophonists, magicians, bird imitators, funambulists, paper-tearing acts and novelty tap-dancers we would take ourselves off on a pub crawl.

Saturday night in the pubs had an excitement all its own, a special flavour you could almost taste, like the tang of salt and vinegar. There was always something going on. In some pubs, nominated regulars would be persuaded to "get up", i.e. sing, to the accompaniment of an out-of-tune piano. There was always someone doing tricks with coins or matches, always someone selling raffle tickets, always someone collecting for a wreath or for a basket of groceries for a poorly pensioner. Often there would be a darts or dominoes tournament. There were regular, sometimes mysterious, transactions: a bookie's runner would furtively pay out on bets, noses were tapped, winks exchanged, a pint or a few cigarettes would be handed over in consideration of a blue cabbage brought in from somebody's allotment.

The kind of hostelry we allowed ourselves to frequent didn't sell food but hawkers would come in off the street selling hot pies and saveloys. Another vendor would peddle a spoof newspaper called *Billy's Weekly Liar* (a publication that, when I was writing a novel called *Saturday Night at the Roxy* some years later, was to suggest a useful alternative title when one Alan Sillitoe threatened to be coming out ahead of me with the not dissimilar-sounding *Saturday Night and Sunday Morning*). Then there was the Salvation Army lassie selling *War Cry*, and treated with the greatest respect even by the taproom's resident comedian (every pub had one, who kept up a flow of patter on the passing show). There would be one more vendor, peddling bags of custard creams and ginger nuts – an unlikely product, one would have thought, but he knew his market: they were snapped up by husbands anxious to take home a peace offering after having stayed for a pint or two too many.

Finally, as "Last orders" were called, the highlight of the evening: the entry of the paper seller with tomorrow's *Sunday Empire News*, hot off the presses of Withy Grove, Manchester, its black headlines always sending an excited ripple through the pub in reaction to the murders, the society scandals, the soccer sensations, the black market exposures, until the landlord's bell cut stridently through the buzz and his cries of "Time, gentlemen, please!" sent us out into a raw Saturday night that whatever the season always seemed to be tinged with fog.

It beat the Moo-cow milk bar.

THREE

In the Mood

'Nothing there was the same as now. All
that happened then, if it happened here,
would be strange and fresh. Everything was
sharper. Cigarette smoke had a pungency it
has since lost. Even stale beer smelled full-
bodied and good. Girls' breasts were whiter.
Like alabaster, we said, though none of us
knew what alabaster was in that long-ago
place. The air was as crisp as apples, and all
the sad songs were sweeter, then.'

— IN THE MOOD, 1983

1 Yet it was not all play. If the two years since leaving the College of Commerce had seemed to be dissipated in the pursuit of pleasure, it was only because there was a powerful disincentive against settling down to anything like a career. Every able-bodied youth could expect, come his eighteenth birthday, to be conscripted into the armed forces for a couple of years. There was, in consequence, little point in laying down roots – most of us were content to coast along in a dead-end job until our call-up papers arrived. So much for the beneficial effects of national service.

But I wanted so badly to be a journalist that from time to time I would fire off letters to the various newspapers listed between neon sign manufacturers and non-ferrous metal fabricators in the local Kelly's Directory, even though I knew it was an all but pointless exercise. Not the great daily and evening papers, of course: they would obviously have no place in their newsrooms for an office clerk in his teens (I was not aware that the position of copy boy existed, otherwise I should have applied for it). But neither, it transpired, did the *South Leeds Advertiser*, nor the *Keighley News*, nor the *Bramley Advertiser*, nor the *Yorkshire Observer Budget*; nor yet the Leeds office of the *New Catholic Herald*, nor of the *Ironmonger*, out in Shadwell near the Reformatory; nor *Laxton's Builders' Price Book*, nor the *Fish Friers' Review*, nor Kelly's Directories Ltd themselves, for whom I offered to work part-time, incorporating my various rent rounds with knocking on householders' doors and asking who lived there, if that was how one set about compiling a street directory. Still, even had any of these publications shown the smallest interest in retraining an undertaker's clerk to become a journalist, only to lose him to the colours, it was to be doubted whether I could expect any advance on the *Leeds Guardian*'s offer of ten bob a week.

All this time I was trying to write – usually courtesy of J.T. Buckton & Sons, in the course of one of whose working days I could conceive, compose (under cover of the postage book), type up and despatch to a periodical a sketch of some 800 words – the maximum requirement at a time of acute paper shortage. There were longer works in progress – at home I was scribbling away at a novel in the manner of P.G. Wodehouse, and every so often I had a stab at a short story; but it was in the 800-word sketch that I pinned my faith.

Humour, I had long ago decided, rashly or otherwise, was my forte: just as professional comedians are given to confessing that they acted the clown at school to gain the approval of their classmates, so I had found that a school essay written in humorous vein always went down well, if for no other reason than that it made a change. Besides, nearly all my models were humorous writers – and had I not already had my great success with that funny piece for the *National Savings News*? Unknown to myself, I did not yet really understand humour – I equated it with facetiousness – but there were in the mid-Forties a score of magazines that used supposedly humorous material, starting with *Punch* and going down through the pocket magazines such as *Lilliput* and *London Opinion* to obscurer, usually short-lived titles with names like *Stag, Pie* and *Wit & Wisdom* (one issue, as I recall).

My market research was conducted at W.H. Smith's railway bookstall in City Station, where I became, in the course of my Buckton's post round, as regular a daily caller as the *Evening Post* van. I also acquired a secondhand copy, circa 1937, of the *Writers' and Artists' Year Book* which for a while became my standard reading on the rocking tram or propped up against the sugar bowl in Betty's Café. Not only did it most usefully list all the markets and their requirements ("*John O'London's Weekly*: A light, anecdotal treatment is desired where possible and humour is welcome. Contributions are paid for on acceptance; usual rate £3.3s per 1000 words. Articles should be typewritten"), but it was packed with information for the budding writer: the addresses of press-cuttings agencies, a list of firms prepared to consider greetings card verses ("if of high standard"), a table of American and Commonwealth journals, notes on serial rights and proof correcting and publishers' agreements, and BBC Requirements and How to Submit a Film Story, and so on and so on, until one began to feel like a member of the writing fraternity simply by turning the pages. The opportunities seemed boundless: with the proper degree of application it could not be long before the cheques for ten and sixpence, a guinea, two guineas, three guineas, were flowing into the bank (I should have to get a bank first).

I pored rather wistfully over the *Year Book*'s advertisements for correspondence courses and schools of journalism, with their genuine-seeming testimonials: "At a rough estimate I have made over £100 in Journalism as a spare-time hobby since taking up your Course 18 months ago. Your help has been money very well spent." Alas, as I found after sending off for their free booklets, I could not afford the fees that would otherwise have repaid themselves several times over.

One of these schools of journalism, indeed a college of journalism, was actually in Leeds, in Upper Briggate, and I took the earliest opportunity of going along and giving it the kind of transfixed stare I normally reserved for newspaper offices and printing works. The college proved to be so far up Upper Briggate that it was practically in North Street where the red light area began, its premises consisting of a room over a sweetshop and tobacconist's, approached by a steep flight of wooden stairs covered in threadbare linoleum. From the sign in the gloomy doorway I learned that as well as being a college of journalism it was also a typewriting bureau, a secretarial agency, a press cuttings service, and the parcels agent for a shipping line. Since it was nearing office closing time I hung around hoping for a glimpse of the college's staff of distinguished journalists who offered their personal specialised tuition based on years of Fleet Street experience, but the only person to descend the worn stairs, and lock the street door after her, was a dumpy, middle-aged lady carrying, unusually for a woman at that time, a briefcase. I guessed it must have contained manuscripts. Despite appearances, I was impressed.

My own manuscripts continued to be returned to me as fast as I sent them out. I didn't in the least mind, or anyway not much. I had read enough writers' reminiscences to know that in the early days rejected stories regularly and monotonously "came home to roost" or "landed with a dull thud on the doormat"; being of their number was like belonging to a club.

Unlike some of my fellow-aspirants, I did not paper the bedroom walls with my rejection slips, although I was getting an impressive collection of them together. But one I did pin up above my bed. It was from *Punch*, and it bore a scrawled note from the editor, E.V. Knox, whose revered pseudonym Evoe had been familiar to me ever since my mother had brought me home a parcel of *Punch* back

167

numbers from Kirkgate Market all those years ago. It read, "Not quite. EVK." It was as good as an acceptance from any other magazine.

This near-miss was a stylised little piece called "Music Hath Charms" — not a very original title for what I thought was a blazingly original piece of writing. I had hit on the idea, or rather the gimmick, of taking a stretch of dialogue — in this case a conversation in a music store — and transposing it into reported speech, as in "Good morning. We were thinking of taking up some musical instrument. Could they recommend the trombone . . . ?" Spurred on by Evoe's two little words, I freshened up my manuscript by pressing it under a damp towel with my mother's flat iron — a tip garnered from the pages of the *Writer* magazine — and sent it out again, this time to the pocket monthly *London Opinion* ("The Editor will be pleased to consider humorous articles, 1000 words and less. Nothing heavy, morbid or neurotic. Payment: immediately on acceptance, at high rates"). It was accepted. The payment, immediate as promised and at high rates as promised, was two guineas.

This was in November 1944, three months before my sixteenth birthday. The little notebook I kept, as advised by the *Writers' and Artists' Year Book*, recording acceptances and rejections — or in my case, rejections and acceptance — reveals that instead of following my success up, I did no more writing at all for the next six months, not even bothering to re-submit those manuscripts that, as the writers' reminiscences would have put it, had "winged their way back like homing pigeons". The fact was that I was too restless. I was so impatient to see my name in print that, absurdly, I was round at W.H. Smith's and riffling through the pages of the current *London Opinion* on the very day I received my letter of acceptance from its editor — an echo of my surrealistic hopes of finding myself in *A Basinful of Fun* even before my proposed contribution had left my hands.

Monthly magazines, I had observed, generally came out in the last week or so of the previous month. This did not discourage me from keeping a feverish eye open for the December number of *London Opinion* from about 5 November onwards. I developed the habit of making a slight detour via City Square on the way to work each morning, so that the established author could drop in on the station bookstall before bringing himself down to earth by way of taking down the office shutters. When, after what seemed like months, I arrived in City Station one morning just in time to find one of W.H. Smith's waistcoated, brillianted young men cutting the string on a pristine pile of December *London Opinions* hot off the steaming London train, my excitement was as intense as if it had been a Christmas parcel. And when my article proved not to have appeared my disappointment was as great as that of Stephen Leacock's Hoodoo McFiggin when, upon opening his Christmas present in the hope of skates, he found boots.

This was to become a monthly mortification. January ... February ... March ... April was the cruellest month: the magazine was several days late for some reason; I was convinced that this added torment had to mean that when the April *London Opinion* finally did appear, my article would be in it at last. It was not.

While I could not settle down to any actual writing during this incubation period, I did try, in a lackadaisical sort of way, to get some work under way by canvassing for commissions. I wrote to the *Yorkshire Evening News* offering a series about the landmark buildings of Leeds. Rejected. I wrote to the *Yorkshire Evening Post* proposing a humorous column on the lines of Beachcomber. Rejected. I wrote to the *Daily Worker* suggesting an exposure of estate agents, to be called "Your landlord's middleman" (and presumably to be written under a pseudonym). Rejected.

I wrote several times to *Picture Post*, a periodical I very much admired. With its black and white photo essays on the small social foothills that form the real backbone of England – commercial travellers' dinner dances, anglers' outings, amateur dramatic nights, street parties, mystery coach tours, mock parliaments, flower shows, market days, jumble sales, pigeon races, whippet races, brass band contests – it had an editor after my own heart. "Fashionable Birmingham has its lager and sandwich in the snack-bar of the Grand Hotel," ran one caption without a touch of irony. Notwithstanding that I had yet to set foot in the place, I wrote suggesting a feature about Whitelock's First City Luncheon Bar. They regretted that they had already devoted three pages to a similar establishment in Liverpool (the Philharmonic, I imagine). Another picture essay was "A Day in the Life of a Fishmonger". I offered A Day in the Life of Kirkgate Market. This they thought such a good idea that they had already done it, several years earlier. Then how about the Leeds arcades? No, they had done those too.

At least we were on the same wavelength. Encouraged, I flicked through back numbers of the weekly for further inspiration. Only *Picture Post* would have dared run a double spread on "The Drama of Cement". I offered The Drama of Quarry Hill Flats – An Experiment in Living. They had done a major piece on Quarry Hill Flats in one of their first issues. I gave up. But I remained affectionate towards *Picture Post*, with its instinctive understanding of the Englishness of the English, even when, a few months later, I opened the latest issue and found to my disgust a picture feature about Leeds Corn Exchange. The editor, Tom Hopkinson, became a friend years afterwards, and I told him the story. "You should have persisted," he said, and he was right.

"Music Hath Charms" by K.S. Waterhouse at last appeared in the July 1945 number of *London Opinion*. To see my name in print was like seeing my name in lights. As, half prepared for another monthly dose of disappointment, I turned the pages with a sort of hopeful hopelessness or hopeless hopefulness, it seemed to catherine-wheel round and catapult towards me like one of those montages of newspaper headlines in a Warner Brothers gangster movie. By K.S. Waterhouse. The typeface was black and bold but to me it was fluorescent.

One hears of reading the print off a particular piece of text. I came close to doing that almost literally. There and then at the railway bookstall I devoured the piece a good dozen times, being mortified at about the third or fourth reading to find a small misprint which, as I re-read and re-read, seemed to grow in enormity like a carbuncle examined in the mirror, until it made nonsense of the entire article. The eyes of the bookstall manager on me by now, I finally purchased three copies of the magazine, for the not inconsiderable sum of two and threepence. From one I extracted my debut freelance contribution (unless you counted the *National Savings News*, which had long ago disintegrated under too-frequent scrutiny) and pasted it into the cuttings book I had months ago bought for the purpose. The second I gave to my girlfriend of the moment. The third I kept in reserve, to send to editors who might want to see examples of my published work.

I had my moment of glory at J.T. Buckton & Sons, although my fellow-clerks were more interested in the tasteful nudes that were a feature of *London Opinion* than in my article. My mother's comment was that the printers had taken their time about it. After that, anticlimax. The whole world, after all, was not held in thrall by the contents of *London Opinion* and no one stopped to congratulate me in the street. There were no letters from editors. As for the girlfriend, while she was impressed, she was not impressed enough to my liking.

The two-guinea fee, of course, had long ago been spent, but at least it had been spent sensibly. I had started buying secondhand paperbacks to supplement *Lettres de mon Moulin*, *Fifty Years of Progress: the Story of Hemingway's Brewery* and the one or two other volumes that comprised the family library. Old Penguins and Pelicans, I had found, could be bought for coppers at Stringer's bookstall in the Market – I acquired Chesterton's *The Man Who Was Thursday*, *The Thin Man* by Dashiell Hammet, a collection of Saki, *A Passage to India*, *The Diary of a Nobody* and many other treasures, all for less than half a crown, together with unread and unreadable Pelicans like Freud's *Psychopathology* which I bought to impress myself and others.

With my two guineas I added the city's two secondhand bookshops to my daily round, and in the course of my browsings unearthed a four-volume *Don Quixote*, *Lamb's Tales From Shakespeare*, Boswell's *Johnson* and several Everyman titles which I still have on my shelves. I also found a good dozen volumes which to my regret were soon to be no longer on my shelves. In the aftermath of the German broadcast episode, my hero P.G. Wodehouse had yet to recover his popularity and you could buy his books in hardback, with dust-jackets, some of them first editions, for a shilling or two. I took home an armful: *Laughing Gas*, *The Heart of a Goof*, *The Clicking of Cuthbert*, *Ukridge*, a batch of Jeeveses, Mulliners and Psmiths. I then did two stupid things. Wanting my acquisitions to look like a proper library I removed all their dust jackets and destroyed them. And then, having devoured all my Wodehouses and needing cash to finance some outing or other, probably with a girl, I sold them back to the shop for about half what I had paid for them. The last time I looked up the Wodehouse titles in a modern first editions catalogue I calculated that I had cleared my bookshelf – my mother's cupboard top, to be precise – of about £2,000. But I still had my Penguins and Everymans. And I had discovered the joy of secondhand-bookshop serendipity.

My article in print and the two guineas gone it was time to buckle to and edge another inch or so up the slopes of journalism. I was sixteen and a half by now, after all, and time was moving on. I tried a few more pieces in the reported speech style of my *London Opinion* success but – rather to my surprise, since I was convinced that I had found an idiosyncratic writing formula to match Damon Runyon's – they failed to find a home. So did everything else. In fact another seventeen months were to pass by before my next sale. My little record book tells the story over a six-year period: 1944: two guineas; 1945: nothing; 1946: £2.19.6; 1947: £11.15.6; 1948: two guineas; 1949: £19.8.6.

The most significant of these sums was the £2.19.6 for 1946 in my seventeenth year, which was entirely made up of threepence-a-line and half-crown and five-shilling payments from the *Yorkshire Evening Post*, and which I invested in one of the new Biro pens that could write under water. The *Evening Post* had started up a magazine page composed of little feature articles, puzzles, bits of verse, and the kind of piece then usually classified as "a lighthearted look" at this or that topic. The page was usually thrown out after the lunch edition to make way for hard news, but it was right up my street. I submitted three or four "lighthearted looks" without success; then one lunchtime at Buckton's, Mr Stead the cashier, who was smoking a pipe over the early edition of the *Evening Post* which we took in for Mr Palmer to check the property column, suddenly exclaimed, "Hullo! This effusion here by one K.S.W. – that isn't you by any chance, is it, young Waterhouse?" They had printed a piece of unremitting facetiousness about tram queues which I had handed in at their offices only the day before while on my Buckton's mail round. It was out of the paper again long before the Final edition but I didn't care – I had already bought six copies.

Better was to come. A few days later there was a letter for me, ill-typed on rough copy paper, from the editor of the magazine page, one Con Gordon. I was impressed, not to say awed, for Con Gordon was world-famous in Yorkshire. As well as a regular and hugely popular "Courts Day by Day" column about the minutiae of life in the magistrates' courts, he turned out regular signed "specials" and droll "lighthearted looks" which made him a favourite with the readers. Con Gordon, in short, was the *Evening Post*'s star writer, and undoubtedly he could have moved on to Fleet Street had he chosen to do so. But he was content to remain where he had fetched up: a big fish basking in a small pond. Every provincial paper has one, though not necessarily with as much talent.

The letter said, "If ever you have time, come in and have a chat. I would like some more articles from you, if they are up to the standard of the tram article. A good time for me to go out for a coffee is between 10 and 11.30 on Mondays and Thursdays, when I am making up the magazine page. Go through the archway and ask for me at the sales counter."

I was through the archway — the magic, faience-tiled archway that led to the Yorkshire Conservative Newspaper Co.'s editorial offices — at 10.01 that same morning, having disposed of my Buckton's post round at record speed. The sales counter, as I was to find, divided its energies between selling back numbers and photographs and filtering the steady trickle of visitors, unhinged or otherwise, who sought audience with the editor or his staff. I was entranced by the sales counter. A young man in a raincoat passed through on his way upstairs and another young man in a raincoat passed through on his way out. Reporters, clearly (I had long ago realised that they did not wear peaked caps, but I did know that they wore raincoats). It was the nearest I had ever been to an editorial floor. Presently a shambling, balding, grey but still tousle-haired figure in shapeless sports jacket, corduroy trousers, fair isle pullover and sandals appeared, and this was Con Gordon. He was gratifyingly every inch the bohemian. He had the faintest of Irish accents but his was the first properly educated, cultured voice I had heard in Leeds outside the pulpit and the stage.

I had thought the Gambit Café might have been Con Gordon's mark but he led me to the basement Lyons at the bottom of Bond Street down from the office, where he stood me coffee and toast. Not at all fazed by my youth or my job as an undertaker's clerk, he treated me as if I were a professional freelance and spoke sympathetically about the difficulties of getting work into the restricted space then available in newspapers and magazines. He gave me what in my callow way I thought were some pretty obvious tips on his requirements for the magazine page — I had, as suggested by the *Writers' and Artists' Year Book*, already studied the market — and then asked if I had brought anything with me. Of course I had — a whimsical sketch about a chapel concert, based on no observation whatsoever, and a series of pawky Yorkshire aphorisms called "Ahr Edward Sez". To my surprise he bought them on the spot.

Even more to my surprise, considering what slender evidence he had to go on, he said he thought I had it in me to become a newspaperman, and asked what I was doing working for Buckton's. Access to a typewriter, I told him, and the fact that I had to mark time until I had done my national service. He agreed that this was a great nuisance but advised me to keep writing and promised that when I got out of the forces, provided I had enough cuttings to show, he would try to arrange an interview with his editor, Barry Horniblow. Apparently Mr Horniblow was a former Fleet Street livewire who had been brought in to shake the *Evening Post* up a bit. He had already taken on one or two inexperienced young men he had liked the look of, so my chances were far from hopeless. But seventeen, I had to agree, was a bit too young. I could wait. I would have to.

I went back to New Station Street enormously heartened, my head swimming with images of myself swaggering around Leeds with a reporter's notebook protruding from my raincoat pocket, a cigarette on my lips and a press pass stuck in the band of my jaunty fedora. To my utter astonishment, the first of my "Ahr Edward Sez" epigrams – "T' chap who sez what wa' good enough fo' 'is grandfather's good enough fo' 'im, would be in a bit of a fix if 'is grandfather 'ad said t' same thing" – appeared on the magazine page that very day, framed in a little box with a drawing of Edward by the staff cartoonist. I got half a crown for it, or fractionally under a penny a word. Evening paper journalism, I decided, was the life.

Edward continued to be inflicted on the *Post*'s readers over the next two weeks, clocking up half a crown a time for me. Of my concert article, however, there was no sign. Then came a setback. One day the magazine page failed to appear, even in the lunch edition. The next morning's post brought another letter from Con Gordon: "Today the editor tore up my magazine page and ceremonially danced on it, and that went for your concert article too. He said it was an old idea and had often been much better done; which is strictly true but if widely applied would stop every printing press in the country. Anyway, I begin to suspect he doesn't like your stuff quite so much as I do. So you had better administer it in smaller doses until he ceases to be allergic . . ."

Luckily for me, besides the now defunct magazine page Con Gordon also ran the Diary of a Yorkshireman, a miscellany column that paid five shillings a paragraph. Had the paper possessed a features editor he would have been that too, and so was in a position sometimes to more or less smuggle the odd short feature of mine into the early editions. More often, he sent my work back, always with a note: "Don't be discouraged. Times are thin for contributors but the wheel will turn. Write all you can. Even if it doesn't see the light of day it will develop your style."

I wasn't in the least discouraged, truth to tell. However peripherally, I now felt in the journalistic swim. My daily perambulations about the city centre were henceforth enlivened by the search for likely five-shilling Diary paragraphs, and I quickly developed a lively eye for quirky little details of the "not many people know that" variety, usually on points of architecture – the legacy, I suppose, of the many hours spent staring at buildings during my white card period. From time to time, by open invitation, I would have morning coffee at Joe Lyons with Con Gordon. To my slight disappointment, I didn't get to meet any of his fellow-journalists who were said to lunch roisterously off beer and roast beef at Whitelock's each day, for he was something of a hermit and avoided their company, and anyway he was a non-drinker and a vegetarian. But he always seemed pleased, or anyway not displeased, to see me. His nuggets of advice, I now began to see, were not as obvious as I had at first thought – or if they were, they were the wood I had up until now been unable to see for the trees. One piece of wisdom I remember particularly: "Write about the Amalgamated Association of Engineers and all the amalgamated engineers will read your stuff. Write about human emotions and all humanity will read it. Journalism's as simple as that."

I continued to bombard Con Gordon with bits and pieces without let-up for a year, and threepenny line by threepenny line and five-shilling paragraph by five-shilling paragraph my earnings rose. They were blown on a week's holiday in Blackpool with Ray Hill, where for economy's sake we slept head to toe in the double bed of our back-street digs like Laurel and Hardy in *Film Fun* on holiday at Shrimpton-on-Sea.

It was my first seaside holiday on the other side of the Pennines since Silverdale, and I wondered why they couldn't have put a poor children's holiday camp slap in the middle of Blackpool. The resort's razzle-dazzle exuberance was a tonic after the dreary war years. The Tower, visible miles away down the railway line so that you were ready for Blackpool long before Blackpool was ready for you, was a symbol of its energy and enterprise. The Winter Gardens was a people's palace out of a Victorian picture postcard, the Golden Mile a Mecca of Thirties concrete gawdy, the promenade a ramshackle succession of architectural styles so that the long, enjoyable single-decker tram ride along the front was like a geological survey, revealing stratum after stratum of the town's developing prosperity since the Preston and Wyre Railway brought the first trippers. All this and the covered market too – plus the Sensational Severed Living Hands of Patma. Ray and I found ourselves a couple of Welsh girls and went on the town.

When I got back home to Halton Moor my calling-up papers for the Royal Air Force were waiting for me behind the mantelpiece clock.

2   After the usual square-bashing nonsense I was required to report to a kind of inland, militarised Silverdale called Wombleton on the North Yorkshire moors, miles from anywhere. The North Yorkshire moors are like Noël Coward's Norfolk, very flat, and even in the driest of summers give out such an impression of being marshland that one expects to see Magwitch staggering across them through the mist.

Even as I humped my kitbag up from the country railway halt I was already plotting my escape via a more congenial re-posting – somewhere reasonably near a city or fair-sized town, or at the very least opposite a bus stop. Such things were possible if you knew someone in the orderly room and were prepared to take on his duty chores in return for promised favours.

There was a snag. RAF Station Wombleton was not a proper RAF station in the sense of having hangars, windsocks, and Spitfires and Hurricanes on the runway – there was no runway, and in fact to my bitter disappointment I was never to set eyes on a taxiing aircraft in the whole of my national service career. It was the transit camp for the RAF Regiment, the Royal Air Force equivalent of the Marines, whose task it is to guard airfields, dig slit trenches and garrotte the enemy – far too like soldiering for my taste. The sprawling camp, swarming with khaki-clad figures bayoneting sandbags or engaging one another in unarmed combat, was administered by a small RAF unit, and it was this unit that I was to join.

Or so I thought. As I was passing a barbed-wire compound where RAF Regiment recruits were stripping Bren guns and polishing fire buckets with Duraglit, I was stopped in my tracks by a bellow of "Idle marching, that man!" from a bulging-eyed, waxed-moustachioed robot on whose knifecrease-pressed battle blouse glistened the three blancoed stripes and burnished crown of an RAF Regiment flight-sergeant. I was marched into the guardroom where

177

my name was taken and checked against a clipboard list; whereafter, by some piece of legerdemain which I do not understand to this day, I found that I had been kitted out in RAF Regiment khaki and was doubling around a barrack square clutching a rifle above my head. In vain did I try to explain that I was a clerk and not cut out for trench-digging. For the next fortnight I spent my days swinging from ropes, clambering walls, learning how to gouge out eyes, and jumping over, or into, slime-infested ditches. It was only when pay parade came around that they realised they had got the wrong Waterhouse. Or so they claimed. My belief has always been that I had been press-ganged, that whenever an RAF Regiment intake was below strength the flight-sergeant simply positioned himself near the gates and waylaid any stray clerks, cooks or other unsuspecting Air Force types who were on their way to the RAF unit. At any rate I was soon out of khaki and back in blue.

I had opted for the RAF for two reasons – I would get to wear a collar and tie and shoes instead of the tunic, boots and puttees of the army; and as a clerk I should have the use of a typewriter. Given that the war had been over for two years and there was nothing whatever for the RAF to do, I should then be well placed to spend my national service career on light short story writing duties. But it proved that one was not allowed access to a typewriter until one had been on a typewriting course. Keeping quiet about my RSA proficiency certificates in shorthand and typing I immediately applied to be sent on one – wherever it was held it could not be in a more God-forsaken spot than Wombleton. After a few weeks of thumb-twiddling my posting came through – it was to a place called Wythall, such a short bus ride from Birmingham that it was practically in the suburbs. I was well pleased.

On York Station I bumped into Willis Hall, now in the army and stationed at Catterick, who was going home on embarkation leave, having been posted to Malaya. We were not to meet again until twelve years later when Willis's play set in the Malayan jungle, *The Long and the Short and the Tall*, was packing the New Theatre, now the Alberry (with another Hunslet graduate, Peter O'Toole, in a starring role), and he rang me to suggest dramatising my new novel about an undertaker's clerk, *Billy Liar*. No one could say that either of us failed to capitalise on his experiences.

While Wythall seemed small beer compared to Malaya it was a pleasant enough billet, a compact former balloon station with comfortable quarters in marked contrast to the Nissen hut wilderness of North Yorkshire. It had two great advantages. One was the presence of a large quantity of Waafs, the first female company encountered in over six months. The other was the proximity of Birmingham, but a ninepenny bus ride away. I had barely unpacked my kitbag before I was opening negotiations with a pretty Waaf to take her to the pictures in Brum, as I had already learned to call it.

From her point of view the outing cannot have counted among her successes, for I was far more interested in the city than in the girl. Birmingham at that time was a larger replica of Leeds, a seething provincial metropolis of trams, blackened municipal buildings in the Italian Renaissance style, steam-enshrouded railway stations, markets, statues of Queen Victoria, department stores, commercial hotels, grills and butteries, and arcades with striking clocks. The evening was damp but that only served to cast the reflections of shop lights and neon signs and yes, the winking Bovril sign, on the glistening pavement, producing a grotto effect, a quality of excited expectation so intense and electric that if the corporation had been able to feed it through a cable they could have lit street lamps with it. It was the same feeling one still gets in New York and San Francisco. What the city had was the spirit of what Arnold Bennett called "get up and go"; and it was as different from the present-day reconstituted Birmingham as a grainy black and white photograph is from a wishy-washy watercolour. But my Waaf, a country lass, didn't take to Birmingham at all; and when, that weekend, I invited her to come and sample the delights of Wolverhampton, which could also be reached easily by bus from Wythall, she declined with thanks. (I travelled to Wolverhampton alone, and found it grimily, and grimly, entrancing.)

The course I had been sent on was not an exacting one. In the mornings one learned the RAF's clerical and filing procedures, a simple system dressed up as a complex one as a work creation scheme; and in the afternoons shorthand and typing. Since no roll-call was ever taken and I already had shorthand and typing, I saw no point in attending these afternoon sessions — there were about sixty of us on the course and I would not be missed. I developed the habit of sneaking into Birmingham directly after lunch, and very pleasant afternoons they were too, occupied as once I had occupied my white card outings into Leeds, in wandering about, exploring and staring at buildings. I had to keep a sharp eye open for the "Snowdrops", the

RAF police, since I had no white card alibi and was technically — or as it was to prove, not so technically — absent without leave, but so long as I kept away from the railway stations and didn't wander around the city with my tunic buttons unfastened I was on pretty safe ground. And I did come to owe the Snowdrops one favour. Espying a pair of them plodding across Victoria Square one afternoon I sought refuge in the Art Gallery, and discovered the pre-Raphaelites. I was a frequent visitor after that. Until . . .

One evening in the Naafi it came to my notice that, egged on by my example, others had started cutting the shorthand and typing classes — either because, like me, they already surreptitiously had these skills or because they wouldn't much mind failing their proficiency test at the end of the six-week course, when all that would happen was that they would have to stay on and take it again — no great hardship since Wythall was an extremely soft touch as RAF stations went. But how many, I asked, were dodging the classes? A good dozen, I was told — and there would be more absentees tomorrow when the local Regal changed its programmes.

A strong, street-life instinct for survival, developed in the course of my juvenile perambulations around Leeds, warned me that it was time to put in an appearance at the afternoon typing session. I did so. Some twenty airmen and Waafs — about a third of the course — failed to present themselves. The instructor reluctantly took a roll-call. He was a mild-mannered education sergeant who wanted only to be left alone at his trestle table to read his *New Statesman & Nation*, but attendance was so sparse that he had no option. The twenty missing trainee typists were hauled up before the commanding officer the next morning, charged with being AWOL, and given three days "jankers" — confined to barracks and put on potato-peeling chores.

Here I thought I would bring my natural cunning into play. The absentees had been brought to book. An example had been made of them and the skiving-off racket nipped in the bud. The shorthand and typing classes, that afternoon, would have a full turnout and the education sergeant, a naturally lazy man, would have neither need nor inclination to take the roll-call a second time. It would be safer than ever to take myself off to Birmingham. I did so, and went and had a self-satisfied stare at the buttery of the Grand Hotel, "where fashionable Birmingham has its lager and sandwich".

My grasp of human psychology was not yet developed. The officer in charge of the course dropped in to check that the necessary lesson had been learned – no doubt he himself had been torn off a strip, as we erks would have put it – and ordered the sergeant to take the roll-call. One name missing. Five days confined to barracks and a lecture from the CO on my confounded cheek and stupidity. I did not venture into Birmingham again from Wythall. The next time I visited the city they had pulled it down and another city of the same name had been put in its place.

The course finished with a jolly Naafi dance followed by a mass exodus to the surrounding allotments where all who retained their virginity now lost it, and preceded by a day of end-of-term euphoria when we all learned where we were to be posted. I had lived in hopes of being sent abroad like Willis – preferably to the staff of the British air attaché in Washington, or failing that, somewhere in Germany where I could go and stare at Munich or Cologne or even Berlin. Another remote possibility was a posting to the Air Ministry in Kingsway where (so good authority had it) you were allowed to wear civilian dress, were billeted in civilian digs in Bloomsbury and other exotic places, and dined nightly at a Lyons Corner House to the strains of a tango orchestra or gypsy violins. In the event I was sent to the RAF Records Office in Gloucester.

I was content enough. My comfortable billet was right across the street from the Records Office and so close to the city centre that I could stroll to Woolworth's in my lunch hour. While Gloucester wasn't Birmingham or Wolverhampton and wandering among its gabled and half-timbered houses and tea rooms and cloisters was, for my taste, a little too much like going for a walk in a jigsaw puzzle, it was a sight more civilised that some of the remote airfields in far-flung parts of the country to which others had been posted. But I would have had to confess that I was less taken with the splendid cathedral than with the Moreland's Match Manufactory, as it still obstinately called itself, home of *England's Glory* red-tipped matches which, with their jokes and sayings on the back of the highly coloured box, were a great favourite in Leeds pubs. (I wondered briefly if they might consider freelance contributions such as my unused Ahr Edward aphorisms. It was not such a wild thought: years afterwards someone opened negotiations with my agent – abortive, as it turned out – for the right to print paragraphs from my newspaper columns on the back of England's Glory matchboxes.)

Exploring further I found that Cheltenham was but a short bus

181

ride away, in fact there was a stop right outside the Records Office. With its Georgian terraces and tree-lined boulevards Cheltenham was more my kind of town – a bit like Harrogate, where I had once ventured on a staring excursion. Cheltenham turned out to have a thriving rep theatre remorselessly ploughing its way through the kind of fare I was used to from the Theatre Royal Court Players back home. With a companionable Waaf called Patricia who shared my theatrical taste, or lack of it, I became a Saturday evening regular, with *The Shop at Sly Corner* or *George and Margaret* following a high tea of poached egg on toast at the Bon Marché department store café.

Life at Gloucester was congenial. There was a camp magazine and a camp theatre with a busy concert party; to both I contributed material regurgitated from the Mill Hill youth club days. There was an abundance of Waafs. The only drawback was that I could not get near a typewriter. This was typical of the RAF bureaucracy: having trained me, as they thought, to type and do shorthand, they placed me in a slot where neither skill was required. My job over at the Records Office consisted of shuffling files about. It was unexacting work with constant tea breaks and there were a great many civilians employed about the place, so that the atmosphere was that of an easy-going provincial insurance office rather than an RAF station. But – no typewriter. The months I was supposed to be devoting to building up a bank of cuttings to impress the editor of the *Yorkshire Evening Post* were dripping away like sand in an hour-glass; so far, since my call-up, I had had only one success – a short story sold to *Boy's Own* for two guineas, which Patricia, working in the orderly room, had typed up for me in her lunchtime. I could not see Mr Horniblow considering a boys' magazine yarn much of a qualification for covering the Leeds coroner's court.

Then one evening in the education hut, where I had gone to do some quiet reading, to my surprise I came across my friend Ray Hill. Ray, like me, had been in the RAF for several months by now but as one posting succeeded another we had lost touch of late. He was studying a sheaf of leaflets in   search of some congenial part-time educational course for which he could volunteer with a view to escaping the tiresome routine tasks of an airman's life such as guard duty and billet orderly roster. The reunion was a serendipitous one for me. In the course of his researches Ray had discovered that if one volunteered to teach an evening class, given that one had the proper qualifications, one was entitled to a payment of one shilling a week per head up to a maximum of fourteen shillings weekly out of the station educational fund.

So I could solve my typewriter problem and be paid for it into the bargain. I reported to the education officer, a naïve young pilot officer, who congratulated me upon my public-spiritedness and initiative and at once set the wheels in motion. A vacant hut was commandeered and equipped with chairs and trestle tables, and the quartermaster's stores prevailed upon to produce a collection of ancient Remingtons, Coronas and Imperials, some of them such early models that you had to lift the carriage to see what you had just typed. Notices were posted on all the bulletin boards, announcing enrolment night for an evening typewriting course under the tutelage of AC2 Waterhouse, K.S.

The trouble was that not a soul turned up. Gloucester was a socially active camp and there were a hundred better ways of whiling away an evening than on self-education – the popular view, when I tried some direct recruiting, was that if the RAF wanted its personnel to acquire particular skills it could teach them in its own time. Fortunately the education officer did not turn up either, and so he was not yet to know that my scheme was a frost.

I think the idea of a phantom typing class was Ray's. It was beautifully simple. I should just take fourteen names and numbers at random off the various duty rosters dotted about the camp and enter them in my official attendance log, placing a tick against each name each week to qualify me for my fourteen shillings. Perhaps from time to time I should mark the odd name down as absent, to lend authenticity.

It was a brilliant plan but very probably a court martial offence. After my brush with authority at Wythall I had grown wily in the ways of the RAF, and I knew that sooner or later, and certainly before any money changed hands, my typing class would have to be produced in the flesh. I therefore modified Ray's brainwave. The fourteen names in my attendance log would be those of trusted friends and collaborators, in on the fraud. When the education officer wished to inspect my typists – he would have to give me notice, for the appointed evening for the mythical class would be a movable feast, changed week by week – I would round them up and sit them behind my battery of typewriters to clatter away as best they could until his arrival. For this service they would be paid sixpence each per week, or half my fourteen shillings between them. Sixpence would buy a Naafi supper. I had no difficulty in raising my phantom army.

The stunt worked perfectly. The typing class was scheduled to start the following week. On the Monday evening after supper I sat alone in the hut assigned to me where, having found the most serviceable (or least unserviceable) of my obsolescent collection of typewriters, I was composing an article aimed at the *Daily Herald*'s new youth page, on advice for new conscripts ("It's not a bad life really, so long as you keep your nose clean . . .") when, as half expected, the education officer walked in.

I snapped to attention and explained that so many men had been detailed for other duties that evening that I had had to change the class to Tuesday. The following night I had my full team on parade, for all that, owing to some mutiny in the ranks, I had had to field two or three substitutes on the promise of Eccles cakes all round in the Naafi later. The education officer duly put in his appearance. Since some of my class of imposters were coal heavers and boilermen who could barely write their own names, let alone type them, I had been rather concerned that he might want to see them in action. I sought to anticipate this by calling them smartly to attention as he entered the hut, knowing that while the rather dim PO would at once order "At ease — stand easy", he would be at a loss how to frame any order that would cause them to sit down again and resume their typewriting activities. So it proved: they remained standing until, after wandering ineffectively up and down the hut for a while, and with a languid "Carry on, airman", he was gone. I never saw him again, for he was soon afterwards demobbed, and no successor ever materialised.

So while I continued to live in spasmodic fear of six months in the glasshouse (I already had my Conscript Prison Hell exposé sketched out in my mind for the *Sunday Pictorial*), my phantom typing class was a huge and profitable success, and my primary aim of having a machine to work on was accomplished with the bonus of a private hut to work in. Furthermore, not only was my *Daily Herald* youth page article accepted — two more guineas — but it was also reproduced in the *Air Reserve Gazette* (another half guinea, for I had remembered the *Writers' and Artists' Year Book* advice to offer First British Serial Rights Only).

I sent the *Daily Herald* cutting to Con Gordon and he wrote back:

"I will certainly do my damnedest to get you an interview with the Editor when you come out of the RAF. I can't undertake anything beyond that, because I'm not going to overshout my hand, but I think there's a sporting chance of getting you taken on. I think you have got the root of the matter in you, but we have to convince the Editor of that."

Galvanised, I threw myself into a flurry of work. Turning my back on the pleasures available to a young man in his prime with two and a half guineas in his pocket, I spent night after night in an abandoned hut at the end of a stretch of tarmac leading nowhere, surrounded by a surrealistic collection of old typewriters, clacking away at articles and stories with increasing if modest success. I sold a whole series of satirical "How to" articles to the *Writer*, a short piece to *Radio Times*, another short story to one of the boys' annuals. With one of my little windfalls I had some letterheads printed: "Writer K.S. WATERHOUSE Journalist. Contributor to: *Daily Herald*, *Yorkshire Evening Post*, *London Opinion*, *Radio Times*, *The Writer* etc., etc." The letters from Con Gordon were encouraging.

Then, just as I was getting into my stride, I was posted again — to Bicester in Oxfordshire. It was tolerable enough. Bicester was a little market town of the worst sort but Oxford was quite near and I spent many Saturdays wandering the High and staring at the colleges and hoping, in my civilian clothes, to be mistaken for an undergraduate. The RAF station, a permanent one with comfortable brick barracks, was the headquarters of No. 40 Group, Maintenance Command, which had something to do with stores and supplies. I was assigned to the staff of a group captain who, upon finding that I had verbatim shorthand, got me promoted to corporal and made me his secretary. Much of the work being confidential I was given my own little office. Since I was often required to work overtime, I also had my own key to the building, so that I could come and go as I pleased. Not only that: two stripes on my arm entitled me to my own private room in the barracks, where I could work and read in peace. Once more I was set up very nicely.

I had reached that agreeable point that eventually came in every conscript's life where one made a demob chart and began to tick off the remaining days to freedom one by one, when to my utter disgust the Russians imposed a blockade on Berlin, provoking the RAF to carry out a round-the-clock airlift of goods and supplies. I knew at once that this was going to affect me and it did. Demobilisation in

Maintenance Command was suspended until the crisis was over. I was mortified.

The setback did have two positive consequences, however. With the planning of the airlift my group captain was thrown into a series of long meetings with all manner of top brass, and I was given the quite responsible task of taking down their deliberations in shorthand, separating the wheat from the chaff and preparing minutes. This gave me invaluable reporting experience. The other consequence was that while waiting for my delayed demob I got another article in print, a significant one.

Browsing through the local newspaper with its front page fatstock prices, the *Bicester Advertiser*, I had hit upon the idea of a piece for *Picture Post* about Britain's market town weeklies, to be called "The World's Greatest Newspaper" (then the slogan of the *Daily Express*). They had turned it down, but I had resubmitted it to a popular rotogravure weekly of the day called *Everybody's*, who accepted it − or rather said they would consider it after I had written it. Taking advantage of the group captain's absence at the Air Ministry I sneaked a day off and interviewed everybody on the *Advertiser* from the compositor to the editor, plus some of the paper's readers and contacts around the market square. I wrote 1,700 words and despatched my piece to *Everybody's*. After an interminable delay − "I am sorry not to let you have the Editor's decision on your article but I assure you that it got a very good recommendation from the Editorial Reading Committee" − I received a letter of acceptance. The fee was twelve guineas, the most money I had ever earned in my life; but what pleased me even more was that I knew I had written a first-rate article. Unlike my previous stuff it was proper journalism, packed with facts, anecdotes, colourful detail and good quotes. It appeared a few weeks before I was at last released from the RAF. It was to do me a world of good.

I was demobilised on a roasting August day from Kirkham in Lancashire with its cheering view of the Blackpool Tower. I rode home through the cotton towns on a slow chuffing train to Leeds Central Station. I was absurdly pleased with myself, full of the joy of freedom and bubbling with anticipation of the heady new life to come. Not for a second did it occur to me that the *Yorkshire Evening Post* might turn me down − the more especially since I had just won one of their short story competitions with a prize of four guineas. I had no plans as to what I should do with myself if I was refused a

186

chance — the possibility simply never entered my mind. I was full of the confidence of youth and had never been happier. I·don't think I have ever been happier since.

It was a Thursday. I rang Con Gordon from a coin box at the station and arranged to call on him the next afternoon at three, after the main edition had gone to press — "to bed", as I had learned to say. I was there punctually at ten to. He took me straight up to see Mr Horniblow, the editor, who sat behind a massive desk in a book-lined room which the Fleet Street reminiscences I had been lapping up for years now would have described as "the editorial sanctum". Mr Horniblow himself, fortyish I would say, looked like an unusually bright bank manager.

He asked me the questions on which Con Gordon had already briefed me .on our way upstairs — education, background, shorthand speed, experience (I rather beefed up my *Leeds Guardian* credentials and mentioned my minute-writing stint at Bicester), and why I thought he should take me on. To this, rather than "Because I might just hang myself if you don't", I replied boldly, as rehearsed, "I consider myself a good risk."

Mr Horniblow then opened the folder of cuttings with which Con Gordon had furnished him and said, like a bank manager reviewing an overdraft, "I have been reading your cuttings and while they are very well written I would have said until recently that you were a feuilletonist rather than a journalist; but now that I have read your excellent article in *Everybody's* I'm persuaded to give you the benefit of the doubt. I'll take you on three months' trial at twenty guineas a month. When would you find it convenient to start?"

"Monday," I said.

I went home and told my mother that I was going to be a reporter. I did not mention the three months' trial. "What do you have to do?" she asked. I could not give her a satisfactory reply — I had little idea myself, that was the truth of it. For the first time I felt a clutch of fear at what I was getting into. I took down my secondhand *Chambers Dictionary* and looked up "feuilletonist".

3 Even at eight in the morning the newsroom was practically invisible under a pall of smoke from cigarettes, cheroots and pipes. The room was L-shaped — along one leg of it ran the long sub-editors' table at which sat half a dozen waistcoated or cardiganned figures, alternately red-faced or sallow-complexioned, pot-bellied or concave-chested according to whether they drank Guinness for strength or milk for their ulcers; but all of them chain-smoking, all of them resembling the Press Club caricatures of newspapermen I had mooned over in my little library of Fleet Street memoirs.

The other leg was taken up by the reporters' table, together with two or three individual desks at which sat the more senior members of the staff such as Mr Mann, the municipal correspondent, who always wore a black jacket and pinstriped trousers and looked more like the Lord Mayor than the Lord Mayor himself. The table was piled so high with books and paper that occasionally a dog-eared street guide or telephone directory would slither to the floor with a crash. Half a dozen typewriters as decrepit as the ones requisitioned for my mythical typing class at Gloucester kept a possible landslide of newspaper files, spiked copy, old notebooks and reference works in check. Two or three reporters, one of them with his hat on the back of his head like the newspapermen I had seen in films, were pecking away at overnight stories for the lunch edition. A couple more sat in the bank of wooden telephone booths at the end of the room, making the regular trawling calls to the ambulance and fire stations, the police and hospitals.

I had been haunted all weekend by the problem of how I was physically to set about starting work. I had no idea where to go or whom to ask for — not the editor, presumably. I couldn't see myself sauntering upstairs past the sales counter, even if I had been allowed to, and blundering around the editorial floor until I found the newsroom. In the end I solved my difficulty by asking for Con Gordon who, rather tetchily – he was in the middle of an article, I guessed – came down and took me up into the newsroom, where he introduced me to the news editor and his deputy, two kindly men named Alan Woodward and Ken Lemmon, and then departed – Con had his own office down the corridor, which he shared with the book reviewer, obituarist and arts correspondent (all the same person).

I was alone in a roomful of journalists. Ken Lemmon, spotting a fish out of water, tried to put me at my ease by introducing me to one or two reporters, but everyone was busy and had little time for this gauche young man in the new Fifty Shilling Tailors suit. To my relief, after five minutes of indecisive hanging about, I noticed Ken murmur to Mr Woodward who looked up from his news diary, took in my situation, and called me over to say, "You'll have seen that we carry the Leeds Market fruit and vegetable prices each Monday. I'd like you to go down to the Market and give me three or four paragraphs by half past nine. You'll find Mr Gomersall on Fruit Row very helpful, and Mr Pollard the self-styled Spud King is a good friend of ours too."

I headed towards Kirkgate in high spirits. My first assignment was a walkover (I didn't realise at the time that it was meant to be), and how appropriate that I should have to write about Market fruit and veg prices! Perhaps when I introduced myself to Mr Gomersall and Mr Pollard they would say, "Ee, it's never Ernest Waterhouse's lad, is it?" (They didn't.) And what bliss to be ambling to the Market on a sunny morning, clutching not a batch of Buckton's letters but a virgin reporter's notebook. The same feeling of liberation that I had experienced on the train home from Kirkham again swamped over me. It never quite left me all the time I remained in Leeds.

I was back at the office in good time – the first occasion ever when I had not loitered in the fragrant streets of my glass-roofed indoor city – where, perched self-consciously on a broken chair in front of a vacant typewriter, I tapped out my copy, remembering to head it with a catchline for the subs and printers as required by the manuals of journalism: "markets 1 . . . waterhouse." I handed it in to Mr Woodward who, having read it without comment, shouted "Boy!" and passed it to the copy boy who came scuttling over to carry it across to the subs' table. I was given nothing else to do and so I sat at the reporters' table pretending to read that morning's *Yorkshire Post* but surreptitiously drinking in my surroundings. I was in a newspaper office. I was in heaven. The reporters' room was empty by now — everyone out on stories. I realised with a lurching heart that if news of a big clothing factory fire came through, I should be the one sent to cover it, or anyway the one sent to do the best he could with the story until a proper reporter could be located. I half wanted and half didn't want the big clothing factory fire to happen.

The morning ticked by. I heard an exasperated sub-editor complain, "Subbing this stuff is like trying to get the Book of Genesis down to two lines!" and hoped he wasn't talking about my copy. At eleven o'clock the copy boy came round with a quire of lunch editions just off the press, and I loftily accepted one, then with casually disguised eagerness riffled through the pages.

My story, my first ever news story, occupied about four inches at the bottom of the City page. Headed "Strawberries cheaper" it began, much as I had written it, "At 8d to 10d a lb, strawberries are cheaper and more plentiful at Leeds Market than they have been all season. Bilberries are 1s 3d a lb, red currants 6d a lb, black currants 1s a lb, English cherries, both white and heart, 1s a lb, gooseberries 5d a lb, cherry plums 9d a lb . . ." This was followed by apple prices, flower prices and the news that peas were cheaper at 3d a lb, while watercress was 2½d a bunch. It was not earth-shattering stuff but it was a start. I was on a newspaper. I was a reporter.

It was a few days before I had met all my colleagues, for there was never a time when they were all in the office at once. Although one or two of them liked to give the impression of being hard-boiled — I was awfully impressed when, on my second day, our crime reporter Frank, upon ringing the Mayor of Dewsbury and being told that his worship couldn't speak to him, rasped, "Why not — has he got laryngitis?" — they were a friendly and helpful bunch.

Like all newsrooms, the *Evening Post*'s housed a cross-section of newspaper types from the suburbanly sedate to the downright eccentric. Our leader writer, Percy, who only ever surfaced to pick up a political speech from the Press Association tape machine, kept a cottage piano in his office which he would play for inspiration in his ceaseless fight against the Attlee government. Our chief photographer, the Falstaffian, ash-bespattered Charlie, who was said to have been the original of the part created by Frank Pettingell in J.B. Priestley's *When We Are Married* (and later played by Priestley himself), was famous for being so drunk when photographing the Archbishop of York that he fell off his stepladder, then picking himself and his broken plate camera up leered, "Come on, yer Grace, give us one of yer big grins!" Ron, a secretive soul who brought his own little Royal portable to the office and wouldn't let anyone else use it, was a cricket fanatic who boasted a lawn made up from sods cut from all the county grounds, and whose garden gate was made up of Test wickets begged from Headingley. Stanley, the one who never took his hat off, had spent a few weeks in the London bureau of the *Chicago Herald Tribune* and spoke with an American accent.

I was not the only recruit to be taken on board that week – a former Fleet Street man named Michael joined on the same day, his brief career on the legendary *Daily Mirror* (legendary, that is, for firing people) having been abruptly brought to a halt when, in skittish mood, he submitted a story in rhyming couplets. Nor was I the youngest: an ambitious sixteen-year-old former editorial secretary called Barbara Taylor – in later life to be better known by her married name of Barbara Taylor Bradford – was being given a trial on the women's page by the chance-taking Mr Horniblow. Barbara was apt to burst into tears from time to time when bawled out for not yet knowing her job to perfection, and I became her hand-holder-in-chief. Little did she know that it was a case of the blinded-by-tears leading the blinded-by-tears.

For a supposedly non-routine job, journalism proved to have a cosily routine core. Each morning I would be sent on two or three minor stories – a chip-pan fire, a small burglary, with any luck a six-car pile-up at Bramham Crossroads, a notorious black spot – which I had to phone in straight from my notes to the copytakers, a phalanx of invisible, schoolmarmish women given to snapping, "Come on, come on!" when I floundered, thus teaching me to think more quickly on my feet. I would then get the tram back to Town – one of the three or four office cars staffed by the van drivers would grudgingly take you out to a job, but wouldn't wait for your return – and make for Perry's café in Commercial Street, where reporters from all three of the city's dailies lounged over coffee and chocolate biscuits each morning in an atmosphere of joshing and raillerie. While at Buckton's, I had once or twice ventured into Perry's and watched this scene of cameraderie from a distant table with a pang of envy. Now I was part of it.

I would then generally be assigned some court reporting, for which with my verbatim shorthand I was a natural. From covering the juvenile court I graduated quickly to the coroner's court, the magistrates' courts, the county court, the crown court and finally Leeds Assizes, where on important cases I would work in tandem with another reporter, the pair of us putting our copy over in alternating ten-minute takes so as to squeeze the last possible drop of juice out of the story before edition time. That was invigorating — one had to stay on one's toes and edit from one's notebook as one went along.

Reporting the courts gave me good practice in using my own editorial judgment, but more importantly from my point of view it gave me access to the coveted Town Hall press room, whose frosted-glass door I had given a wistful stare on my first quick circumnavigation of the Town Hall corridors back in the white card era. The smoke-filled press room, with its cigarette-burned old table, roll-top desks, men in hats, packs of greasy playing cards and candlestick telephones, was all I could wish for — straight out of the film of Hecht and MacArthur's *The Front Page* with Lee Tracy and Adolphe Menjou, or *His Girl Friday* with Cary Grant and Rosalind Russell.

It was here, against a background of urgent shouts down the telephone of "Copy, please . . . There were gasps from the public gallery in Leeds No. 1 Court today when . . .", that I learned to play serious poker. The card school was especially lively during the Assizes "black list" — cases of, for instance, South Yorkshire miners buggering sheep equipped with wellington boots (to stop their feet slipping), which at the time were deemed unreportable even when smothered in euphemism — when I would make desperate efforts to remain solvent until a policeman popped his head round the door and announced that the court was back to the relative wholesome normality of a good meat-axe murder.

Lunchtime would find me in the Victoria Family and Commercial Hotel behind the Town Hall for a beer and a sandwich, where, if the case across the road was big enough, I might rub shoulders with, or anyway be in the same mahogany saloon bar as, the local correspondents of the *Mail*, *Mirror* and *Express* and even some of the big boys over from Manchester. Or if there was some exclusive story the *Evening Post* was shielding from the opposition, one might seek refuge behind the pink terracotta façade of the Jubilee Hotel out in the Headrow, a splendid, five-storey authentic gin palace with art nouveau windows. The last time I ventured into it the brewers had converted it into a replica of a zoo.

If there was nothing much going on in the courts after my brief lunch I would wander back to the office when, unless there was an accident or some other hard news story to follow up, I would be given a "special" to do for the next day's lunch edition — perhaps I might be trusted to do an interview with a minor visiting celebrity (I interviewed Lana Morris in the belief that she was Lana Turner), or with a particular district's oldest inhabitant who was "99 years young".

The working day finished with the final edition going to press at four — unless, that was, you were on "late stop" duty, left in charge of the Stop Press for, where the news justified it, the occasional Late Final — the "Special" that I used to be sent running out for in my stockinged feet as a child in Middleton; or unless you were covering some evening event such as a concert or a public meeting. A small gossiping band of raffishly inclined reporters did hang on anyway, whether they were on duty or not, waiting for the pubs to open. I was as often as not of their number, for at the day's end I could not bear to tear myself away from the office — it would have been like leaving a party early.

We would sprawl around the reporters' table, feet up, smoking and talking. I had never heard proper talk before. Anecdotes were told — I had read anecdotes in books but never heard anyone telling them — only jokes, and that badly. Here we had raconteurs. A favourite story was that of an Edwardian editor of the *Yorkshire Post* who wrote to a female applicant for a reporting job, "Dear Madam, So long as I am Editor of this newspaper, the frou-frou of a woman's skirts will not be heard in its corridors. Besides, there is not sufficient lavatory accommodation." Then there was the news editor who, upon hearing from a reporter on another paper that rumour had it there was a newsroom vacancy, replied, "Dear Sir, Rumour, so often a fickle jade, errs again." I lapped this kind of thing up, and was practically open-mouthed with admiration when some of my colleagues proved to be wits in their own right — as when, reading a story about how a crowd of four hundred had been led in prayer by a kneeling clergyman while an old-age pensioner leaped from a blazing third-storey window, our religious affairs correspondent remarked drily, "I'd rather have four atheists holding a blanket."

Which pub I found myself in come opening time would depend on whose company I was in. One or two sophisticated souls preferred Polly's Bar across the street, a proper American bar with subdued pink lighting and cocktail shakers, the first such establishment I had ever set foot in, and one that in an earlier existence had seemed so much out of my social stratum that I had only once ever given it the barest flicker of a stare. Here, over gin-and-Its and Americanos, one might meet long-legged mannequins and junior fashion buyers from Marshall and Snelgrove's on the next block, as well as reasonably exquisite young women with an expensive taste in drinks who looked as if they might be mannequins but were not.

I was on safer ground in Whitelock's, with its long marble-topped bar, iron tables and snug settles, and old etched mirrors advertising soup and bread for a penny and the names of breweries long gone. Betjeman was to call it the Leeds equivalent of Ye Olde Cheshire Cheese in Fleet Street. In that somewhat orthodox era, Whitelock's was regarded as the city's hotbed of bohemianism, which was why I had for so long been so curious about the place.

It certainly lived up to its reputation. It was much used by artists, or anyway shag smokers who looked like artists, by university students trailing long scarves, and by bearded men wearing corduroy jackets with Penguin books stuffed into their pockets, who I was told either worked for the BBC or had had worked commissioned by the BBC, or were hoping to have work so commissioned. So this was what writers, producers and actors looked like! But of the select number of my colleagues who favoured Whitelock's as a drinking resort, none seemed to know any of this exotic crew and so I was not yet introduced into their charmed circle.

I did, however, meet one real live, full-time poet − R.C. Scriven, or Ratz as he signed himself, a regular contributor of light verse to the paper. As well as having a considerable local talent Ratz had a national one too, for not only was he the author of a much-acclaimed, prize-winning radio play called *A Single Taper*, about someone undergoing an operation to try to save his sight, but he frequently appeared in *Punch*. A line of his describing the advent of spring, "My foot covered five daisies", had always stuck in my mind. In true bohemian style Ratz was usually penniless, and so it was my privilege to buy him a drink. Conversation, however, was difficult, for not only was he four-fifths blind, as I had deduced from *A Single Taper*, but he was almost totally deaf and utterly reliant on an erratic battery-operated hearing-aid that only seemed to work when he was being asked what he was going to have. Although I was to become quite a chum of Ratz's in various hostelries about town, our Whitelock's acquaintanceship was short-lived. At that time Whitelock's lavatories were out in the yard, next to the kitchens. One night after a prolonged bout of hospitality from admirers and sympathisers, Ratz went out to relieve himself and was found by an outraged chef urinating against the white-tiled kitchen wall. Barred for life.

But the authentic working journalists' pub was the Pack Horse, down one of the ginnels leading into Briggate, a smoky old pub much used by both the *Evening Post* and *Evening News*, and the place for good newspaper talk about scoops and stunts and circulation wars. The Pack Horse was opposite the Empire and had accumulated a gallery of signed photographs of the stars to rival the Varieties circle bar; but I never saw any of them in there, except for a novelty act known as Kardomah, whose slogan was "Fills the stage with flags", and a mind-reading turn called Maurice Fogel, who told us that he had once got off jury service on the grounds that he might know what the accused was thinking. Fogel's visit to the Empire coincided with a poltergeist story out of which all the papers were getting much mileage, concerning a couple up in Headingley who, while decorating their new house, were hampered by paint pots floating off on their own accord, stepladders crashing down the stairs and electric light bulbs detaching themselves from their sockets and smashing against the walls. One night in the Pack Horse someone suggested getting Fogel along to investigate. It was very late and no one had any clear idea what a mind-reader would have to say to a poltergeist; but the *Daily Express* had already got a team of psychic researchers in the house and our own religious affairs man had brought in a vicar to try his hand at exorcism, so the presence of Fogel could only add to the merriment.

Everyone was rather drunk – I, still very new to this game of journalism, intoxicated twice over at being allowed in on such a lark – and we all trooped across to the Empire stage door and had Fogel brought out. He was, of course, all for the stunt, especially upon being told that the national press were already camping out in the house. Taxis were called and by midnight we had a nice little seance going, with a dozen reporters, four photographers, a clergyman, three psychic researchers, the scared couple and Fogel's publicity agent standing in a circle in the attic of the Headingley haunted house. Fogel himself sat tied to a chair in the middle of the ring with a tambourine on his knees. The door was sealed and the lights put out, then the tambourine bounded across the room. Someone put it back on Fogel's knee, when it began to shake out a message – from none other than Houdini, according to one of the psychic researchers. Fogel thereupon confessed that he had himself been working the tambourine, claiming, rather inconsequentially, that here was proof that the poltergeist was a hoax. A violent argument broke out between Fogel, the psychic researchers, the vicar, Fogel's publicity man and the afflicted householders, in the course of which some of the sozzled reporters remembered they had deadlines to keep and departed.

It was all marvellous nonsense, and I was in such a state of bliss after my night's adventure that I walked all the way home. And to think that the staid old Yorkshire Conservative Newspaper Co. were paying me twenty guineas a month to live this sort of life – had they only known, and had I had the means available, I should willingly have paid twenty guineas a month to them.

To walk home, in fact, would have been no great hardship even without the spring of exhilaration in my step, for home by now was on the Headingley side of town. Twenty guineas a month was a good sum of money to be earning – to be paid by the month at all seemed to me a sign of prosperity and on top of that there was the odd five shillings for any Diary paragraph I got in the paper, plus, I discovered, seven and sixpence for amateur drama reviews. I could well afford a small flat, and accordingly I found a modest apartment in the university district by Woodhouse Moor, within walking distance of Town.

So as well as putting clerking behind me I had now said goodbye for ever to council house living. Although I had been weaned off my mother's council house by two years in the forces, it was still something of a wrench to leave Halton Moor – not the estate, which I detested, but the essentially late-Edwardian home I had been brought up in. My little flat was by no means modern but moving into it was like stepping out of a time machine upon returning from a bygone age. No more soot-encrusted kettle simmering on the hob, no more flat irons resting in the hearth, no more blacklead, no more donkey-stone. No cobbler's last (for home boot repairs), mangle, copper (for boiling clothes), wicker clothes basket, zinc watering can, wireless accumulator, earthenware milk cooler, chimney rods.

No more loaf tins in the oven, no bread cakes the size of hub caps cooling on the windowsill. I had been familiar with these objects all my life but within days I felt as if I had been passing my life in a Five Towns story by Arnold Bennett but had now stepped into a post-war novel by J.B. Priestley.

It was, as I was not yet to realise, the beginning of a general move upmarket for the Waterhouse clan. My brothers had long ago come home from the war with as little fuss as they had departed (when Kenneth got back from the Western Desert my mother, who after all had not set eyes on him for five years, asked only "Is it still raining?" before laying out his supper) and settled into their peacetime jobs – Kenneth at the Yorkshire Copperworks in enviable Hunslet, Dennis as a car repair shop storeman, Stanley as a plasterer. Now sister Stella and Dennis married (Stanley and Kenneth did not) and produced children who, thanks partly to the Butler Education Act of 1944, were to become teachers or technological whizz-kids of the property-owning kind. Whatever stray gene had produced me stayed in the family system to upgrade the Waterhouses out of the artisan class for ever. From total illiteracy to letters after one's name and a car in the garage in two generations – no mean feat of social engineering.

Of course, I went to see my mother regularly, religiously, every Sunday, when the trams criss-crossing the city were jam-packed with young men in their best suits and young women in their powder-blue or lilac "costumes" and matching little hats, on their parental pilgrimages, and when in Richard Hoggart's memorable phrase all the dustbins of Leeds were covered with a thin top coating of John West salmon tins.

I enjoyed my walks down into Town each morning and would often vary my route, a favourite one being through the university and down through the Civic Hall, to which my brand-new National Union of Journalists card bearing my Polyfoto and the word PRESS in big letters now gave me access (I had been refused entry by the commissionaire in my white card staring days), then through the Town Hall and along Park Row past all the banks with their legions of ex-College of Commerce clerks all toiling away. I congratulated myself frequently on the fact that no building in Leeds was now denied me, from the Council chamber to the humblest working men's club, from the Territorial Army barracks to the Leeds Library; I could walk the iron-railed balcony of Kirkgate Market to seek out the Markets Superintendent, or the marble halls of the Yorkshire Penny Bank to keep an appointment with the manager; my press pass would take me past any stage door or into the very parlour of the Lord Mayor himself; I had access to the cocktail bars of the Queen's and Metropole hotels, and even to Albert Cowling's cavernous, subterranean Wine Lodge. The last veil of the city had at last been torn away; but more than that, I was now a part of Leeds life − I was living it rather than merely looking at it.

In short, I was thoroughly enjoying myself, and never more alive − so much so that I quite forgot I was only on three months' trial and could be pitched back into clerical serfdom on the editor's whim. What I would have done then I had no idea, but as things turned out I had nothing to worry about − not that I had been worrying in the first place. Mr Horniblow, it seemed, was too innovative and unsettling for the conservative board of the Yorkshire Conservative Newspaper Co. He departed abruptly for Fleet Street whence he had come, and was succeeded by the benign news editor, Mr Woodward. If Mr Woodward knew of the three months arrangement, he never let on. Indeed he once stopped me in the corridor and congratulated me on settling in nicely.

Towards Christmas I got notice of an unexpected four guineas a month rise. I celebrated my new affluence with a pub crawl from Polly's to Whitelock's to the Pack Horse, in the course of which I consumed fourteen bottles of Guinness. Back at the office I fell asleep in the lavatory and awoke at seven in the morning, just time enough before starting work for a canteen breakfast and my first ever barbershop shave. Another adventure.

4 While the euphoria had not worn off (nor has it since), after about a year of this idyllic existence I began to grow restless. I had realised that becoming a newspaper reporter was not the summit of my ambition. It had seemed such a difficult goal from the view of a half-educated undertaker's clerk in a council house that I had never thought beyond it.

Now I set myself two fresh targets. The first was to get to Fleet Street, perhaps via Manchester — but less because I saw myself pursuing a lifelong career on national newspapers than because I had made up my mind that I wanted to live in London.

I had already paid one brief and confused visit to the capital, on the proceeds of my twelve-guinea windfall from *Everybody's* in the last weeks of my national service, and I was completely hooked. Like Birmingham, London was still a monochrome rather than a Technicolor experience, still essentially a Victorian-cum-Edwardian metropolis (Romano's had only recently closed its doors), with only the odd stunning modernistic edifice such as Broadcasting House, the black glass *Daily Express* building, a handful of Jazz Age hotels and restaurants and Frank Pick's elegant tube stations to indicate, as some of us naïvely hoped, the shape of things to come. This was a London of Lyons Corner Houses with palm court orchestras and wandering violinists, of coffee stalls and ABC (for Aerated Bread Company) teashops and Dickensian chophouses, of flower girls and streetwalkers and costermongers, of trams along the Embankment and chunky red buses and black cabs like truncated hearses, and bomb craters.

I stayed at the Union Jack Club, the forces hostel by Waterloo Station, and sallied forth to find Soho which, confusing it with W.W. Jacobs's Limehouse, I looked for on the river with the result that I was soon hopelessly lost south-east of Tower Bridge. I didn't mind at all: the cindery smoke of London was in my nostrils and "the roar of London's traffic" as they called it on the *In Town Tonight* wireless programme was in my ears, and I was as happy as the days were long.

And long they were, for I was up at five in the morning to discover Covent Garden market, whose cloisters I wandered for hours, marvelling at the criss-crossing ballet of porters with their own height in fruit baskets balanced on their heads. In the afternoon I perched on a shelf of the Westminster Theatre to see Flora Robson in *Black Chiffon*, and in the evening on another shelf somewhere in Shaftesbury Avenue to see my first ever revue, in which Hermione Baddeley did a Restoration comedy sketch by Alan Melville where all the s's were pronounced as f's: "Come fit on the fofa and feduce me, you filly fod." I walked all the way home to the Union Jack Club trying to compose a revue sketch in my head. There was fog coming up from the river, and the mournful hoot of lighters, and out in the trolley-bus-hissing suburbs there would be dapper henpecked husbands boiling down flypapers to make arsenic, and there would be human heads in hatboxes in the left-luggage office at Victoria Station. This was the place to be, all right.

On my last morning I made the pilgrimage to Fleet Street, had half a pint of ale at Ye Olde Cheshire Cheese, the Whitelock's of the south, and went and stared at the plaque to Edgar Wallace on Ludgate Circus where he sold newspapers as a boy: "Edgar Wallace, Reporter. Born London 1875, died Hollywood 1932. Founder member of the Company of Newspaper Makers. He knew wealth and poverty yet had walked with kings and kept his bearing. Of his talents he gave lavishly to authorship – but to Fleet Street he gave his heart."

About giving my own heart to Fleet Street I was not so sure, for the second of my targets was to become a serious writer of novels and plays. I was still turning out the odd magazine feuilleton as Mr Horniblow would have called my modest successes, and I had been paid the unheard-of sum of £25 as winner of a competition in a boy's paper, the *Champion*, for, of all things, a football story. But my heart was no longer in writing just for the sake of getting published – perhaps my few daily inches in the *Evening Post* fulfilled that need. I wanted now to become a proper writer, not just a hit-or-miss churner-out of froth at a guinea a thousand words. I saw myself set up in an attic flat in Chelsea, wherever that might be, interviewing starlets for the *Daily Express* by day and working on the great British novel, or even the minor British novel, by night.

The trouble was, what to write? While I was slowly learning to write from my own observation, I had yet to write a single word from my own experience. When my mother, not all that many years ago, had brought home for me the collected plays of J.M. Barrie, I had failed to follow up my newly acquired interest in this versatile author by reading his book *When A Man's Single*. This account of his life on the *Nottinghamshire Journal* and as a freelance writing magazine pieces gave, as I too belatedly discovered, the best advice possible for the aspiring journalist: "Do not fruitlessly aspire towards international travel and the drawing rooms of the mighty in your search for a topic, but write about the small everyday events of your own existence, and these accounts will sell." Con Gordon had said much the same thing. But even had I read Barrie in time for this wise counsel to be of any use (in the event, the only thing I learned from him, and quickly unlearned, was how to write infuriatingly arch stage directions), I might have reflected that it was all very well for him, he hadn't been brought up on a flat council estate where nothing ever happened. Arnold Bennett had his Five Towns, Lawrence his Nottinghamshire pit villages, but all I had to fall back on was a dormitory suburb and a surrogate interest in Hunslet.

But then one day I picked up at Stringer's bookstall in the Market a Guild Books paperback of Dylan Thomas's *Portrait of the Artist as a Young Dog*, a collection of short stories based on his boyhood in Swansea. It was an eye-opener. Thomas came from a world as remorselessly ordinary as my own. He was a grammar school boy, from the semi-detached end of town rather than the smoky terraces; nothing desperate had ever happened to him, he hung around with a crowd of other boys and they did the things that boys do – the kind of things I had done. The stories brought my own childhood back to life and made it seem what I had never remembered it to be – exciting.

And so there was my lesson, and my model. I began to think back over my own childhood and the small change of my upbringing in Middleton, which now seemed crowded and full of incident. I remembered a fight I had stupidly got into at the Wolf Cubs. For years it had been nothing but a tiny, rather painful half-memory, but now I let myself drift back into the past and it became vivid in my mind again. I put it down on paper and for the first time, outside of newspaper reporting, something I'd written seemed to be about something. I never tried to publish the piece because although it had life it didn't have form – it was an incident rather than a story. But I knew I was on the way to something now, and I began to excavate further. These childhood episodes, the first real things I had ever written, were to surface in due course as fragments of my first novel, *There Is A Happy Land*.

At around this time I also wrote my first radio play, stimulated largely by the circumstances that every morning on my way to the office I passed the BBC Leeds studios, housed in a former Quaker meeting house in Woodhouse Lane, and I was curious to see inside them. By giving the Pack Horse and Whitelock's a miss for a few evenings and working at a newsroom typewriter when the others had all gone, I managed to produce an Ealing-type romp called *The Town That Wouldn't Vote*. I never seriously expected this to be accepted, but I did think it showed enough promise to warrant an invitation to the BBC where I might with luck be taken under the wing of a producer who would point me in the right direction. To my surprise, after a routine postcard acknowledging receipt of the script, the next thing I heard from the BBC was a contract in duplicate, requiring my signature in acceptance of "the fee mentioned above and on the terms and conditions stated". The fee mentioned above was sixty guineas, a fortune – it bought, among other luxuries, my first ever typewriter, an Imperial portable.

A few days later I was summoned to the BBC to meet my producer, Guy Stephen Deghy, a heavily built, voluble Hungarian I recognised as one of the bearded bohemians of Whitelock's. He took me straight across to the BBC local, the Fenton Arms, showed me the framed cheque for a pound from Wilfred Pickles with its accompanying instruction, "Break glass in case of emergency", bought me a half of Tetley's bitter and then got me drunk on talk. T.S. Eliot, J.B. Priestley, Tennessee Williams, Graham Greene, Evelyn Waugh, Norman Mailer, Ratz Scriven, Con Gordon, the pre-war Berlin cabaret, Blackpool, the quality of Leeds fish and chips, the London theatre, apartheid, *Passport to Pimlico*, *Citizen Kane*, the rival merits of Tetley's and Younger's beer, Hunslet Feast, the Spanish Riding School, the works of Hank Janson and Louis MacNeice's "Bagpipe Music" were among the subjects touched upon before closing time. Despite a twenty-year age gap, Guy and I hit it off from the start, and we were to become lifelong friends and collaborate on several fruitful projects.

Guy had no faults to pick with the play at all. I was rather disappointed — I had expected, in the best Hollywood tradition, to be required to go away and do hurried rewrites, working far into the night with a cigarette on my lips. He did not even trouble to mention that my play presented something of a challenge in that it had no fewer than sixty-three characters including three real-life London BBC announcers and the commentator from *British Movietone News*. Even if we could have got these celebrities up to Leeds there was not enough studio space to hold them, or indeed for more than a couple of dozen of the cast; in fact the only way my play could be put out at all was by linking up three studios, Leeds, Manchester and London. Guy invited me to the transmission and it all went so much like clockwork that I had not the slightest inkling that manipulating sixty-three characters in three separate studios was in any way out of the ordinary. It was only at the party over at the Fenton later that I had some glimmer of the technical miracle my producer had just achieved when he said casually, "That seemed to go awfully well and I should like to commission another Thursday Play from you, but do you think next time you could keep it down to about half a dozen characters at most?"

Alas, the commission never came. A few days later Guy was arrested for drinking a few minutes after hours in Whitelock's with his friend the then landlord. Fined ten shillings. In those Reithian days it was not precisely a firing offence but it was enough to put the block on his future prospects with the BBC. Guy took off for London to act, write and generally continue the bohemian life — the fact that he was down there mingling with actresses and drinking in the French Pub was a further spur to my ambition to reach my Chelsea garret.

In the meantime, I had settled in nicely at the *Yorkshire Evening Post* as the editor Mr Woodward had put it, even though I did not intend to settle there for all that much longer. It was a wonderful if, as I now recognised, temporary way of life. There was a Press Ball at the Town Hall to which, in a dinner jacket hired from Rawcliffe's where my mother had bought my School Cap, I escorted Barbara Taylor. There were functions to cover — dinner dances and banquets for this or that federation of this or that trade or calling, where I was indoctrinated into the mysteries of the fish knife, the cigar cutter and the grape scissors, and where I stylishly made my notes on the back of a menu card.

By now, by virtue of taking on the amateur theatre reviews when

205

nobody else wanted to do them, I had established myself as second-string drama critic. The senior critic, Mr Bolton, got the Grand Theatre, the Empire was the perquisite of the chief sub-editor who had a taste for music-hall, and my beat was the Theatre Royal and the City Varieties – Theatre Royal Monday first house, City Varieties second house. It could have been the other way round but Ray Hill, with whom I often shared my pair of complimentary tickets, was convinced that I had droit du seigneur over the chorus girls. Thus Monday night would often end with our hanging around the stage door to escort two peroxide blondes – any two peroxide blondes, the first pair out – to a fish and chip supper and then back to their theatrical digs in the North Street area. There our stage door Johnny dalliance would abruptly end, for in that district self-respecting chorus girls would not hang about on the doorstep for fear of being mistaken for ladies of the night, and theatrical landladies had a strict policy of No Gentlemen Callers.

As for my reviews, attempts to emulate Ivor Brown of the *Observer* were blue-pencilled as clever-clever and I quickly learned to write in the then house style of the entertainments page – that is to say, generously. The theatres were, after all, regular advertisers. My Theatre Royal review invariably praised the Court Players' *ingénue* with whom I was in love; and I usually had a good word for the consistent, i.e. always the same, performance of the leading man who never failed to get an exit round by shouting "Good night!" and slamming the door regardless of what the stage directions might have required.

My Varieties reviews were practically written for me by the proprietor, Mr Harry Joseph, who over a liberal drink in the circle bar would literally mark my card: taking my programme he would scrawl through some names and asterisk others with a running commentary on the quality of the acts – "He's no good . . . I shan't be booking this one again . . . Now these fellows are top class – they'll be back here in six weeks on their way down from Sunderland, so give them a good write-up, son . . ." While I was hardly likely to emerge as a rival to Ken Tynan with this kind of stuff I was thrilled to be almost a part of the City Varieties' backstage life, and thus by extension of the backstage life of the city itself.

By now I was becoming something of a hardened reporter. I had seen my first murderer sentenced to death, the prisoner clutching the same spiked dock from which Charlie Peace had been despatched to the scaffold, and had been repelled yet fascinated by the black cap ritual and the dreadful formula of the sentence of execution. My hands were still so shaky after I had phoned in my story that during the press room poker session later I dropped my cards. The old Press Association hand who had seen it all before said gruffly, "It takes everybody like that the first time, young 'un.''

I had covered grisly accidents where the firemen were still cutting bleeding victims out of their vehicles, I had interviewed bereaved mothers, and I had been sent up in a Tiger Moth like the one that did a loop-the-loop over the Murder Woods when I was a child, to report on the snowed-up Dales. And I had got my tram scoop.

The way of my tram scoop was that Mr Mann, the municipal correspondent, was off on his annual holidays to Whitby and it fell to me to cover the Council beat in his absence. Mr Mann was perfectly happy to leave the city's municipal affairs in my whippersnapper hands: like all specialists he was always careful to take his holiday when there was nothing very much going on in his particular field, and in any case he was well aware that I knew no one in civic circles above the rank of waitress in the Town Hall basement restaurant. I was unlikely to upstage my august senior.

Little did he know. Little did I know. After a week of ineffectual meanderings around the corridors of power I was descending the stairs of the civic restaurant for a coffee one morning when I encountered the Chairman of the Transport Committee, a blunt-speaking Alderman to whom I had been briefly introduced at the bar of the Victoria Commercial Hotel. The Alderman walked with a pronounced limp and was having difficulty mounting the stairs and so it seemed only civil to help him up. He thanked me, enquired as to the whereabouts of Mr Mann, and upon learning that he was away said, "Never mind – tha'll do. Does tha want summat to write about?" Putting his arm around my shoulders the Alderman led me out to the Town Hall steps and pointed to the junction of Park Row and the Headrow, where a great log-jam of trams, eight or nine of them queuing up behind one another like lighters waiting to enter harbour, was causing total gridlock, the first of them having broken down.

"Tha sees yon trams, lad? We're getting shut of the buggers."

Sensation. Scrapping the trams was akin to scrapping Kirkgate Market or Headingley cricket ground or the Town Hall itself, and I had it first. I sprinted over to the Civic Hall and got a quote from the Alderman's Conservative opposite number, to the effect that covering fifty miles of tram track with asphalt would put a shilling on the rates. I did not bother to note his additional comment, to the effect that the Alderman was merely flying a kite — so he was, and it was to be four or five years before the trams were finally condemned, but it was still a scoop. I telephoned the story through and went about my business. I could not understand why it did not make the early editions, to give me something to crow about in the saloon bars, but then I realised they were holding it until the Final so that it would be too late for the opposition to follow it up. And there it was, all over the front page. My first real exclusive.

Mr Mann duly returned from holiday, when he was not best pleased. Nevertheless, he was gracious enough to congratulate me. Waving away my thanks he added, "Did you by any chance notice, when you interviewed the Alderman, that he walks with a bit of a limp?" I confirmed that I knew the Alderman was minus a leg.

"Correct, laddie. And do you know where he lost that leg?"

"Passchendaele?" I hazarded.

The municipal correspondent tucked his thumbs into his waistcoat pockets. "If you'd looked up the Alderman's details before writing your brilliant exclusive," he said, "you would have seen that he was run over. By a tram."

Nevertheless, my tram scoop stood me in good stead and I was given bigger and better stories to do. These I diligently clipped and filed each evening, as did every other ambitious reporter, for when you wished to change to another paper your cuttings were your passport.

And I was by now positively in the mood for change — not only because I wanted to get to Fleet Street and London but because I felt I had lived long enough in Leeds. The Alderman might have been premature about the trams but there was no doubt that the city was stirring out of its pre-war, post-Edwardian sleep. While it would be a long time yet before Leeds declared itself the Motorway City — it would be a long time yet before we even saw the first motorway – there was a civic restlessness about, a growing clamour for clearing away the old, for comprehensive development and social engineering, and the high cranes were gathering on the horizon. From what I heard of the plans for Leeds in its transition from the provincial to the regional I didn't think it was going to be my kind of place. I had been growing up in an industrial Atlantis that was about to be submerged. Time to move on.

5   Things had gone so smoothly for me so far that it came as
    something of a shock to realise that getting out of Leeds
    was not going to be the easy ride I had anticipated. Our
crime man Frank came back from an interview with the *Daily Mirror*
in Manchester with the report that the news editor had openly
scoffed at his impressive set of cuttings, pointing out sceptically that
they could be anybody's work. This was perfectly true – indeed, I
had been banking on that fact in venturing to augment my own
meagre collection of cuttings with stories by other hands. In those
days only two staff members' names appeared above their work –
Con Gordon's and the pseudonym of the plump and pompous sports
editor who for reasons of his own chose to call himself Little John.
Everyone else was identified simply as *Evening Post Reporter*. It was
clear that if I were to stand any chance of battering down the doors
of Withy Grove or Fleet Street I should somehow have to start
getting my name in the paper.

But how? With the connivance of Ray Hill I hatched a plot. We
had for months been planning a holiday in London, mainly with the
object of discovering Chelsea, reputedly the haunt of poets, painters
and artists' models with loose morals. I proposed a stunt: that we
should set off and walk to London, covering the 210-mile journey in
one week flat, I phoning in a daily account of our progress. It was
perhaps a rash notion. While I had whiled away many an hour
wandering the streets of Leeds I had no particular love of strenuous
walking, and the prospect of tramping thirty miles a day was a
daunting one. But it would be a lark, and if the paper agreed to go
along with it they could hardly confine my daily byline to *Evening
Post Reporter*.

The ruse worked. The editor was enthusiastic, and after Ray and I
had had great fun plotting a route with the aid of a Bartholomew's
map spread over the big dining table in Whitelock's, my opening

story featured not only my name but also a photograph of the pair of us striding out from City Square at the start of our trek.

We walked briskly through the familiar streets of Hunslet and were soon on the A1, still romantically known as the Great North Road, reaching Doncaster by nightfall. So far, so good: the only countryside yet encountered was that semi-urban scrubland of allotments, rhubarb fields and potato patches, slag heaps, car dumps and sooty fields with grazing pit ponies which was the only type of greenery I could abide. We now had to find a place to sleep. "Barns and the lee of hedges will be our makeshift beds," I had rashly promised, but it was spluttering with rain and the lights of Doncaster beckoned. We ditched our resolution to emulate W.H. Davies and the knights of the open road and established a routine of finding rooms in modest pubs. In my despatches I referred to them as inns: it seemed so much more Chestertonian.

The second leg of our journey took us through the Dukeries, a seriously wooded beauty spot that seemed to stretch for hundreds of miles. From time to time motorists or lorry drivers would slow down to offer us a lift through this uncompromising forest and I for one was tempted, but any one of them could have been a potential spy for the rival *Yorkshire Evening News*, ready, for half a guinea tip-off money, to denounce our 210-mile walk as a fraud. I pined for the line of factory chimneys, like plane trees on the horizon of Picardy, that would tell us we were nearing Nottingham. Not for the first time, it came home to me that I was an acute sufferer from rural agoraphobia.

But I was getting twelve inches or so into the paper every day, each account of our small adventures being headed "From Keith Waterhouse". For some reason, perhaps because there was not usually much room in the papers for escapist stuff, the story was generating a fair amount of interest, and pressmen on our route, tipped off by the *Evening Post* news desk, would turn out to interview us and wire back pictures of us bathing our sore feet.

The original idea was to finish up in Trafalgar Square, but in the event we completed our Leeds to London marathon at Broadcasting House, where we were to be interviewed on the popular Saturday evening wireless programme *In Town Tonight*. The visit, for me, was more of an adventure than the actual broadcast – setting foot in that hallowed Bauhaus lobby was like staying at the Savoy Hotel. While the scripted interview – bafflingly, unscripted talk was completely banned at that time — was incredibly stilted ("I must say you both look pretty well. Just how long did your walk take you, Keith?"), it did me no end of good. *In Town Tonight*, in those pre-TV days, was the equivalent to one of today's prestigious chat shows, and the *Evening Post* was heavily plugged, an unheard-of boost.

I returned to the gothic turrets of the Yorkshire Conservative Newspaper Co. to something of a hero's welcome. Apparently my series had put on sales, the paper was basking in unaccustomed publicity, congratulations had filtered down from the boardroom to the editorial floor, and I was to get a ten-guinea bonus. Nor, somewhat to my dismay, did it stop there. Mr Woodward, the editor, cashing in on my little success, took it into his head to appoint me the *Evening Post* Walking Reporter. I was to be taken off the news desk diary of courts and meetings and chimney fires and given a roving commission to roam the broad acres breathing fresh country air into the smoke-ridden pages of the newspaper.

To anyone who loved the countryside it would have been a dream assignment. To me, it was a case of being hoist by my own petard. I spent the entire summer traipsing around the Dales, following all the main Yorkshire rivers from their source high in the curlew-swirling hills, along their meandering route down through the sheep-infested moorlands to the green valleys below. The scenery was breathtaking but for me never more so than when I could see wisps of smoke rising from the mill chimneys far, far below the rooftop of England. Staying in reasonably picturesque inns or, in the more remote regions, youth hostels, I always found the golden dawns heart-lifting, but the sunsets dipping behind the hills into the unseen industrial landscape beyond were depressing — it was with a sense of yearning that I would watch the last West Yorkshire single-decker pulling out of a cobbled market square, bound for Leeds, Bradford or even the comparative hustle and bustle of Ilkley. I would compensate myself by looking for a back-street fish and chip shop, its vinegar and batter scents smothering the stench of heather and evoking a Proustian remembrance of Hunslet.

I finished this season of forced labour tramping the entire length of the newly established Pennine Way ("the walkers' Great North Road", as I called it) from the Cheviots to the Peak District — possibly the only rambler ever to follow these 250 switchback miles in suede shoes. While the prose of my Walking Reporter articles tended towards the purple — "The wind that blows tin cans down the city streets is the same wind that moans tonight along the crags and heather of the Dales, howling round peak and scar, and wresting piccolo tunes from the reed patches near Kettlewell, nestling under Great Whernside's protective wings" — I was at the same time picking up some good solid feature stories, a particular success being a talking Labrador in Bishopdale that could do sums and play dominoes. All these made impressive signed cuttings to lay before editors.

Settling back in the office I found that I was now regarded as the paper's star feature writer. Con Gordon was running so many regular columns that he no longer had time to do the colour stories he had made his speciality, and so — to his relief, he said, since he had no longer anything new to say about the bank holiday weekend at Scarborough or the St Leger race meeting in Doncaster or Children's Day in Roundhay Park — I was to step into his shoes.

Since my name now automatically went on everything I wrote, pretty soon I felt in a position to start pestering Fleet Street for a job. I had heard that the mercurial Mr Horniblow was now editing a popular tabloid, the *Sunday Graphic*, and so he was the obvious first candidate. I sent off a batch of cuttings and to my astonishment received a telegram the very next day: CAN OFFER YOU THREE DAYS A WEEK AT FOUR GUINEAS DAILY — HORNIBLOW. I showed it to Con Gordon. He explained that what Horniblow was offering me, in his flamboyant way, was casual shift work. He advised me to turn it down — the newsprint shortage was still as bad as ever and these were perilous times for Fleet Street casuals whose services could be dispensed with at a second's notice. Pointing out that I had neither the experience nor the contacts to survive on that basis, Con sought to temper my disappointment with the words, "Never mind — the day is coming when you'll be earning forty pounds a week on a national." A far-fetched prediction, I thought. Left to myself, I should probably have accepted Mr Horniblow's impetuous offer, but I bowed to Con Gordon's journalistic wisdom. Anyway, it was an encouraging start.

I began methodically petitioning the London dailies, Sundays and the three evenings. They were unanimous: in the long, austere aftermath of the war when the broadsheet papers were down to six pages and the tabloids twelve, they were simply not taking staff on. One or two of them offered a ray of hope — "It is clear from your cuttings that you are destined for an early move to Fleet Street and I wish I had an opportunity to speed it — '' but none of them offered work.

In desperation I even applied for a reporting vacancy in Bermuda, on the *Hamilton Star*, advertised in the *World's Press News*. I was interviewed in London but heard no more. Very many years later I met an executive on the paper who showed me the report on me that had been sent back to Hamilton: it said that while my credentials were excellent, my thick Yorkshire accent would present a social challenge in the yacht clubs and bridge circles of the islands.

As the rejection letters piled up it was beginning to look as if I ought to forget London for a while and think about Manchester, a city I had still yet to visit. Just as I was coming round to this decision I happened to meet, in Whitelock's one day, a reporter from the Manchester edition of the *News Chronicle* who had come across the Pennines on some story or other. Over a drink or two I was flattered to learn from him that the northern editor of the *News Chronicle* had been much taken by my piece on the talking dog that could do sums and play dominoes. That was interesting: I had always had a feeling that my talking dog would do me some good one day (although when in the fullness of time I joined the *Daily Mirror* as a feature writer and was instructed in my first week to go out and find an animal story, I was told upon proudly presenting the talking dog of Bishopdale, "Shit! We need circulation in the West Country. See if you can find a talking dog that does sums and plays dominoes in Cornwall").

While I had begun to think about Manchester I had not yet begun to think about the *News Chronicle* — I knew that my strength was as a descriptive writer and the *News Chronicle*, a literate as well as a Liberal newspaper, already had more excellent descriptive writers than it could find space for. But if the northern editor had expressed admiration of my stuff, it was worth a try. I wrote off at once, and received a reply to the effect that while there were no vacancies at present and there would be little point in making a special journey, when next I happened to be in Manchester I might care to call in for a chat. Naturally I was over the Pennines like a bat on my first available day off.

The northern editor was cordiality itself and very complimentary about my work. But it was the usual story of newsprint starvation and getting quarts into pint pots. However, should a vacancy occur I could regard myself as being high up on the waiting list. Meanwhile, had I thought about London?

Diplomatically, anxious not to spoil my chances but even more anxious to learn what was behind this intriguing question, I said that while as a northerner Manchester was of course my first choice, I had never entirely ruled out Fleet Street. The northern editor went on to say that he happened to know that the *News Chronicle*'s London office would shortly be looking for a feature writer. If I had no rooted objection to living in the south and cared to write to the editor, he would be only too happy to support my application.

I went out into Derby Street with a song in my heart and spent an enchanted afternoon exploring Manchester. Another vibrant, black-and-white city: I so much took to Manchester that it almost seemed a shame to have to live in London, whither I was supremely confident I was at last on my way. Perhaps I would get back up north to write the odd feature, staying at the Midland Hotel and spending an evening at the Opera House.

I wrote to the *News Chronicle* in Bouverie Street that very night and after a couple of days on tenterhooks was highly satisfied to get a reply that could not have been more encouraging in its businesslike terseness: "Dear Mr Waterhouse, I have provisionally booked 3 p.m. on Wednesday next in order to see you. Should an emergency arise I will notify you, and suggest another date. Yours faithfully, N.S. Cursley, Asst Editor."

The cinder-bespattered, steam-belching journey to London, as I was chugged past the rhubarb fields of Middleton with the still collapsed drystone wall that had earned me my white card passport to city life, was as euphoric as the train ride from Kirkham in Lancashire on the hot day of my demob, when the *Yorkshire Evening Post* was my oyster. I would live in Chelsea, when I could find it (Ray Hill and I had been unable to locate Chelsea on any tube map), or perhaps in Bloomsbury, or Fitzrovia. I would lunch at Ye Olde Cheshire Cheese and dine at a Lyons Corner House or in one of the charming little Italian restaurants I had seen in what would turn out to be Soho. I would be no stranger to the West End theatres or the Tate Gallery or the Royal Academy. I would take Sunday morning walks to Speakers' Corner.

The *News Chronicle* being owned by the Quaker Cadburys I thought I had better not arrive for my interview with Cheshire Cheese alcohol on my breath, and so I lunched abstemiously at the

Kardomah at the bottom of Fetter Lane. I walked along Fleet Street past the *Telegraph* and the *Express* and Reuter's and the Press Association to pay my tribute to Edgar Wallace on his corner of Ludgate Circus; then I crossed over and walked down Bouverie Street where great reels of newsprint were being unloaded from lorries on to the rollers of the *News of the World*'s delivery bay. A basement roar of machinery told me that the Late edition of the *Star* was coming off the presses. And a few doors away was the *Punch* office. Oh, yes, this was where I belonged.

Mr Cursley was a homely northerner somewhat in the Alan Woodward mould. I felt at ease until the moment he said, "While I remember, you must be sure to send me an account of your expenses," when I knew that something was amiss. There was no vacancy for a feature writer. Rumour, that fickle jade, had erred yet again. But Mr Cursley had heard about my work and was impressed with it − that was a good feature story about the talking dog that did sums and played dominoes − and wanted to have a look at me. When the newsprint situation improved, he would certainly agree that my cuttings entitled me to consideration. But when that day would come he found it impossible to say.

I had shaken hands and was back out in Bouverie Street with the newsprint reels circling above my head before I realised what had happened to me, or rather what had not. I had been so certain, so cocksure, that in immediate retrospect the interview seemed almost an affront. Not since my rejection by Cockburn High School had I encountered such a setback. In shock, I blundered up into Fleet Street, past El Vino's that I had read so much about, past the Cock Tavern, past the Wig and Pen Club, all without a glance. Presently I found myself on Waterloo Bridge where, leaning against the parapet, I broke down in such shuddering sobs of rage, frustration and disappointment that passers-by stared at me.

All, in these few stinging moments, seemed lost. How was I to know then that within months I should be established in Fleet Street, that within three years I should be more familiar with New York, Washington, Moscow and Leningrad than I now was with London, that within four I should be turning down the post of the *News Chronicle*'s chief reporter, that within five I should be publishing my first novel, and that within ten I should see my name in lights on Shaftesbury Avenue and on the cinema posters of Leicester Square?

A sauntering policeman had his eye on me, perhaps discerning a possible candidate for the Thames. I pulled myself together. After all, I was only just turned twenty-two — there would be other times, other opportunities. I dried my tears and strode out to the Strand, then skirted Trafalgar Square and walked up the Haymarket. It was winter and getting dark already and all the lights were lit and there on Piccadilly Circus, along with Wrigley's Spearmint and Gordon's Gin and Schweppes was the Bovril sign all spelled out in electric light bulbs — an exact replica of the one I had first seen in Town on the way to the Mickey Mouse show at St James's Hospital, and with the same man in his little room behind flicking his light switch on and off. Home again.